CO...
KINGDOM CHALLENGE

CONFRONTING KINGDOM CHALLENGES

A CALL TO GLOBAL CHRISTIANS TO CARRY THE BURDEN TOGETHER

GENERAL EDITOR

SAMUEL T. LOGAN JR.

CROSSWAY BOOKS

WHEATON, ILLINOIS

Library of Congress Cataloging-in-Publication Data
Confronting kingdom challenges : a call to global Christians to carry the burden together / Samuel T. Logan, Jr., general editor.
    p. cm.
    ISBN 978-1-58134-863-7 (tpb)
    1. Mission of the church—Congresses. 2. Church and social problems—Congresses. 3. Church—Unity—Congresses.   4. Church—Catholicity—Congresses. I. Logan, Samuel T., 1943–   . II. Title.
BV601.8.C654   2007
261.8—dc22   2007002685

VP		17	16	15	14	13	12	11	10	09	08	07
15	14	13	12	11	10	9	8	7	6	5	4	3	2	1

CONTENTS

PART FOUR
A FINAL CHALLENGE

CONTRIBUTORS

Dr. Robert C. (Ric) Cannada Jr. is Chancellor and CEO, Associate Professor of Practical Theology, Reformed Theological Seminary. He received his B.A. from Vanderbilt University and his M.Div. and D.Min. from Reformed Theological Seminary (RTS). A Presbyterian pastor for twenty years, Ric served First Presbyterian Church in Clinton, South Carolina before starting Covenant Presbyterian Church in Little Rock, Arkansas. From 1986 to 1993 he served as Senior Pastor of the First Presbyterian Church in Macon, Georgia. In the summer of 1993 he moved to Charlotte, North Carolina to lead in the establishment of the Charlotte campus of RTS. Under his leadership, RTS Charlotte grew substantially. Ric has taught courses in church polity and in sanctification at Charlotte as well as courses at seminaries in the Ukraine and Brazil.

Dr. Wilson Chow is President and Professor of Biblical Studies at the China Graduate School of Theology (CGST) in Hong Kong. CGST was founded in 1975 and currently has more than 200 full-time and more than 300 part-time students. It has just launched a Ph.D. program. Dr. Chow received his M.Div. from Westminster Theological Seminary and his M.A. and Ph.D. degrees from Brandeis University. He has served as a visiting professor at Fuller Theological Seminary, Westminster Seminary California, and Regent College, and he has also taught in Croatia, Russia, Japan, South Korea, and the Philippines. Dr. Chow has written numerous articles on theological education in and for China, he has lectured in China, and he is regarded as one of the world's experts on Christianity in China.

Charles Clayton is National Director of World Vision Jerusalem. Prior to his present position, Charles served as the Executive Director of World Vision United Kingdom and then as Group Chief Executive of Shaftesbury Housing and Care. He holds degrees in civil engineering and in theology (the latter from Westminster Theological Seminary). He has coauthored a volume on biblical hermeneutics entitled *Let the Reader Understand* and numerous papers on leadership. He is a past member of the American Management Association, the Management Centre Europe, and the UK Chartered Management Institute. He is currently a Fellow of the Institute of Directors and a Fellow of the Royal Society of the Arts, both in the UK; and he has served on a variety of boards in the commercial, nonprofit, and education sectors.

Dr. Victor Cole is Professor of Educational Studies at the Nairobi Evangelical Graduate School of Theology (NEGST) in Kenya. Dr. Cole received his theological training at Dallas Theological Seminary and his Ph.D. from Michigan State University. From 1999 to 2004, he was Deputy Vice Chancellor for Academic Affairs at NEGST. Among his publications are *Perspectives on Leadership Training* and *Training of the Ministry: A Macro-Curricular Approach*. Dr. Cole also serves as a Consulting Editor for the *African Journal of Evangelical Theology*.

Dr. David R. Haburchak is Program Director of the Internal Medicine Residency Program and Professor of Medicine at the Medical College of Georgia. Dr. Haburchak was a Distinguished Military Graduate of the ROTC Program at the Johns Hopkins University, where he earned his B.A. degree as well as his M.D. He has pursued a twenty-four-year career in the United States Army Medical Corps, holding many leadership positions in academic military medicine, including chairmanship of departments of medicine and program directorships in internal medicine at three Army teaching hospitals. He is board certified in internal medicine and infectious diseases. He has received numerous awards for teaching and leadership in the Army Medical Department and was awarded the Laureate Award of the Army Chapter of the American College of Physicians. Dr. Haburchak has had extensive experience with medical faculty of the former Soviet Union, Cuba, Kenya, and Yemen while on short-term medical evangelism mission trips and visiting lectureships. He is a member of the American Osler Society and has attempted to promote the best traditions of personalized patient care in the competency-based and measured practice of the twenty-first century.

Archbishop Peter Jensen is Anglican Archbishop of Sydney, Australia. Canon Jensen was inaugurated as the eleventh Archbishop of Sydney in June 2001. Archbishop Jensen did his theological training at Moore Theological College in Sydney, Australia, and at London University in England. He earned a D.Phil. at Oxford for his research on Elizabethan Anglicanism. He was appointed Curate at St. Barnabas's Broadway in 1969 and worked with unprivileged youth and with students at the University of Sydney. In 1985 Archbishop Jensen was appointed Principal of Moore Theological College, a position that he held until his elevation to Archbishop in 2001. Over the past thirty years, Archbishop Jensen has been heavily involved in the theological debates within the Anglican Communion, serving as a member of the Sydney Diocesan Doctrine Commission since 1980. In the Anglican Church of Australia, he has been a member of the General Synod Doctrine Commission (now Doctrine Panel) since 1982. He has contributed to a number of publications of that body, including the recently published *Faithfulness in Fellowship: Reflections on Homosexuality and the Church*.

Dr. Peter Jones is Executive Director of CWIPP Ministries (Christian Witness to a Pagan Planet) and Scholar-at-Large of the World Reformed Fellowship. Dr. Jones is a former Professor of New Testament at Westminster Seminary California where he continues to serve in an adjunct capacity. He is an internationally recognized author and speaker. Among his many books are *Cracking Da Vinci's Code*; *Capturing the Pagan Mind*; *Gospel Truth, Pagan Lies*; and *Spirit Wars: Pagan Revival in Christian America*. He earned his Th.M. at Harvard Divinity School and his Ph.D. at Princeton Theological Seminary. He taught for eighteen years at the Faculté de Théologie Réformée in Aix-en-Provence, France.

Dr. In Whan Kim is President of Chongshin University and Theological Seminary in Seoul, South Korea. Dr. Kim has been on the faculty of Chongshin University since 1982 and has also served as Dean of Academic Affairs and Vice President. He did his undergraduate work at Chongshin University (B.A.), his seminary training at Chongshin Theological Seminary and Westminster Theological Seminary (M.Div. and Th.M.), and earned a Ph.D. from the University of Wales, Lempeter, Great Britain. He served as chairman of the committee to found the Society of Reformed Theology and now serves as the chairman of its Department of Old Testament Studies. He has been ordained by the Philadelphia Presbytery, Presbyterian Church in America, and he is now an ordained minister of the Presbyterian Church in Korea (Hapdong).

Dr. Diane M. Langberg is a licensed psychologist in private practice in Jenkintown, Pennsylvania. Dr. Langberg is an internationally recognized author and speaker whose books include *On the Threshold of Hope: Opening the Door to Hope and Healing for Survivors of Sexual Abuse*, *Counseling Survivors of Sexual Abuse*, and *Counsel for Pastor's Wives*. She founded "The Place of Refuge," an inner-city nonprofit trauma and training center in Philadelphia. She is Section Editor for the *Journal of Psychology and Christianity* and is on the Editorial Board of *Marriage and Family Journal*. Dr. Langberg is Chair of the Executive Board of the American Association of Christian Counselors and is Adjunct Professor of Practical Theology at Westminster Theological Seminary and Associate Professor of Practical Theology at Reformed Episcopal Theological Seminary. She received her Master's and Ph.D. degrees from Temple University and is affiliated with the Initiative Against Sex Trafficking.

Rev. Jimmy Lin is Minister of Chinese Broadcasting for the *Back to God Hour* radio program, a ministry of the Christian Reformed Church. Rev. Lin and his staff preach the gospel weekly (in both Mandarin and Cantonese) to listeners throughout the People's Republic of China (where one fifth of the world's population lives), Southeast Asia, Australia, New Zealand, and North and Central America. Many of his messages are available online, and extensive written materials are published as well. Rev. Lin is a graduate and a former member of the Board of Trustees at Westminster Theological Seminary.

Dr. Samuel T. Logan Jr. is President Emeritus and Professor of Church History Emeritus at Westminster Theological Seminary and Executive Secretary of the World Reformed Fellowship. Dr. Logan served on the faculty of Westminster beginning in 1979 and, from 1991 to 2005, served as President of that institution. He has served on the Executive Committee of the Association of Theological Schools in the United States and Canada (ATS) and has chaired accreditation teams for both ATS and the Middle States Association of Schools and Colleges. He did his undergraduate work at Princeton University and his seminary training at Westminster, and he earned a Ph.D. in Theology and Literature from Emory University. Dr. Logan edited and contributed to *The Preacher and Preaching: Reviving the Art in the Twentieth Century* and *Sermons That Shaped America: Reformed Preaching from 1630 to 2001*. He has written numerous articles on British and American Puritanism and on the life and work of Jonathan Edwards. He is an ordained minister of the Orthodox Presbyterian Church.

Dr. John Nicholls is Chief Executive of the London City Mission (LCM). The LCM was founded in 1835 (when London was the largest city in the world) as a joint venture of Christians from many different Protestant denominations. It has maintained its original aim ("to go to the people of London, especially the poor, to bring them to an acquaintance with Jesus Christ as Saviour, and to do them good by every means in our power") and today employs some 140 evangelists and many volunteers in a wide range of ministries. Dr. Nicholls (who served as Director of Training before becoming Chief Executive) co-authored the definitive history of the LCM, entitled *Streets Paved with Gold*. He is a minister of the Free Church of Scotland, received his D.Min. in Pastoral Ministry from Westminster Theological Seminary, and previously served as Pastor of Cole Abbey Presbyterian Church in London.

Dr. Manuel Ortiz is an author and Professor Emeritus of Ministry and Urban Mission at Westminster Theological Seminary in Philadelphia. Dr. Ortiz received a B.S. from Philadelphia College of the Bible, an M.A. from Wheaton Graduate School of Theology, and a D.Min. from Westminster. He is a church planter, having planted five churches in Chicago and two churches in Philadelphia, and he is in the process of starting three more church plants in Philadelphia. He is widely called upon by denominations for consultation in church planting, leadership training, and ministering in communities facing transitions. He has also taught courses in a number of other seminaries both in the United States and in other countries and has been asked to consult with numerous seminaries that have recognized the need for beginning urban mission programs.

Dr. Ron W. Scates is Senior Pastor of Highland Park Presbyterian Church in Dallas. Dr. Scates served pastorates in San Antonio and Baltimore before taking his present position at Highland Park. Ron holds positions on the boards of The Assistance Center of Towson Churches, Youth for Christ of Metro-Maryland, Regeneration Ministries, Chesapeake Habitat for Humanity, *Reformed Worship Journal*, Christian Assistance Ministry of San Antonio, San Antonio Metropolitan Ministries, Spiritual Advisory Board of the Greater Baltimore Medical Center, Presbyterian Hospital of Dallas Board of Governors, and Presbyterians for Renewal. He is also currently affiliated with Evangelicals for Social Action.

Dr. Yusufu Turaki is Professor of Theology and Social Ethics at the Jos Evangelical Church of West Africa Theological Seminary (ECWA) since 1980. He studied theology and ethics at Gordon-Conwell Theological Seminary, he holds a Ph.D. in social ethics from Boston University, and he did postdoctoral Research at Yale University. Dr. Turaki has been involved with church administration and leadership at various levels and has done extensive research and publication dealing with theological education, Africa's contemporary sociopolitical issues and problems, church ecumenics in Nigeria, culture and modernization, Christian-Muslim relations in Africa, and Christian missions and colonial legacies in Africa. He has held various leadership positions such as provost of Jos, General Secretary of the ECWA, Vice President of the Christian Association of Nigeria (CAN), Executive Secretary of the Ethics, Peace and Justice Commission of the Association of the Evangelicals of Africa (AEA), and Director of Education of ECWA. He is currently involved with Bible translations with the International Bible Society (IBS), Nairobi, Kenya and is an adviser to the Africa Bible Commentary (ABC). Dr. Turaki's publications include, among others, *The British Colonial Legacy in Northern Nigeria: A Social Ethical Analysis of the Colonial and Post-Colonial Society and Politics in Nigeria*; *Tribal Gods of Africa: Ethnicity, Racism, Tribalism and the Gospel of Christ*; *Christianity and African Gods: A Method in Theology*; *Theory and Practice of Christian Missions in Africa*; *Foundations of African Traditional Religions and Worldview*; and *The Unique Christ for Salvation: The Challenge of the Non-Christian Religions and Cultures*.

INTRODUCTION

The articles in this volume are edited versions of presentations given at the Second General Assembly of the World Reformed Fellowship (WRF) in Johannesburg, South Africa, March 7-10, 2006.

The World Reformed Fellowship is a growing network of church denominations, associations, local congregations, institutions, agencies, and individual leaders working together to complete Christ's Great Commission. It seeks to link those in the historic evangelical Reformed tradition of Christ's church in order to facilitate communication, collaboration, and cooperation for mutual encouragement, support, and advancement of kingdom concerns.

The WRF is not a council but rather, as the name affirms, a fellowship. Leaders and groups within the evangelical, Reformed tradition of Christ's church get to know and trust one another within this fluid network of relationships, developing mutually beneficial partnerships and assisting local believers with their vision of reaching their regions or nations for Christ. In many ways the WRF fulfills the dream cherished by John Calvin in the 1500s, the Westminster Divines in the 1600s, and George Whitefield and Jonathan Edwards in the 1700s of truly worldwide cooperation among the Reformed branches of the church.

The WRF seeks to embody one of the clearly stated but often neglected themes of the great Reformed confessions of the church. For example, the Westminster Confession of Faith (XXV, 2) affirms that there is "a visible universal church" that "consists of all those throughout the world that profess the true religion." The Belgic Confession (Article 27) emphasizes that the "one single catholic or universal church . . . is not confined, bound, or limited to a certain place or certain persons. But it is spread and dispersed throughout the entire world."

While specific regional or national expressions of the universal church do, in many ways, embody characteristics of the body of Christ, there are other characteristics of that body that transcend those expressions. It is those other characteristics that the WRF seeks to set forth in its commitments and in its activities.

The World Reformed Fellowship affirms that:

The essence of "the true religion" is adoration and worship of the Triune God, Father, Son, and Holy Spirit. . . .

This Triune God is worthy of the praise and service of all of creation. . . .

Christians in many places and many denominations who share these first two commitments will find their worship and service of the Lord God enhanced by contact with others of like mind.

Therefore, the WRF seeks to provide:

A network for communication and sharing of ministry resources among such Christians
    A forum for dialogue among such Christians on current issues
    Opportunities for such Christians from one region of the world to share their unique spiritual and theological perspectives with such Christians from other regions of the world, all within the framework of the evangelical Reformed faith
    Regular occasions, some for such Christians in specific regions of the world and some for such Christians worldwide, to come together for worship and dialogue and resource-sharing

The formal doctrinal commitments of the WRF are as follows:

The Scriptures of the Old and New Testaments are the God-breathed Word of God, without error in all that they affirm;
    The following creeds represent the mainstream of historic orthodox Christianity: The Apostles' Creed, the Nicene Creed, and the Chalcedonian Definition;

Every voting member of the WRF affirms one of the following historic expressions of the Reformed Faith: The Gallican Confession, The Belgic Confession, The Heidelberg Catechism, The Thirty-Nine Articles, The Second Helvetic Confession, The Canons of Dort, The Westminster Confession of Faith, the London Confession of 1689, or the Savoy Declaration.

The articles in this volume represent well the kinds of issues with which WRF members are concerned. The theme of the Second General Assembly, at which these papers were delivered, was "*Masibambisane*," a Zulu word meaning "Let us carry the burden together." We invite you, the reader of these materials, to join us in carrying the burdens and in seizing the opportunities described herein.

To give you some idea about the present membership of the World Reformed Fellowship, below is a list of members as of May 21, 2007.

Membership in the WRF is free; for information about joining, contact me at samueltlogan@aol.com or at 430 Montier Road, Glenside, PA 19038 USA.

I hope you enjoy and benefit from these materials, and I look forward to hearing from you.

Samuel T. Logan Jr.
Executive Secretary

PART ONE

THEOLOGICAL
FOUNDATIONS

CHAPTER ONE

THE EVANGELISTIC CONTEXT OF BURDEN SHARING

PETER JENSEN

When the Gentiles heard this, they were glad and honored the word of the Lord; and all who were appointed for eternal life believed.

ACTS 13:48, NIV

Last Christmas a friend of mine gave a couple of his non-Christian friends a gift. They unwrapped it and found that it was an evangelistic book, a book about Jesus. He was watching their faces, and they seemed so disappointed, as though they had rejected him and his gift. Despite their rejection, it was what I call "a mission moment."

There are times in the history of the church when there seems to be a hunger for the gospel, and fruit falls easily off the tree. But, in the West at least, we are not living in that sort of moment. Many times, though, we may come across a mission moment like the one my friend experienced, if we are involved in evangelism. In fact, most of us don't like getting involved in evangelism because most of us like to be liked, and most of us prefer a quiet life.

Even the business of giving our friends an evangelistic book is sometimes, so it seems to us, a bridge too far. And yet, those mission moments, those evangelistic moments, have a sort of typical quality.

As we commend Christ to the world there is a typical quality of disturbance. The gospel of Jesus Christ asks so much of us that when we commend it truly we create turmoil.

Indeed, we can trace this experience of the mission moment right back through history to the New Testament itself. There is nothing strange about it. So the passage that appears at the beginning of this chapter, Acts 13, is at that point a typical mission moment. It was unique, of course, but it is also commonplace.

It was unique because there were unique persons in a unique place at a unique time. But it was unique in another sense: it was primary, it was the first time, it was the early days, when evangelism was just beginning to occur, and every evangelistic opportunity was more or less a first time. It was also one of the moments when decisions had to be made about whether the gospel was for the Jews only or also for the Gentiles. Of course, it became perfectly clear that the gospel had to go to the Gentiles as well as to the Jews. This was the moment when the Christian faith was ceasing to be merely a Jewish thing and began to be a worldwide thing.

The point of issue, you'll find as you look back further in the passage, was that those Jews rejected the teaching of the Lord Jesus. The apostle says in verses 38–39 (NIV) of this passage, "My brothers, I want you to know that through Jesus the forgiveness of sins is proclaimed to you. Through him everyone who believes is justified from everything you could not be justified from by the Law of Moses." Here is a moment in which the Law of Moses came under attack as a means of justification. The apostle made it perfectly clear that what Jesus offered by way of forgiveness of sins was something that could not be offered under the Law of Moses. The consequence was that this whole gospel movement was going to spill out over and beyond those who gave adherence to the Law of Moses, into the world. What we are looking at here is a little snapshot of the beginnings of a "grace-quake." An extraordinary event was just occurring here with effects that go on and on to this very day.

It was unique, and yet, on the other hand, it is commonplace. After all, what we have here is the Word being spoken, the speakers of the Word, Paul and Barnabas, and the listeners to the Word. In every mission moment we follow the same pattern as they did. We too speak the disturbing Word, perhaps beginning with an evangelistic book as my friend did, or perhaps by saying the Word that will lead someone to say, "Yes, I believe in Christ." In any case, there are a messenger, a message, and a hearer. What they did there has been successively done down through the years and down through the generations. They started that which we are continuing. You can trace all the way back to where they were from where we are. We are simply doing what they taught us to do. This unique event is also a commonplace event.

As we think about what a mission moment may entail then, let us see what they did and learn from them, the pioneers. I note three things in particular: First, that this mission moment was verbal—there was much human speech; second, that it involved interaction—there was much human listening; and third, that despite all the human activity, the mission moment belonged to God.

First, it was verbal. I make such an obvious point for a key reason. Many Christians have lost their nerve when it comes to words. When the Bible came under sustained assault in the eighteenth and nineteenth centuries, many Christians found their authority in religious experience. They preferred the path of mysticism—of a wordless encounter with the divine that can only be described, if at all, in stumbling, error-filled, human words. Commending the way of Christ is turned into living the life, without words. The result is that there is no gospel to preach and no assurance or certainty about the things of God. Not surprisingly, in many Western countries, Christianity appears to be in its death throes, since the Christians do not understand that we make Christians through the verbal gospel, and we may have confidence in the words that God himself has spoken.

Acts 13 reveals that a lot of words were spoken in this classic mission moment. Indeed, the reason they were able to preach the gospel was that the ruler of the synagogue invited them to speak, to have a message of encouragement. As a result, Paul gave the most extraordinary message of encouragement that those hearers had ever encountered. He announced that the Son of David, Jesus, had come, and although David was still in his tomb, this One had risen from the dead. Here was a new and living King demanding a full allegiance. He finished in the most startling way, by saying that through Jesus there is forgiveness of sins—you may be justified from all the things that you cannot be justified from by the Law of Moses. It was an electrifying, turbulent sermon.

The apostle himself called it the word of the Lord. Look at verse 44, for example: "the whole city gathered to hear the word of the Lord." Verse 48 as well: "when the Gentiles heard this, they were glad and glorified the word of the Lord." It is also called "the word of God" in verse 46 of the passage. Paul and Barnabas answered them boldly, "we had to speak the word of God to you first."

Here is a word of unsurpassable authority. The Word of the Lord, the Word of the living God—there is no other word greater or more authoritative than this Word. When the Christian evangelist shares the gospel, whether in a quiet one-to one occasion or before a large crowd, it is shared as a Word of the Lord. It doesn't come with some lower authority; it doesn't come tremulously as though it is just an opinion. On the contrary, this gospel we share is the Word of the Lord, or it is nothing, and it comes therefore with his authority. In that we may take great confidence in our evangelistic work.

We are not simply sharing human opinions, but we are sharing that which has come to us from the Lord himself and is all about the Lord. It is the Word of the Lord because it comes from the Lord, and it is the Word of the Lord because it is about the Lord. He is the content of this Word as well as the author of this Word. And yet it comes through human messengers.

How did they communicate it? I'm sure they did it with a smile. I'm sure they did it with their lives. I'm sure they were aware of the limits of their knowledge of God. But in the end you communicate the Word by speaking.

There are a number of different words used in and around this passage describing verbal communication:

> They spoke the word of the Lord;
>   they talked to people.

There is an interesting word in verse 43: "the congregation was dismissed," and "Paul and Barnabas talked with them and urged them to continue in the grace of God." They "urged" or "persuaded" them to continue in the grace of God. Here is a sense of urgency, of strong speech.

Or look at verse 46: "Paul and Barnabas answered them boldly." They spoke with great assurance and great boldness.

Of course, they had to speak thus because it was in the face of contradiction and rejection. They spoke, they talked, they persuaded, they urged, they spoke boldly. Look more widely in the Book of Acts, and you will see all sorts of words used for this activity of transmitting the Word of the Lord. They debated, they lectured, they preached, they spoke boldly, they chatted, they conversed. They were immensely flexible in method; they used all sorts of words to serve the Word of the Lord and to bring it home to the listeners. But, of course, it remained a word, and the Word of the Lord at that.

When they spoke, God spoke. When they gave his Word, the listeners, if they responded favorably to the Word, if they were persuaded by the Word, heard not the human messenger but God himself speaking. They received not, as it were, simply the word of human beings, but they received it as the Word of God himself.

And yet this Word of the Lord didn't come, so to speak, from the heavens. As we know, the way in which the Lord almost always speaks is through human messengers. He uses ambassadors—ambassadors for Christ—to transmit his messages. We see in the apostles, and the apostles' friends and their fellow missionaries, all sorts of different words used in the service of the Word of the Lord.

That is to say, it is God's usual method in dealing with us to use human messengers and to use the human resources of the human messengers. He makes full use of the way in which we human beings communicate with each other. He doesn't bypass us in this, but gloriously he incorporates us. How graciously he does so. We don't think for a moment, presumably, that God needs us to transmit his message. God is the master of language. He invented language. I take it that if God wished to evangelize the world using his own voice, so to speak, he could do so whenever he pleased. But in the kindness and mercy of God in his plans for how the world is to be evangelized, he takes up and uses and incorporates our foolish efforts in his great work.

A small number of people have spent their lives translating the Scriptures into some of the languages of the Australian Aboriginal people. They have been giving their lives to the transmission of the Word into the languages of what is, after all, only a small group of people. This is one of the most loving of projects. Does God need it? I don't doubt that God knows all the languages and is able to speak as he will in any language directly. But in his grace and mercy he uses our feeble efforts and even overrules our feeble efforts. Feeble though they are, he still enables us to be the bearers of his good news.

What a mercy from God! What a privilege we have to be the bearers of his gospel. How foolish we are when we become shy, and diffident, and unwilling to speak. How foolish we are when we fear rejection. How foolish we are when we want to be liked and therefore we don't speak. How foolish we are when we don't trust God's words, and don't trust God to bring salvation through his words. How much we deny ourselves the enormous privilege that God has given us to be part of his work. In this, we are not following the apostles. *The mission moment was verbal.*

Second, notice that the whole occasion of this mission moment involved very human interactions—the audience did not sit still. There was listening, and there was response. The speakers were met with acceptance, as verse 42 tells us, for example. The people invited them to speak further about these things the next Sabbath. There was a great deal of interest in what they had to say. They were met with hearing. On the Sabbath "almost the whole city" gathered together, we are told in verse 44, to hear the Word of the Lord. What a thrill that must have been, to see everybody there to hear the Word of the Lord.

They were met with a welcome, but they were also met with contradiction and slander. Look at verse 45—"when the Jews saw the crowds, they were filled with jealousy and talked abusively against what Paul was saying." They contradicted and slandered the Word of the Lord. So amidst the words of this gospel, the Word of the Lord being spoken, there is this human anger being expressed, human jealousy, nasty words, malicious words, strong words against what was being said, not just against the messengers, but also against the message.

And then later there was an incitement to persecution. If you look at verse 50, the "Jews incited the God-fearing women of high standing and the leading men of the city." They stirred up persecution against Paul. All these words were being spoken too. There is a lot of talk going on in this whole passage, and some of it is pretty nasty talk. There was an incitement to persecution. They did not like the Word of the Lord. And eventually, of course, as we know, there was rejection of Paul and Barnabas, and they were actually expelled from that region.

The gospel word is a gracious word. The gospel word is a word of God's love. The gospel word is a word to be spoken where possible with grace. But the rejection of the gospel is an immensely serious matter. There comes a moment of decision against the hearers: "so they shook the dust from their feet in protest against them and went to Iconium." That phrase "they shook the dust from their feet" was a sort of reverse sacrament. It was a visible word of the judgment of God.

The gospel preachers, with the gospel of the grace of God on their lips, also spoke the word of judgment. For the gospel word of grace only makes sense in the context also of judgment. And when the people rejected the preachers, and expelled them, and did not want to hear them anymore, then the judgment of God came upon those who expelled them. They judged themselves, and in judging themselves they were paving their way to the judgment of God himself.

The words in which we deal are not just words. They are mighty and powerful words. They are tremendously significant words. They are words of make or break. They are words of life-changing significance. They are words on which eternity hangs. The rejection of the words, and the rejection of the minister of the words, is not personal. It is really, in the end, a rejection of God himself. And the rejection of God will lead to the judgment of God. The issues are that significant.

Yes, evangelism is hard, isn't it? It's hard for us. Here is a mission moment, and it is pretty typical of mission moments around the word, full of tension, full of disagreement, full of joy as people become Christians, but full of anger as well. Full of welcome, but full of rejection. That's very typical of mission moments. That is why we don't want to get involved, because we don't like hostility, and we don't like rejection. We want to be liked.

We ask ourselves sometimes, why is it so hard to share the gospel with others? Why is it so difficult? Why doesn't God come right in and make it a great deal easier? There doesn't seem to be any detour. But remember there was no detour back then either. It wasn't as though Paul drew himself up to his full height and said, "I'm an ambassador of the living God, stand back. I'm staying here whether you want me or not." It wasn't as though Paul had a 100 percent rate of converting people. You know as well as I do that his missionary efforts were marked with rejection, with pain and suffering, with shipwreck, and sore feet, and being stoned and imprisoned. In all that he was simply following the path of his Master.

In the end, you see—and this is the third point—the mission moment, like the gospel itself, does not belong to us, even if we think that we have initiated it or spoken it. God graciously allows us to be part of it, but it belongs to him.

Even the nature of the gospel itself stands as a testimony, not to human effort, but to the kindness of God, the grace of God, both in giving us the gospel and in sending forth the gospel. Remember, the gospel was a message of the grace of God. We have seen that already in those verses I've quoted. "Through him everyone who believes is justified from everything you could not be justified from by the law of Moses. . . . Through Jesus the forgiveness of sins is proclaimed to you." That is the message, the essential message, the essence of the message of the grace of God in the death of our Lord Jesus Christ who died as our substitute on the cross to take away our sins. That is the most wonderful message in all the world. It is the message of the grace and mercy of God. It only makes sense, of course, if you understand the judgment of God.

The very word "justified" reminds you of that. How are you going to be justified? Only through the mercy and grace of the Lord Jesus Christ, who bore the punishment for sin, bore the judgment that we should have borne.

Receiving this means continuing in it. Look at what the apostle and Barnabas say in verse 43—"who talked with them and urged them to continue in the grace of God." *Continue* believing in the forgiveness of sins. *Continue* believing in the love of God. *Continue* believing that you are justified, despite the fact that you cannot be justified by the Law. You are justified by the grace of God through the simple act of faith in God, repentance. The gospel is a gospel of grace. Receive the gospel, continue in the grace of God in the gospel. *Continue* trusting in your heavenly Father who has been revealed to you through the powerful Holy Spirit in the gospel of the grace of the Lord Jesus Christ. *Continue* in grace. The gospel, of course, belongs to God because it was under his command.

Here we see that for all the human turmoil and speaking and acting and accepting and rejecting, the whole mission moment belonged to God and was under his control. The Jews, even the Law-abiding Jews, did not deserve the forgiveness of sins and the mercy of God. The Gentiles—so far outside the boundaries of the mercy of God, so degenerate and idolatrous—certainly did not deserve any part in the forgiveness of sins and the mercy of God.

But look: here was a crucial, pivotal moment in the history of the gospel because it was in and through these events when the Jews stirred up controversy and rejection that the Gentiles began to hear the gospel. Have a look at verse 46: "Since you reject it and do not consider yourselves worthy of eternal life, we now turn to the Gentiles." They judged themselves, didn't they? Those particular hearers did not consider themselves worthy of eternal life, and the judgment of God would follow upon the judgment they laid upon themselves. But even in the catastrophe of judgment and rejection we see the triumph of God's mercy. For this is what the Lord has revealed, that it was in the rejection by those who heard first that the light of the gospel went forth to the rest of us—"I have made you a light for the Gentiles, that you may bring salvation to the ends of the earth."

We are looking here at another of those little crucial moments in the history of God's people, where suddenly the gospel is going to spill the banks and go forth until the whole world is encompassed in the gospel of the Lord Jesus Christ, so that it even reaches Tasmania. The gospel has reached to the ends of the world, and here we see the beginning of that process as those people rejected Christ, and in their rejection there came the spilling out of the gospel among the Gentiles. And God directed it. The apostle says, yes, it's happened, and God said it would happen. You see, even the rejection of the gospel, painful still to hear about and painful for the apostles to experience, did not frustrate God. Just as he did at the cross, God used the rejection itself to set his great saving work forward.

He has directed that the Jewish apostles now go to the Gentiles, that from Israel would come the saving truth. And why did this happen? Because it was the nature of the gospel itself. Because the gospel is grace: "you are justified from the things that you cannot be justified from by the law of Moses." Because of the absolute gracious heart of the gospel, it could not be for the Jewish nation alone. It had to be for men and women of all nations all around the world.

And that, dear brothers and sisters, is precisely why we are here at this General Assembly of the World Reformed Fellowship. We are here not just to feed our souls and to enjoy our fellowship. We are here because we are committed to the gospel going to all the world. Our love ought to reflect the love of God in the gospel and therefore be for all people. The gospel belongs to God. And ultimately we come to the text in verse 48: "when the Gentiles heard this, they were glad and they glorified the word of the Lord; and all who were appointed for eternal life believed."

Yes, in the end, it is true that God graciously uses us. Yes, it is true that we have to bring our best to his service. It is true that we have to spend thirty years translating the Bible into the language of just a few peoples, relatively speaking. Yes, it's true that we must give our best for this. Yes, it's true that he graciously uses our feeble efforts and our somewhat better efforts sometimes to bring people to himself.

But the truth of the matter, the underlying truth, is that it is all his work. Note this: "all who were appointed for eternal life believed." Not all; it wasn't universal. There were many who still rejected it, and the apostle says they don't count themselves worthy of eternal life—they bring their rejection upon their own selves. But underneath it all, by the powerful work of the Holy Spirit of God, in line with his determination before the foundation of the world, his elect are being summoned home. And when God summons the dead to life, they come to life, not by any power within themselves, but by the mighty power of his Holy Spirit taking his Word and bringing his Word to life in the hearts and souls of people. When we see the Gentiles full of joy and glorifying God's Word, we know it is not because the better people have chosen God, or the cleverer people have chosen God. No, we know it is because God has chosen them.

If you are here tonight as a believer, as one who belongs to the Lord Jesus Christ and rejoices in the grace of God and glorifies the Word of the Lord, if you are here tonight as one who has chosen the Lord, I trust you realize you have chosen the Lord because he has first chosen you. You belong to the Lord because he has chosen that you belong to him, because he has appointed you to eternal life. If you are here tonight rejoicing in the grace and mercy of God, that he has saved you, unworthy as you are, then you must see too that there is no point thinking that there is a little bit of worthiness in you, namely, that you chose him. Indeed, your choice only reflects his choice of you. Continue in that grace. All is of grace, dear brothers and sisters. All is of grace. In the end it has nothing to do with you. God chose you, and that is why you chose him.

> *O the love that drew salvation's plan!*
> *O the grace that brought it down to man!*
> *O the mighty gulf that God did span at Calvary.*
> *Mercy there was great and grace was free,*
> *Pardon there was multiplied to me,*
> *There my burdened soul found liberty—*
> *At Calvary.*

I hope you have lots of mission moments. I hope you take courage. We live in desperate times. People need to know about Jesus, and God's appointed method is to use you and to use me. I hope you have lots of mission moments in the next month and the next year. Despite the fact that you don't like rejection, and the fact that you do like to be liked, and the fact that you like a quiet life, I hope you won't let those fears stand in the way.

How are you going to be encouraged to do it? What's going to keep you going in the face of rejection and hostility and people looking at you with that look when they unwrap their Christmas present? What's going to keep you going? Only God's grace. Only the fact that it is God's gracious gospel that has saved you. God's grace has captured your heart, and you want others to know that grace—not because you are better or because you are a spiritual giant or because you are a wonderful person or a moral person. None of these things is true. It is just that you have received grace, and you want others to receive it too.

And what will keep you going is that you can trust God for it all. In the end you are not going to convert anybody. In the end it is not your business. It is God's. He will use you, but he will use you graciously to allow you to be part of his purposes as he brings home his own people. In the end, the mission moment doesn't rely on us, but on him: For as many as were appointed unto eternal life *will* believe.

CHAPTER TWO

THE BIBLICAL MANDATE OF UNITY IN BURDEN SHARING

RIC CANNADA

Behold, how good and pleasant it is when brothers dwell in unity! It is like the precious oil on the head, running down on the beard, on the beard of Aaron, running down on the collar of his robes! It is like the dew of Hermon, which falls on the mountains of Zion! For there the LORD has commanded the blessing, life forevermore.

PSALM 133:1–3, ESV

Psalm 133 is one of those psalms or songs that we refer to as the Psalms of Ascent. These were psalms that the people of God would sing especially on their way to Jerusalem for one of the three great feast days of the year as they would ascend toward Jerusalem. As those who have visited Israel realize, Jerusalem is elevated compared to the land around it, so you ascend toward Jerusalem from any direction. Most of the people would have been walking or riding on a camel or a donkey, or some perhaps riding in a chariot. Still, they would all be going up, ascending to Jerusalem and singing as they went, gathering with people from other tribes and villages along the way.

I believe that one of the psalms they would have loved most was this one, because it speaks about the unity they had together as they came from various backgrounds. They often did not know one another; but they were all gathering for the same purpose, to worship the one true and living God.

UNITY IS GOOD AND PLEASANT

Notice that there is a proverbial statement at the beginning of this psalm—"Behold, how good and pleasant it is when brothers dwell in unity!"—and then two illustrations of this proverbial truth. That sense of blessing when brothers dwell together in unity is like oil and like water. One of the illustrations may seem strange to us at first. The other illustration is easier to understand and appreciate.

The first illustration is the strange one. The good and pleasant feeling when brothers gather in unity is like precious oil being poured on the head of Aaron so profusely that it runs down his beard and even down to the edge, the hem, of his robes. That does not sound good and pleasant to us. It sounds dirty and messy. We need to remember, however, that the oil was perfumed and that they did not bathe often in those days. Perhaps that is why they saw this as a blessing. Or as someone else has suggested, perhaps it seemed so good and pleasant because the oil was poured on Aaron and not on them!

We should remember that oil itself in the Scriptures is a symbol of blessing. Here the blessing is poured on Aaron as the representative of the people of God. If they had ever seen one of Aaron's descendants ordained as a priest, they would have seen oil perhaps sprinkled or even poured, but never poured profusely, not this way. Here we have the image of the oil poured out so profusely that it runs down his beard all the way to the hem of his robe. This is a symbol of God's great blessing upon them as the people of God through his blessing of their representative. That would certainly be a good and pleasant thought. That is what the psalmist says it is like when brothers dwell together in unity. It is like the blessing of God poured all over Aaron as our representative and therefore his blessing poured all over us.

The psalm provides a second illustration of this sense of joy and blessing when brothers dwell together in unity. The second illustration makes a little more sense to us, using water, not oil. The blessing when brothers dwell together in unity is like the dew of Mount Hermon coming down on the mountains of Zion around Jerusalem, for there the

Lord commanded the blessing, life forevermore. Hermon is a mountain approximately one hundred miles north of Jerusalem. It is a very high mountain, and it is snow-covered much of the year. This affects the weather patterns in that region. The area around Mount Hermon is more lush and green than is true farther south around Jerusalem.

Whether you have been to Israel or have merely seen pictures of it, you realize that the area around Jerusalem is very arid, rocky, and dusty. It is amazing what the modern Israelis have done with irrigation. You can see very green fields and then right next to them fields that are very rocky and dry. Actually, if you look very closely even at those green fields you will see that they are full of rocks. How in the world agricultural equipment gets through those fields without being badly damaged, I do not understand. The illustration in the psalm is one of the heavy dew around green Mount Hermon falling instead around dry Jerusalem.

Apparently they have a weather pattern in Israel similar to our jet stream that will occasionally pick up the weather pattern around Mount Hermon and carry it as far south as Jerusalem. Once when we were in Israel, I asked our Israeli guide about this weather pattern, and she confirmed that this would happen from time to time. Even small amounts of moisture would immediately cause things to sprout green in those desert areas around Jerusalem. You can imagine these families traveling to Jerusalem for one of the great feast days, perhaps traveling a long distance and having to spend the night on the road along the way. The land is dusty and arid, and the air is hot. Then they wake up the next morning, and the dew of Mount Hermon has fallen, and the ground is moist and wet and the air is cool. What a joy, what a blessing that would be for the rest of their journey into Jerusalem. That is what the psalmist says it is like when brothers dwell together in unity.

UNITY IN THE FAMILY OF GOD

Consider two primary lessons from this psalm. First, the psalmist is encouraging us, urging us, about the importance of unity among the *brethren*, unity in *the family of God*. The psalmist was not encouraging the Israelites to be unified with their pagan neighbors. He was not urging them to be unified with the Egyptians, or the Assyrians, or the Babylonians, or the Philistines, or the Canaanites. Instead, they were to be separate from those people and their idols and to focus their worship on Yahweh (Jehovah), the only true and living God. Also the Lord is not urging us through this psalm to be unified with other religions. We in the Reformed faith are especially known for our commitment to the truth. We do not believe in unity at all costs. We do not believe in unity at the expense of truth, particularly essential truth.

My pastor in my youth was Dr. John Reed Miller. Through much of his ministry Dr. Miller tried to meet with the youth in the church when they were seniors in high school to spend some time with them individually before they left home. I remember during my senior year we had breakfast together at the Holiday Inn on Interstate 55 in north Jackson. I was planning to move to Nashville and had enrolled at Vanderbilt University. We talked about my future, and he told me one of the wisest things anyone has ever said to me outside of the Scriptures. Dr. Miller said that when you start looking for a church, you will know the liberal preacher not so much by what he says as by what he does not say. Normally what that preacher says will be okay. It will be what you can hear at any civic club: be nice, be kind, be loving, and don't kick the dog or the cat. It is what he does not say that is the problem. He will not get to the heart of the matter—the reality of sin and salvation, of heaven and hell, of the absolute uniqueness of Jesus Christ and his virgin birth, his substitutionary death on the cross and his bodily resurrection, and the essential importance of trusting Jesus Christ alone for our salvation. It is not so much what he says that is the problem; it is what he does not say. In this way and others, Dr. Miller taught me the importance of standing for truth.

During my twenty years as a pastor, I became convinced that the greatest heresy in our day is summarized in a phrase that sounds good and right. We hear it so often that it sounds like motherhood and apple pie. How could it be false? It is the phrase, *the fatherhood of God and the brotherhood of man*. It sounds great and true, doesn't it—the universal fatherhood of God and brotherhood of man? We hear this statement from the media. We hear it from the politicians. We hear it from many preachers. We hear it in many different places, and we hear it often, but it is exactly the opposite of what the Bible teaches. It is a statement straight from hell.

John 1:12 (ESV) says, "But to all who did receive him, who believed in his name, he gave the right to become children of God." If we become children of God through our faith in Jesus Christ, what were we beforehand? Obviously we were not children of God. What were we then? Children of Satan? Surely not, and yet that is exactly what the Bible teaches. It is what Jesus said to the Pharisees: "You are of your father the devil" (John 8:44, ESV). We are all children of Satan, children of wrath, until we become children of God through our faith in Jesus Christ, until we are adopted into his family. God is not, therefore, the father of everyone. He is the father of those who are in the family, those who are Christians. We are all his creatures, even his highest creation created in his image, but we are not all his children.

Also, we are not brothers and sisters with everyone, only brothers and sisters with other Christians. Can we then treat non-Christians any way we desire? Of course not. The Bible says, "Love your neighbor as yourself" (Matthew 22:39, NIV), Christian or non-Christian, whoever he or she is. The Bible also says, in Galatians 6:10 (ESV), "let us do good to everyone, and especially to those who are of the household of faith," those who are in the family. There is a difference between those who are in the family and those who are not. One of the major problems with the phrase *the fatherhood of God and the brotherhood of man* is that it subtly teaches and implies universalism. If God were the father of everyone, would he send any of his children to hell? Of course not. But that is not what the Bible teaches at all. It teaches that we are not all in the family, that we must be adopted into the family of God through faith in Jesus Christ. Psalm 133 is encouraging us to be unified, but in a spiritual sense only with those who are in the family of God.

Those in the USA today live in a pluralistic society where we properly allow people to worship in different ways or to have no religion at all. Thankfully, we have a government that is historically theistic. In our founding documents a government is based on a belief in a Creator God, and we are united in this sense as Americans. We put this on our money, and we say it in the Pledge of Allegiance to our flag along with people from other religions, that we are one nation under God. We even sing along with others, "God bless America," acknowledging a Creator God. We can also use this as a witness to our fellow Americans, as Paul did in Athens when he talked about the unknown God they worshiped there. We can say, "This Creator God to whom we refer on our coins and in our pledge, you can know him personally through Jesus Christ as you come to know and understand who Jesus is."

There is a distinction, however, that we need to remember: there is only one true and living God, and we come to know him in a saving way and come into his family in only one way, through faith in Jesus Christ. In this sense, we are urged to be unified, in this special way, only with other believers in Christ, with those who are truly our brothers and sisters spiritually.

THE WORK OF UNITY

There is a second lesson to notice in Psalm 133, that we are to remember the importance of *unity* among the brethren. Why does the psalmist even need to say this? Aren't we already unified since we are in the same spiritual family, without any problems or conflicts? Well, we are still sinners, although saved by grace. The church, the people of God—his family—are filled with divisions, strife, heartache, difficulty, and conflict. We grumble and complain, we envy and covet, we are full of jealousy and greed and malice and strife and anger and wrath. Every book in the Bible asks us to believe truth, to get our minds straight. Every book in the Bible also teaches us to get our hearts and lives straight as we promote love and unity. Why is this necessary? Because we are still sinners, and we still need to work on love and unity in the family of God. It does not merely happen automatically among Christians. That is why the psalmist taught them to sing this psalm to one another, to encourage them to think about unity and to work on unity. He reminds us of the blessing of unity but also that this unity does not just happen. We must work at unity.

In the first half of his letter to the Ephesians, Paul teaches about the dividing wall between the Jews and the Gentiles that has been torn down in Christ to bring unity between these two groups in the one family of God. Then Paul has to spend the second half of Ephesians telling both groups to live and act like it, to display their unity. He begs them to be forbearing, to be patient with one another, to work at love, and to remember that they have one faith and one baptism. Paul urges them not to lie to each other or steal from one another, not to have malice or greed, but to forgive each other. Why does he have to say all of that?

Because of their sin and our sin. We, too, have to work at unity in the family of God.

I tell our students at Reformed Theological Seminary that in some ways it is more difficult today to be a pastor than ever before. Thankfully, in the United States today we are not faced with physical persecution in the sense of being put in prison and beaten or killed for our faith, although we may face this again in the future even in our country. We do face great difficulties, however, in terms of social pressures, and I think this is primarily for two reasons.

One reason for our difficulties is the variety of expectations within every congregation today. It used to be that everyone stayed generally in the same location and in the same church generation after generation, and the job description for the pastor was clear even when it was not written. The pastor knew what he was supposed to do, and the people had a clear understanding of the pastor's role, but that is not true anymore. Every congregation everywhere in the United States is a mixture of people from all sorts of backgrounds with very different and deep-seated preferences in worship style, music style, and ministry style. They have differences over what the minister is supposed to do and whether he is to spend more of his time in study and prayer or in administration and pastoral work. I am sure it has always been true that a preacher could never please everyone. Now it is true, however, that whatever a preacher does or says, a significant minority in the congregation will deeply disagree with him. Since this is the case, we have to work hard at unity.

A second major reason for the difficulties facing pastors today is the super-high expectations in every church. Because of communication and the media and travel today, we are aware of what everyone else and every other church is doing. We, therefore, are aware of the best preachers and the best music programs and the most varied ministries, including outstanding youth and children's programs, and we are always comparing our church and our pastor with others. When you put those two things together, a wide variety of expectations and super-high expectations, you can see why it is very difficult to be a pastor today. It is a challenge to be unified as a congregation. We must work at love, caring, forgiveness, understanding, patience, and many other virtues. What a blessing, what a joy, how good and pleasant it is, however, when brothers do dwell together in unity!

When I think of this blessing of unity, I do not think of the illustrations the psalmist uses in Psalm 133. I certainly do not think of oil being poured all over me or over anyone else. I might think of water and how grateful we are for water after a long time without rain, but we are usually blessed with water where I live.

The illustration of unity that comes to my mind is one of a family reunion. I have a large extended family with many cousins and aunts and uncles. We have our differences as all families do, but it is really a great family. We generally love to get together at weddings, and even funerals, and on all sorts of occasions. It is a joy to be together. That is not true of every family. Some people come from families that are so divided that when they do have to get together they dread it for weeks or months ahead of time and hate to have to go to the family event. Then when they do go, they hate it the whole time they are there and cannot wait to leave. How sad that is! How good it is when families are united! Isn't that what heaven is going to be like?

One of the most beautiful pictures of heaven in the Bible is one of a great big, joyful family reunion, at the wedding feast of the Lamb and his bride (Revelation 19). In a sense, when we gather for worship each Sunday, it ought to be a mini family reunion, a foretaste of heaven, as the family of God is gathering to worship him. As we drive in our cars to worship with our families, instead of walking or riding on donkeys or camels as the Israelites did, we ought to be singing this psalm with our children, reminding ourselves and our children how good it is when brothers dwell together in unity. What a joy it is when that unity is present, and how hard we should work at it!

BECOMING UNIFIED

What about you? If I asked the person who normally sits next to you or behind you or your family in your church to tell of your impact and influence in your congregation, how would that person describe you? Would they describe you as one who is full of criticism and complaint, always grumbling about something, always causing problems and division and strife and conflict? Or would that person describe you as a unifier, as an encourager, one who is supportive and joyful?

There is a time for speaking the truth, even when it causes problems—speaking the truth in the right way, speaking the truth in love. The first part of this message emphasized the importance of truth. Also, the Lord loves variety and does not insist on uniformity, on all of us being just alike, but he does want unity. How important is it for us to be in unity as the people of God? Jesus prayed fervently in his high-priestly prayer the night before he died that we might be one, as he and the Father are one. In Proverbs 6:16–19, KJV there are seven things listed that the Lord hates, and the climax of those things that the Lord hates is "he that soweth discord among brethren." What about you? Are you one who stirs up dissension among the brethren?

Years ago my wife and I were privileged to travel to Israel with an organization called The Fellowship of Evangelical Seminary Presidents. It is a group from many different backgrounds and denominations. On this trip there were Presbyterians and Methodists and Baptists and Nazarenes and Episcopalians. There were seminary presidents representing two different denominations of The Church of God and the Assemblies of God and others. We came from very different backgrounds, but we all were evangelical Christians who loved the Lord Jesus Christ. We had a special time near the garden tomb celebrating Communion together.

Then on Sunday morning we were in the "upper room," and we shared this psalm, Psalm 133. We stood in a circle, held hands, and prayed together. Then we sang, "We are one in the Spirit; we are one in the Lord. We are one in the Spirit; we are one in the Lord. And we pray that one day all unity will be restored, and they will know we are Christians by our love, by our love. They will know we are Christians by our love." It still gives me chills when I think about that time, a special time, when in spite of our differences there was a palpable sense of God's presence and of joy as we experienced the blessing of unity among the brethren. We had all kinds of differences among us, and at times we would be honest and discuss these differences. More importantly, however, we were unified in our love for our Lord Jesus. We are a part of the same family, and what a joy it is when we can experience that together.

If this blessing of unity can be true of Christians from many different traditions, how much more so should it be true for those who share the same commitments in our Reformed heritage! As Reformed Christians who are historically orthodox and evangelical and confessional, we should be unified and enjoy the blessing of that unity at this General Assembly of the World Reformed Fellowship.

But this doesn't just happen. We are called to work at unity and to remind ourselves of the importance of it. We are to seek to understand and appreciate each other, to forgive one another, and to love one another, to speak the truth in love, and also to love in such a way that our love covers over a multitude of sins.

Finally, I appreciate what Derek Kidner says in his commentary on this psalm, that no matter how hard we work at unity, it does not merely come from our efforts. True unity must come from the Lord. Kidner points out that the Hebrew word sometimes translated here "descending" or "running down" or "falling down" is actually used three times in Psalm 133. The oil descends on Aaron's beard and on his robe, and the dew of Mount Hermon descends around Mount Zion. The blessing of unity ultimately descends from the triune God. "It is a gift from above. It is bestowed rather than contrived, a blessing far more than an achievement." So we look to our Lord for the blessing of unity as we pray to him together.

CHAPTER THREE

THE DANGER OF DISUNITY IN BURDEN SHARING

IN WHAN KIM

We who are strong have an obligation to bear with the failings of the weak, and not to please ourselves. Let each of us please his neighbor for his good, to build him up. For Christ did not please himself, but as it is written, "The reproaches of those who reproached you fell on me." For whatever was written in former days was written for our instruction, that through endurance and through the encouragement of the Scriptures we might have hope. May the God of endurance and encouragement grant you to live in such harmony with one another, in accord with Christ Jesus, that together you may with one voice glorify the God and Father of our Lord Jesus Christ.

ROMANS 15:1–6, ESV

The late Dr. Seung Man Rhee was the first President of the Republic of Korea, and when Koreans were fighting one another after their liberation from Japanese rule, he urged his countrymen to set aside their relatively minor differences in order to create a genuine national unity. His words were strong: "If united, you shall prosper; if dispersed, you shall perish."

This truth has been demonstrated over and over again, not only in the lives of our nations but also in our personal lives. This is exactly the point that Solomon makes when he says, in Ecclesiastes 4:12 (NIV), that "Though one may be overpowered, two can defend themselves. A cord of three strands is not quickly broken."

In the passage from Romans 15, the apostle Paul asks God to give his church the spirit of unity *so that*, with one heart and mouth, the church may glorify the God and Father of our Lord Jesus Christ. Such a prayer is most appropriate to us today because we, as Reformed and evangelical Christians, have gathered from all over the world specifically to strengthen our unity. In fact, our gathering in this General Assembly of the World Reformed Fellowship represents a partial fulfillment of Paul's prayer, but just a *partial* fulfillment. It is our biblical responsibility, in light of Romans 15, to commit ourselves to strengthening this spirit of unity further among Reformed believers around the world so that our churches and our theological schools and our other church-related organizations can respond to the challenges facing all of us in such a way that the God and Father of our Lord Jesus Christ will be glorified.

With this in mind, and as we move into the last full day of this General Assembly, I would like to have us consider together exactly what the Bible does and does not mean by *unity*. I would then like to suggest some possible applications of this biblical definition.

First, we must always remember that unity was one of the hallmarks of the original creation. The creation narratives envision an essential and critical unity of all of God's creatures in terms of origin and accountability: the heavens and the earth, man and woman, and all other creatures under the sovereign lordship of the Creator. Further, since the creation is the revelation of the triune God and since he, three persons in one Godhead, embodies unity in diversity, all of creation must somehow also reflect unity in diversity, even if that reflection is not yet fully understood.

Therefore, the unity of the people of God is neither accidental nor a production of human need. It is rather a fundamental and God-ordained order of human life. To the degree that we are living out the *imago Dei*, to that very degree will we, and must we, live lives of unity with others under his sovereign lordship.

But not only is unity a creational reality, it is also a covenantal reality. When God created man and woman in his image, he made a covenant with them and united man and woman into one body in terms of the marital bond. He gave them a single covenant mandate to fill the earth and to subdue it as his vicegerent so that mankind and the world together in unity might be his kingdom and dwelling place. Even though the first man and woman rebelled against him and broke this covenant, God never nullified his creation covenant mandate. He rather renewed his covenant relationship with them to continue to fulfill his single creational purpose. Under this renewed covenant, which we call the covenant of redemption, God stipulated that the fallen man and the fallen woman would fulfill the mandate "by his grace." It is still the same mandate—that all things be brought under his kingdom authority.

The sealing process of covenant making under the covenant of redemption functioned to make this unity visible. God appointed circumcision to be the seal of the Abrahamic covenant. The circumcision sealed either aliens or descendants of Abraham to be the legitimate members of the body of the seed of Abraham. The circumcised were all legitimately capable of inheriting the covenant blessings of Abraham and formed one covenant community.

When God entered a covenant relationship with his chosen people, the twelve Israelite tribes, at Mt. Sinai, Moses sprinkled the sacrificial blood on the people to seal the twelve tribes of Israel as being one united body of the people of God. Baptism plays the same function for the people of the new covenant. One faith and one baptism in the name of Christ unite God's people into one body of Christ, whether they are Greek or Jew, man or woman, lord or servant, black, white, or yellow. This unity, sealed by the sprinkled blood of Jesus Christ, the mediator of the new covenant, embraces generation to generation of the people of God—those here on earth and those in heaven (Heb. 12:22–24).

Therefore, as long as we are living as the covenant people of God, we must faithfully commit ourselves to maintaining this unity in Christ. God has bound the members of his people into one another to be one single body of Christ, and we call him, in one voice, *our* Father and *our* Lord.

Of course, we recognize that there is extraordinary diversity within the one body of Christ. There are gender diversity, ethnic diversity, linguistic diversity, cultural diversity, and many other types of diversity too numerous to mention. Such diversity sometimes creates (or contributes to) disputes and quarrels among God's people and may lead to schism and division, possibly leaving the impression that there are many different kinds of people of God in the world. However, the Scriptures are clear: there is only one people of God, and there is only one church and one kingdom of God in the world, which is the dwelling place of God.

The fact of diversity does not disprove the fact of unity. The fact of diversity rather demonstrates one crucial characteristic of true biblical unity—its dynamic nature.

Ephesians 4 expresses this truth powerfully. At the beginning of the chapter, the apostle Paul exhorts the church to maintain unity: "Make every effort to keep the unity of the Spirit through the bond of peace. There is one body and one Spirit—just as you were called to one hope when you were called—one Lord, one faith, one baptism; one God and Father of all, who is over all and through all and in all" (Eph. 4:3–6, NIV). The apostle then moves immediately to describe the diversity of gifts with which God has blessed his church—"He gave the apostles, the prophets, the evangelists, the pastors and teachers. . . ." But that diversity has a dynamic and unifying purpose: "To equip the saints for the work of ministry, for building up the body of Christ, until we all attain to *the unity of the faith* . . ." (ESV).

So the fact of diversity itself serves the goal of unity. What none of us can be by ourselves, we can be together—the body of Christ.

Thus the Scriptures establish the agenda for churches and Christians in a way that both recognizes and builds upon various diversities within and among churches and Christians. We don't ignore our differences; we use them to make us strong and mature and complete. "Then," Paul says, "we will no longer be infants, tossed back and forth by the waves, and blown here and there by every wind of teaching and by the cunning and craftiness of men in their deceitful scheming. Instead, speaking the truth in love, we will in all things grow up into him who is the Head, that is, Christ. From him the whole body, joined and held together by every supporting ligament, grows and builds itself up in love, as each part does its work" (Eph. 4:14–16, NIV).

We cannot be all our Creator would have us be without other

diverse members of his body. But that diversity must always be understood in the context of the essential unity of the body of Christ, which is itself built on the unity of God's creating, covenanting, and redeeming work.

So how exactly do we live out this biblical understanding of unity? Does this agenda apply only to the churches built up by the apostles? No, it does not. Our local churches today are all "built up" as we live out this same apostolic confession. So how do we live it out?

First, of course, our Reformed churches must constantly seek to maintain the integrity of their Reformed confessions.

I am confident that Reformed theology provides the best overall system for interpreting the Scriptures and for presenting a biblical worldview. However, Reformed churches frequently have a tendency today to ignore the distinctives of the Reformed Faith in their practice. Reformed churches often maintain the "brand name" formally but fail actually to *be* distinctively Reformed in practice.

In some countries, there are churches and theological institutions that call themselves Reformed but that have, in fact, left the orthodox Reformed faith to such a degree that they have made the term *Reformed* a term of opprobrium within the broad evangelical community. In such places, the "World *Reformed* Fellowship" struggles to win a hearing among those who do continue genuinely to honor historic biblical orthodoxy. As Archbishop Jensen noted in his opening address to this General Assembly, when we talk about Reformed theology, we are not talking merely about Reformed *opinion*. Reformed theology deals with the Word of *the Lord*, and it is the Word of the Lord both because it comes from the Lord and because it is about the Lord.

Paganism and relativism have challenged and will continue to challenge this commitment of historic Reformed theology, and we must help one another deal with these challenges. Otherwise, we will be defeated by and absorbed into movements that actually deny the fundamental truths for which Reformed theology has historically stood. Reformed Christians in the United States need Reformed Christians in South Korea; Reformed Christians in Brazil need Reformed Christians in Nigeria; Reformed Christians in Indonesia need Reformed Christians in Scotland. We need one another in order to build up the total body of Christ in our faithful understanding of the Word of God.

Two speakers at this General Assembly have addressed specifically the challenge of paganism in the twenty-first century—Dr. Peter Jones from the United States and Dr. Yusufu Turaki from Nigeria. We—the Lord's people from all over the world—need the perspectives of both of them if we are to be mature and wise in our faith and if we are to maintain the integrity of our various Reformed confessions. No single national body of Reformed believers can do it alone. We recognize the diversity among us culturally and ethnically, and we use that diversity to make us together stronger in the Lord.

But second, we live out the biblical unity that we have been discussing by making certain that "the strong" relate appropriately to "the weak."

In Romans 15, the apostle Paul was dealing with this relationship between the strong and the weak. The church at Rome was made up mainly of Gentiles, but it included a number of Jewish Christians as well. Commentators have argued for years about which group was "strong" and which was "weak." D. G. Miller reasonably distinguishes three groups within the Roman church who seemed to have been the subjects of Paul's attention here: 1) legalists or moralizers, 2) libertines or antinomians, and 3) spiritualists. The activities of each of these groups are strong in certain ways and weak in others. One might, in fact, say that each of the three groups was both strong and weak.

The problem, of course, was that each group tended to regard itself as "strong" and to criticize and even to despise, in a spiritually self-righteous manner, those who were "weak." Regardless of which was actually stronger and which was actually weaker, Paul's exhortation was clear—the strong were to bear with the failings of the weak *in order to maintain the unity of the church.*

We have, of course, the identical situation today. There are strong and weak members (however one identifies strength and weakness) within every local Reformed church. There are strong and weak congregations (however one defines strength and weakness) within every Reformed denomination. And there are strong and weak denominations (however one defines strength and weakness). Every individual, every congregation, and every denomination is in the midst of the process of sanctification. Not one of them is perfect—yet!

I personally believe that, all things considered, orthodox, Reformed churches tend to be the strongest churches. But sometimes we have allowed Satan to turn that very strength into weakness. We "glory" in our particular denominational or congregational heritage, and we criticize and even despise, in a spiritually self-righteous manner, those whom we see as "weak." Please remember my first point of application. We absolutely must seek to maintain the integrity of our Reformed theological convictions. But we must do so with humility and in the genuine desire that, as Paul stated in Romans 15, we together may "with one voice glorify the God and Father of our Lord Jesus Christ."

And, therefore, all of the actions we take with respect to those we regard as weak, and all of the words we speak to and about them, must be taken or spoken with the conscious intention of melding our voices with theirs in one chorus of praise to God. Further, our words and actions must have that intention in such a dramatic way that those who hear and those who see are led immediately to comment, "Behold, how they love one another!"

Reformed Christians—those who know best of all that whatever good we have, we have purely by the grace of God—must be humble and sacrificial in extending the fellowship of Christ to other Christians until we all grow together into the maturity of Jesus Christ. In certain cases this might even mean that we strategically withhold, for a time, our Reformed distinctives for the sake of that ultimate united Christian maturity.

For example, those who are biblically Reformed in their theology seem often to emphasize the formal aspects of worship, in the correct belief that Scripture prescribes reverence as an essential characteristic of worship. Other Christians—not usually Reformed—emphasize the spontaneous aspects of worship, in the likewise correct belief that joy and delight are essential characteristics of worship. How do we Reformed Christians relate to such other Christians? What exactly would characterize a relationship that had as its ultimate, clear intention the melding of all of our voices in one chorus of praise to God?

If we are to live appropriately in obedience to Paul's teaching in Romans 15, we must avoid the extremes of both the WCC (the World Council of Churches) and the ICCC (the International Council of Christian Churches). The WCC has abandoned any commitment to the authority of Scripture and has attempted to achieve unity through syncretism. It succeeded in building up the political unity of the church but failed to build up the biblical unity of the church and therefore secularized the church. Its counterpart, the ICCC, attacked the WCC (appropriately) for these errors but soon broadened its attacks to include any churches that refused to support fully all that the ICCC said and did. In the end, the ICCC also undermined the kind of unity the apostle Paul was promoting in Romans 15.

We are here at this General Assembly of the World Reformed Fellowship to affirm our commitment both to historic Reformed ortho-doxy (as taught in the absolutely authoritative Word of God and as expressed in the great Reformed confessions of the church) and to the specific teaching of the Westminster Confession of Faith that there is a universal, *visible* church (XXV, 2). We affirm the truth of Reformed theology, and with the same vigor we extend the hand of our fellowship to other biblically committed churches, church-related organizations, and theological institutions toward the goal of establishing a Romans 15 unity. This means that we genuinely desire and seek to learn from them to rectify blind points or weaknesses in Reformed faith. And it means that we genuinely desire and seek to share with them what we see as the biblical strengths and insights of Reformed theology. We do all of this in order that we together might become mature, attaining to the whole measure of the fullness of Christ (Eph. 4:13).

A radical thought in conclusion—when Jesus Christ comes again to us to consummate his kingdom, there will, among his people, be no Calvinists, no Arminians, no Presbyterians, no Baptists, no Methodists, no Americans, no Koreans, no Africans, etc. There will be only children of God, the holy and glorified sons and daughters of God. And that fact should thrill us!

As the day of the Lord comes nearer, the fight between the king-dom of God and kingdom of Satan will become more and more intense. The Lord God—Father, Son, and Holy Spirit—tells us both how to fight and what the outcome will be. We fight best as the *united* people of God, because that way of fighting actually prefigures and embodies the goal and the promised outcome of that fighting.

May the God of endurance and encouragement grant you to live in such harmony with one another, in accord with Christ Jesus, that together you may with one voice glorify the God and Father of our Lord Jesus Christ.

PART TWO

PRACTICAL APPLICATIONS—SHARING CHALLENGES

CHAPTER FOUR

SHARING THE BURDEN OF ETHNIC CONFLICT IN THE MIDDLE EAST

CHARLES CLAYTON

We are all aware of the ethnic and religious strife that seems to be growing in the world today. No doubt we are also aware that it is seldom purely *that*; it is seldom merely ethnic or religious. For many people, religion is a convenient coat to disguise the underclothes of greed, politics, or, at best, a response to injustice.

When people come to visit the work of World Vision in the Holy Land, we sometimes have to help them prepare for their own emotional responses. They might see things that are different from the stereotypical images in the media, but more disturbingly, they might discover that their own deeply held assumptions need revision.

So we ask visitors to treat everyone they meet with courtesy and respect, no matter what their religion, race, or nationality. We ask them to listen to both sides of the conflict and to take time to understand the genuine concerns of each. You might already be thinking that I have stated the obvious, but it is surprising how often it is necessary in the context of strife. As Christians, we have a special responsibility to take this trouble.

The Middle East conflict also seems to get people thinking about the big issues of the world. One day you are enjoying coffee with friends and your mind is focused on the little nuances of etiquette in an unfamiliar culture, when a passing remark makes you think about *geopolitics*. So let's start there. I see two large fault lines appearing in today's world.

FAULT LINES IN THE MODERN WORLD

The first fault line is a pragmatic one. It is a *power struggle over resources* such as water, oil, and gas. While the U.S. aims to "make our dependence on Middle Eastern oil a thing of the past" (George Bush, reported by CNN, January 31, 2006), Russia aims "to be the world leader in the energy sector" (Vladimir Putin, reported by BBC News, February 13, 2006). Many see an emerging war about water, which in some places is more precious than oil. This division is all about who has the power over the resources.

The second fault line is more philosophical. It is an *uncertainty*, a growing lack of confidence in the justice systems, a cynicism about who can be trusted, a question about authority. The events in Abu Ghraib, Basra, or Guantanamo Bay—or the furor over the Danish cartoons—might have been small in relation to global politics or the scale of operations of their respective nations, but they are pebbles in the world's shoe. So it is that the conflict between the Israelis and the Palestinians is a focus, or an excuse, for strife in other places. It raises questions worldwide about the ethics and fairness of the world's great nations. People see Gaza, and they question America.

These fault lines are often linked to religion. The "Christian West" is becoming divided from the "Muslim East." Last month Andrew White, the Chief Executive of the Foundation for Reconciliation in the Middle East, said, "Sadly, the Coalition has not taken seriously the religious dimensions of the war in Iraq . . . religion is not only the key to what is wrong in Iraq, but taking it seriously is the only thing that will prevent the nation slipping into civil war."

Are these concerns too big for us as Christians? Not at all. We have an opportunity to address them—to demonstrate what a living Christian faith can really mean—and I believe this is a core challenge for the world's churches today. Speaking personally, it is one of the reasons I have chosen to serve with World Vision in the Middle East.

WHAT IS DEACONAL MINISTRY ALL ABOUT?

It is about incarnating the love of Christ.

This is the essence of a ministry of reconciliation, one that promotes justice and peace, as well as expressing care and compassion for those who suffer. Such a ministry has to include a prophetic role, calling people to act justly as well as to love mercy.

The Israeli–Palestinian conflict is no ordinary strife. It is a heady mix of theology, history, geography, economics, and politics. As I am sure you know, the theology includes an emphasis on eschatology in all three of the world's biggest religions. Two-thirds of the world's religious people, at least nominally, regard Jerusalem as a spiritual center.

This is one of the world's longest continuous conflicts, and it has created the world's largest and longest-running refugee problem. The UN Security Council's resolutions have been ignored in this situation more than anywhere else.

The Palestinian economy has collapsed in the last five years. Some analysts have called it the steepest economic decline in modern history. International aid to the area has become one of the highest per capita in the world. The current political upheavals have brought fears of deepening poverty and violence.

Israel and the Occupied Palestinian Territories are often the focus of international interest, especially in the Western Hemisphere, where our own history and theology are intimately linked to these lands. As the journalist Tom Friedman has remarked, most local conflicts go unnoticed, but when a stone is thrown at a tank in the West Bank it is on headline news. He said that Israel, even in quiet times, has played host to "one of the largest foreign press contingents in the world, with some 350 permanently accredited news organizations stationed in Jerusalem and Tel Aviv" and that the Palestinians "have received more attention and visibility than any other refugee community or national liberation movement in the world."[1]

There are suffering and a profound need for healing on both sides, whether the sufferers are Israeli or Palestinian, Jewish, Muslim, or Christian, and rich or poor in material terms. The stated mission of World Vision should, in my opinion, be the mission of every Christian—"to follow Jesus Christ in working with the poor and

---

[1]Thomas Friedman, *From Beirut to Jerusalem* (London: HarperCollins, 1998), 426, 443.

oppressed to promote human transformation, seek justice, and bear witness to the good news of the Kingdom of God. . . ."

There are two primary challenges that Christians will face, especially in the Middle East, if they adopt and seek to live by this mission. They are *the battle for truth* and *the meaning of reconciliation*. It is poignant that we are considering these two themes at the WRF General Assembly here in South Africa, because this is the place where the phrase "truth and reconciliation" first caught the modern world's attention.

THE BATTLE FOR TRUTH

The first casualty of war, it is often said, is truth. Everyone in this room, including myself, has a preconceived notion about the Middle East dispute. If three of us discuss it, we will probably end up with four opinions. Where is the truth? Many people arrive in the Middle East with one particular view in mind, whichever side it is, and then look for evidence to reinforce that view.

This is no accident. For a start, there is a huge amount of propaganda. One side demonizes the other, other side responds in kind, and we have, in effect, a media war.

I once met a Christian journalist who had just spent a whole week visiting only the Israeli side. As we talked together with a colleague, he showed surprise when hearing that there were Christians living in the West Bank. "Have they been there long?" he asked, and my colleague politely answered, "Yes, quite a while; many can trace their Christian heritage back for centuries, possibly millennia . . . and I think the first Christian here was called Jesus." Fortunately, our guest was able to laugh with us, and he vowed to visit some Palestinian Christians next time.

Then there is the problem of theological systems that have been built around a few assumptions. The holders of such a system can't afford to question any part of the system in case it all comes tumbling down, threatening their confidence in the very existence of God.

You will not be surprised to hear that the religious aspect of this conflict is a problem of hermeneutics and, therefore, of epistemology. I publicly thank Westminster Theological Seminary, where I studied, for introducing me to the meaning of those words. It isn't just one particular text in Scripture that trips us up—it is a whole set of assumptions and methodologies.[2]

Ethnic and religious strife is often sustained by people who build up myths about each other, attaching to those myths hair-trigger stereotypes and using both to cause hatred to explode. At times it seems that the racism we encounter is as ingrained and subconscious as the epistemology that gave birth to it. I suppose most diaconal ministries in such contexts have to grapple with this subversive battle.

I faced it only last week when an individual said to me, "What's wrong with *these people*?" and went on to say that "these people" have a fatal flaw, that they are not "normal" simply by virtue of their ethnic identity.

In the Holy Land, an ordinary discussion can very quickly slide toward the Third World War. Criticism of Israel evokes bitter accusations of anti-Semitism or even an anti-Christian bias. Criticism of the Palestinians brings accusations of being anti-Muslim . . . or even an anti-Christian bias (again!). There are raw nerves everywhere.

Let me illustrate this battle for truth with two topics.

First, the statistics of violence: Who is suffering most in this conflict? In the twelve months between February 2005 and January 2006, Israel killed more than five times as many Palestinians as vice versa.[3] The number of *children* killed is even more alarming when we consider Israel's claim that every attack is carefully targeted.

It is not a conflict of equals. One side has large numbers of sophisticated weapons, while the other has fewer weapons, most of which are primitive by comparison. It is tempting, therefore, to hold one side more accountable than the other. But a "deeper truth" should govern our thinking here.

Both sides have operated with similar values, killing and injuring civilians as they go about ordinary life such as shopping or attending school. Every act of violence is atrocious and condemnable, and there is a need for protection on both sides. But whereas the statistics point to an unequal struggle, the culpability is more than mathematical. Both sides need to retreat from violence, both need to uphold international

---

[2]For a detailed exploration of this thought, see Charles Clayton and Dan McCartney, *Let the Reader Understand* (Phillipsburg, NJ: Presbyterian & Reformed, 1994).
[3]Report of the United Nations Office for the Coordination of Humanitarian Affairs, January 2006.

law, and both need to respect the Geneva Conventions. In the business of killing, one mother's heart is just as broken as any other.

My second illustration concerns the Separation Barrier. The Israelis say it is a security fence or anti-terrorism fence. They point to Israel's right to protect itself from violence and the fact that the number of suicide bombers has decreased dramatically during the period of its construction so far. About three hundred kilometers have already been built, and its final length will be seven hundred or eight hundred kilometers.

The Palestinians say it is not about security (or at least not primarily about security), but it is about Israeli confiscation of Palestinian land and Israeli devastation of the Palestinian economy. Palestinians point out that the barrier is often not a fence but a nine-meter-high concrete wall; that in most places it doesn't separate Israelis from Palestinians but Palestinians from Palestinians; that only 20 percent of its route is on Israel's internationally agreed borders; that the remainder meanders inside the West Bank; and that it prevents Palestinian movement but not Israeli movement. They point to the International Court of Justice resolution in July 2004, which condemned the barrier not for its existence but for its *route*.

So the arguments go on. Is it a security fence or something else? Is it about defense or land? One thing is sure: it is not a solution but a *failure* to find a solution.

In the battle for truth in the Middle East, those who seek to be Christian peacemakers face unanticipated spiritual shocks when they encounter other "Christians" who actually try to justify violence against Palestinians using eschatological arguments, as if the violence is some kind of "regrettable necessity." Such ethical perversions are no better than the logic of a terrorist bomber, but they do demonstrate again that the problem has major hermeneutical dimensions and, in my judgment, unconscionable results.

It is also a challenge for pastoral ministry. Try telling a bereaved mother that her suffering is justified in the eyes of some Christians. Try telling it to the four-year-old who saw her deaf father bleed to death after being shot for no apparent reason other than that he was born of the wrong race in the wrong place. Those grieving their losses have found a tragic equality, whether they live in Nablus or Tel Aviv, east side or west side.

Those of us who have a ministry in such an environment must first rid ourselves of our own insidious stereotypes or we will attempt our work with a reticence and fear, perhaps with an air of condescension, and possibly even racism in our hearts.

"Oh no, not me!" you are quietly saying to yourself. "I don't have that problem. I *know* the real truth about those people."

And I respond, "No, wait a minute. I live there. I really *do* know!"

And hearing this, the great Reformed apologist Cornelius van Til, if he were here today, would be biting his knuckles and pulling out his hair in frustration with us.

It reminds me of the Presbyterian who said to the Baptist, "It's OK to be different. We can each have our own style; you worship in your way, and I in *His*."

Brother Andrew once said: "I deny anybody the right to an opinion on the Middle East situation if they have not shed real tears for those in trouble." Perhaps the first step to knowing the truth is not an intellectual one, but something more visceral and volitional. It is striking that Jesus said, "If you hold to my teaching . . . Then you will know the truth . . ." (John 8:31–32, NIV). He seems to be suggesting that knowledge begins with obedience, not vice versa.

Recently I met the head teacher of a village school in the West Bank. Their land is being taken by two nearby settlements. Although she watches the children struggle every day with the harshness of life under occupation, she is trying to teach them how to love.

As we drank mint tea and ate little pastries in her office, she said, "Walls only build hatred . . . so let's try to see the *person* on the other side." I noticed that the classrooms were filled with children's paintings of friendly scenes, and she explained that the theme of the week was to learn how to love. But there was a poignant end to our conversation; when asked if she would be willing to be quoted by name, she declined. Even with such a non-violent message, she did not want to risk losing the villagers' travel permits, preferring instead to concentrate on teaching the children quietly.

The times are indeed evil when an admonition to see people as people can be regarded as a dangerous admonition. But as we know, there is nothing new under the sun. Hear these words from the prophet Amos:

> *You hate the one who reproves in court and despise him who tells the truth. You trample on the poor and force him to give you grain. Therefore, though you have built stone mansions, you will not live in them; though you have planted lush vineyards, you will not drink their wine. For I know how many are your offenses and how great your sins. You oppress the righteous and take bribes and you deprive the poor of justice in the courts. Therefore the prudent man keeps quiet in such times, for the times are evil.*
>
> **AMOS 5:10–13, NIV**

THE MEANING OF RECONCILIATION

The second big issue we face is this: what does true reconciliation look like? When people have become deeply divided, what can be done to bring them together? Israel's first prime minister said, "There is a gulf, and nothing can fill this gulf. . . . We, as a nation, want this country to be *ours*; the Arabs, as a nation, want this country to be *theirs*."[4]

Is work toward reconciliation a hopeless task, going back to the enmity between the ancient sons of Abraham? Are the people permanently divided? How do we find peace with justice? Should we even try? Is it possible only between individuals? Is it possible only between *Christians*?

These profound questions raise even deeper questions about the church's role in secular society. Though there are challenges and difficulties, I still believe that the Christian church holds the key to societal change. Yes, an entire nation can achieve reconciliation with another nation as a result of a movement between individuals, and the Christian message is at the heart of this possibility.

Let me illustrate my point by referring directly to the three great monotheistic religions that have significant presence in Israel today. Of course, as I do so, I recognize that I am employing some fairly broad and sweeping generalizations, but I do believe they are valid.

The Jewish faith is characterized by many laws. It engenders a culture of systems and legal procedures, and *justice* is a strong theme.

---

[4]Quoted by Colin Chapman in *Whose Promised Land?* (Oxford, UK: Lion Publishing, 2002), 262.

As a result, there is a lot of accountability in Israeli society today, mixed with complex methods for actually *avoiding* the impact of the law. New laws are being written all the time and, conversely, with the new laws come new ways of technically satisfying the laws while, at the same time, avoiding any personal inconvenience from the laws. Fortunately, many of my Israeli friends have a sense of humor about this, and there are many smiles about it at times like Pesach (Passover). In this kind of context, reconciliation is very much a legal matter, to be decided by the courts.

The Muslim faith is characterized by something different, but equally a conundrum. There are constant references to the character of God as "merciful," yet in daily life the societal emphasis is more on retribution, on satisfying honor rather than putting aside dissension or trying to end a conflict—and then, surprisingly, overturning this very principle by floods of sheer pragmatism.[5] Fortunately, many of my Muslim friends have a sense of humor about this too. In this context, reconciliation is all about honor in the community.

I still chuckle at the memory of a man in Gaza who, at dead of night, stole a very large greenhouse that had been built with help from World Vision. The next day he was brought before an array of community leaders seeking retribution, and he was required to rebuild the whole thing within forty-eight hours, concrete bases and all. Then, finally, they brought him to me for the last word, and as we stood solemnly in the dusty field, it felt as though his execution were in my hands. As soon as I was assured of his repentance and reparations, and when he had promised to treat it as community property in the future, I offered the hand of friendship. Then every face burst into smiles, we were immediately offered tea, and we sat down together under some shady olive trees to drink it like old friends. When community honor was upheld, reconciliation was possible.

Christianity brings yet another perspective. When Jesus said, "Blessed are the peacemakers . . ." (Matthew 5:9, NIV), was he referring primarily to Christians? Yes, I believe he was. For a start, he was speaking to his *disciples,* while the crowd was simply listening in (vv. 1-2). Furthermore, the designation "for they will be called sons of

---

[5]For further discussion of this subject, see Raphael Patai, *The Arab Mind* (New York: Hatherleigh Press, 2002), 116, 241, 287.

God" was a label that can be given only to those who are his by faith (John 1:12). Yet it is clear from the totality of Scripture that those who make peace are seen to represent the heart of God, who took the painful initiative of sending his Son to die to accomplish peace with his people. In this context, reconciliation is about mercy and grace as well as justice.

I am speaking on this occasion to Christians, and I therefore am bold to urge us all to live lives worthy of our name. We must not allow the world to diminish our unique identity and the unique contribution we can make in the work toward reconciliation! We do not merely *love* peace; we seek actually to *make* peace. We take the initiative—sometimes the very painful and costly initiative—to seek to make peace happen. We, the church of Jesus Christ, can influence the culture of our nations to be characterized by an awareness of right and wrong, guilt, repentance, *and forgiveness*. Christians know that an apology is not a sign of weakness but of strength. Therefore, while legal precision and community honor may be signs of "common grace," we, by the power of God's Spirit, have the privilege of bringing to the discussions the "special grace" of *grace*. This point was well made at a Christmas Eve service I attended last December in Bethlehem when the preacher called for "unarmed love" to visit our troubled world.

Of course, we must ourselves embody the grace that we speak. One of the things that embodying grace in a Middle Eastern context involves is the private and public recognition of the significance of both legal precision and community honor. Even as we seek to bring a uniquely Christian contribution to the work of reconciliation, we do so openly recognizing and affirming the values that Muslims and Jews will bring to this work. This is the kind of gracious initiative that we must take if we are to live up to our name and if we are to have any hope of actually making progress.

In terms of specific steps that must be taken in any work of reconciliation, I would identify three.

First, reconciliation must begin with truth-telling. In my consideration of "the battle for truth," I have outlined some of the things that this involves in today's Middle East, and I won't, therefore, repeat those things other than to reemphasize that the *full* story needs to be freely and openly told.

Second, reconciliation takes place between people who place themselves on the same moral plane. In the gospel this happens because we are raised up to God's presence by the righteousness of Christ and he is "not ashamed to call us brothers" (Heb. 2:11, NIV). On any merely human level, it happens when two people (or two peoples) bow together before the same authority and humbly recognize their equal accountability to mutually accepted standards. As Curtiss DeYoung points out, "Reconciled relationships can occur only when each individual believes and perceives that he or she is an equal partner and in need of the other."[6]

One small hint at how this might happen occurred once at midnight, at the notorious Qalandyia checkpoint near Ramallah, as my wife and I were returning from a ministry opportunity within the Palestinian West Bank. It was my sixteenth checkpoint in two days, and I was getting weary of them. There were long lines of frustrated people. When at last our turn came we switched off the lights, as required, and edged forward slowly.

The young Israeli soldier yelled, "Identity!" in English. He was dressed in full marine-style outfit, with a big helmet, flak jacket, all kinds of equipment, and machine gun ready. He scanned our faces and asked, "Are you Christians?" (Our little plastic ID cards say we work for a "Christian, international, humanitarian organization.")

"I mean are you *believers*?" he clarified. "Well, yes, we are followers of Christ," we replied. There was a pause, then he explained that he was also a Christian and said, "What is it like for the churches there?" We replied, "Well, it's hard, it's really hard for them." He said, "Yes, it is hard for them because they are surrounded by Muslims." We wondered if he knew that most of the church's suffering in the West Bank is caused by the occupation, but we realized that he might have known this already and perhaps couldn't say anything because his colleague was standing beside him.

He continued, "We pray for the churches in the West Bank and Gaza. We pray for our sisters and brothers there." We felt he was genuine. We thanked him, then exchanged a few more pleasantries and mutual God-bless-you's. As we drove on, looking in the mirror, I could

---

[6]Curtiss DeYoung, *Reconciliation: Our Greatest Challenge, Our Only Hope* (Valley Forge, PA: Judson Press, 1997), 74.

see him holding his gun toward the next car and shouting "Identity!" He was doing his job again.

This may a bit superficial, but to us it was a glimpse of "level ground." We never knew that soldier's name, but for a couple of minutes we shared something quite transcendent in extraordinarily stressful conditions. He showed compassion for his Palestinian "brothers and sisters." They (Palestinians) and he (Israeli) and we (British) were united in our bowing before Christ.

So reconciliation starts with truth, and then it demands a leveling attitude, an equality of moral positions. For Christians "there is neither Jew nor Greek, slave nor free, male nor female, for we are all one in Christ Jesus" (Gal. 3:28, NIV, replacing "you" with "we"). If it is true (and it is!) that "*All* have sinned and come short of the glory of God" and if it is true (and it is!) that "the wages of sin is death, but the *gift* of God is eternal life in Christ Jesus our Lord," then none of us is intrinsically morally superior to anyone else. Of course, we know this. But somehow it must become one of the first things that people see about us—that we live it! We will do precious little reconciling until we ourselves show that we genuinely do see others as our brothers and sisters . . . in the sense that we all are equally created in God's image and that we all equally need the same Savior.

We must do this, and we must *be* this before we even start to think about trying to bring reconciliation to others. And once we *are* this, we may possibly begin to see ways in which this sense can be offered to and urged for others we want to help to reconcile. If we seek to urge any separated peoples toward equal submission to mutually accepted standards, we must first show that *we* have submitted to those standards.

Third and finally, it takes *hard work* in the details. Any damaged relationship results in a tangled mess of problems. How far back do these tangled messes go? Those in the Middle East go back a few thousand years. Sometimes the key is not to try to untangle anything, but to dispense with the tangle itself, to apply "sweeping grace" and simply agree to start again.

You can probably write the rest yourself, because the Middle East problem is not only a problem of the Middle East. It is in your country and mine. It is in our churches. It is in our own hearts.

I have talked about the battle for truth and the meaning of reconciliation, two things that exercise us every day in Jerusalem. I will close with a story that illustrates both:

CONCLUSION

Recently my wife and I met with members of the Bereaved Parents Family Circle. These are people who come together from both sides of the Israeli-Palestinian conflict to give each other comfort and to work for peace. World Vision has supported their work, and we have published a booklet with them called *Who Will Wipe Away Their Tears?* It lists children who have been killed on both sides and simply documents the information as a way of calling attention to the need for a nonviolent solution.

On this recent occasion there was an especially meaningful encounter. We had dinner at a local restaurant with two bereaved fathers, one an Israeli, a secular Jew, and the other a Palestinian Christian who was accompanied by his wife and seventeen-year-old daughter.

Israeli: "My parents were Holocaust survivors. Their pain will always live with me. Seven years ago, I lost my thirteen-year-old daughter to a Palestinian suicide bomber. It felt like a finger poked me between the eyes, and I can never forget the moment when my whole life changed forever. But, although I cannot forget or forgive, since then I have chosen to turn my anger and grief into efforts for peace, to call for an end to the violence."

Palestinian: "My family has lived under occupation for decades, and then two years ago I lost my twelve-year-old daughter to an Israeli gunman."

He then described the dreadful day when he and his family were driving down a street in Bethlehem only to find themselves suddenly riddled with bullets by Israeli soldiers. They were all injured, and their younger daughter was killed. "Since then I too have chosen to turn my grief into efforts for peace, to call for an end to the violence."

There was a silence, then he continued, "But, my friend . . ." At this point he reached over and held the other man by both arms. They held each other, their eyes meeting and sharing something only two bereaved fathers can ever share.

" . . . my friend, there is something more you need." He explained that he and his wife had been able to come to the point of forgiveness. He said, "You will only really be free when you have been able to forgive as well." His wife agreed, saying it was something she had to do not once but every moment of every day. I asked her how it was possible, and she replied, "Only by God." Poignantly, their seventeen-year-old said she was not yet able to forgive, and this added even more authenticity to her parents' dramatic statement.

There was a moment when the two men seemed frozen in time, their faces showing a depth of feeling that simply cannot be described. We wept with them, and in that moment we could really see how the cycle of violence can be ended. It has to start with forgiveness—the only sure route to reconciliation.

After a little more conversation they parted with handshakes and hugs, and their friendship seemed to have deepened even further.

Forgiveness—how rare, and yet how powerful!

CHAPTER FIVE

SHARING THE BURDEN OF GLOBAL SEX TRAFFICKING

DIANE LANGBERG

Many centuries ago—twenty to be exact—baby girls were considered a liability. Demographics in the first century in certain parts of the world were stunningly imbalanced male to female. Female infanticide was not uncommon. Infant girls, often considered the equivalent of deformed, were killed by exposure. In essence, it was permitted by law to leave them outside the city on the dung heap to die. That is about as clear a judgment of "worthless" on a human life as can be made.

There was, however, a growing group of people who seemed to think the judgment was an error. Rather than accepting the culture's assessment regarding the value of females, they went outside the city to the dung heaps to find and rescue the abandoned baby girls. The decision was both risky and sacrificial. It required standing against the mainstream and making a judgment that ran counter to the culture of that time. It meant the giving of life, time, and goods to someone else's discarded baby girl. It meant extending the circle of one's responsibility. It meant being devalued and disdained for stooping so low as to treat what was deemed worthless as precious instead.

Who were these people? They were the church, the body of Jesus Christ. They followed the Lamb who went outside the city gates to make the ultimate sacrifice and give his life as a ransom for many who were deemed worthless. By his death, he judged them precious. His first-century body followed him outside the gates to the garbage heaps of those days to rescue baby girls. The call that our first-century brethren answered is not unlike a call that now sits before us in the twenty-first-century church. The question that remains to be answered is whether or not we too will follow the Lamb outside the city gates to pursue and rescue those found worthless in the eyes of this world and sacrificially work among them because they are precious in his sight.

THE EXTENT OF ABUSE

According to Amnesty International, worldwide one in three females—nearly one billion—are beaten, coerced into sex, or otherwise abused in their lifetime. One in three—think about that statistic the next time you sit in an airport or walk through a crowded marketplace or sit in church. In my country, the United States, though reports vary, most studies suggest that one in three or four females is sexually abused by the age of eighteen. Rape, one of the most underreported of all crimes, is believed to happen to one in four women. Nearly 5.3 million domestic abuse victimizations occur each year among U.S. women aged eighteen and older. In the United States, where there are many laws protecting women on the books, being born female is still something of a risk.

The rates increase exponentially if you look at worldwide statistics. The most brutal and destructive manifestation of the anti-female bias is female infanticide, a practice not limited to the first century. There are countries today where baby girls are left in the jungles to die, given poison at birth, or buried facedown in the ground right after birth. There are no overall statistics, but a minimum estimate would place the casualties in the hundreds of thousands. Sex-selective abortions count for an even higher number of missing girls. Demographics suggest that between sixty and one hundred million females are missing.

One of the most brutal and large-scale destructive forces against girls and women in the world today is that of sex trafficking. The U.S. State Department, in its Trafficking In Persons (TIP) report, defines sex trafficking as "commercial sexual acts induced by force, fraud, or coercion, or when the person induced to perform such acts has not attained eighteen years of age." The Trafficking Victims Protection Act of 2000 states that trafficking involves recruitment, harboring, transportation, or obtaining a person for the purpose of commercial sexual exploitation. Commercial sexual exploitation simply means that a sex act is performed in exchange for something of value such as money, clothes, drugs, food, or shelter. Included are prostitution, pornography, child brides, stripping, and live sex shows. Trafficking victims can be found in brothels, "cage" brothels, massage parlors, saunas, escort services, nightclubs, some aromatherapy clinics, and, of course, the streets. Victims are also found by way of the Internet, which has been dubbed an "electronic red light district."

The U.S. State Department (DOS) report estimates that approximately seven hundred thousand women and children are trafficked annually across international borders. Of that number, 80 percent are female, 70 percent are trafficked for sex exploitation, and 50 percent of them are children. Though as an underground activity sex trafficking is very difficult to measure accurately, it is thought that in order to supply this global sex trade, a woman or girl is sold in the developing world every ten minutes. The DOS reported that about fifteen thousand victims are trafficked each year into the U.S. (others say as high as fifty thousand).

The problem is that we are not very good at identifying victims of trafficking. The Department of Justice states that four hundred thousand children in the U.S. are lured or forced into prostitution each year. Most of these are white, working, middle-class runaways from troubled families who begin selling their bodies at about age thirteen. Some organizations estimate about two million child prostitutes globally. UNICEF estimates ten million child prostitutes worldwide. Whatever the numbers, we are facing a staggering, global problem.

Victims enter the trafficking world in one of four ways: they are kidnapped, coerced, sold, or they leave home voluntarily with the promise of a better life elsewhere. Girls and women are considered a commodity to traffickers. They run low risks for big money. In most countries the penalties for sex trafficking are less severe than those for drug trafficking.

THE ABUSED

Who are the purchasers of trafficked victims? Many are pedophiles.
Others fall into one of two categories: *preferential exploiters*, those
looking for something in particular; and *opportunistic exploiters*,
businessmen, travelers, those who purchase a victim because of the
anonymity afforded them in another country. There is no profile
for a user. Customers cut across every division such as age, socio-
economic status, ethnicity, or profession. In essence, "everyman"
is a potential user. We tend to delude ourselves into thinking we
can discern who such people might be. In fact, we cannot tell. To
paraphrase a British law enforcement official: There are three components to sex trafficking: an endless supply of girls and women,
an endless supply of ruthless traffickers, and an endless supply of
clients and customers.

What factors make a woman or girl vulnerable to becoming
trafficked? Obviously, gender is primary. Those who are orphans or
refugees, have experienced prior sexual abuse, or are widows or ethnic
minorities are very vulnerable. Poverty is also a major factor. Violence
against females is a global human rights scandal. It is one of the most
pervasive and ignored human rights violations around the world. To
loosely quote a character in the movie *Hotel Rwanda*, "If we could see
souls, we would see that the streets of this world are littered with the
souls of women and children."

Let us put some faces on these overwhelming statistics and get
some glimpses into what is really happening to women and girls
around the globe.

Manna lived with her brother in South Asia. She was often beaten
by him and eventually decided to run away when she was fourteen.
A young woman found her crying in the train station and offered to
help. She promised her a job selling fabric and took her to a place
to sleep. When Manna awoke, the woman was gone and another
woman came and told her that her life was no longer her own. She
would not sell fabric. She would instead be selling her fourteen-year-
old body. She refused her first three customers, but the brothel owner
beat her repeatedly until she gave in to the men who came to rape
her. She tried to run away and begged the men who raped her to call
the police. Two years later, while hidden in a soundproof dungeon,

she was rescued by International Justice Mission and now lives in an aftercare home. In her words, "I was in prison . . . but God took me from that place."

We are standing at dusk on a dirt road in an African country. We see a young mother walking while holding her toddler's hand and carrying an infant on her hip. It is a lovely sight. Suddenly that view is shattered as we see her speaking to a man who has approached her. She sets the children down off the road and speaks to the toddler. She disappears behind the brush, and when she returns we see money placed in her outstretched hand. She takes the toddler's hand and picks up the infant and proceeds on her way. We watch this scene occur three times. When asked about the transactions she quietly says, "It is how I feed my children."

A young girl named Siri lived in a small village in rural Thailand. She attended four years of school and then was required to stay home and care for her three younger siblings. At fourteen, she was sold for the equivalent of two thousand dollars to a well-dressed woman visiting the village and promising Siri's parents that she could get their daughter a well-paying job. The trafficker sold her to a brothel owner who initiated her into prostitution by immediately raping her. She escaped to the police, who were paid well by the brothel owner, and so she was returned to her pimp for another beating. Her earnings were the equivalent of four dollars per customer, and to cover her so-called rent she had to service over three hundred men each month. It did not take long for Siri to be convinced of her worthlessness.

Marika was desperate for work. Her mother was sick and her father a drunk. A woman in a recruitment agency in her hometown in Ukraine told her of a waitress job in Tel Aviv. She agreed to take the job to help her family. She was not flown to Tel Aviv but found herself in the Cairo airport and then transported by van to a village. Two men mounted camels and forced her, along with other women, to set out into the Sinai on foot. They eventually came to the Israeli-Egyptian frontier and were taken by pickup to a deserted house. They were ordered to disrobe so they could be inspected. They were informed that they had been purchased for the equivalent of ten thousand dollars each and they would work off their debt by servicing clients. The first night she was given eight men.

A young woman from Latin America was told there was a good restaurant job for her in the United States. Her family was desperately poor, and she longed to help. She was smuggled in and found herself in a trailer with many other women and forced to service over forty men a week. She was not allowed to leave the premises nor given medical attention. The women were eventually freed when investigators arrested the brothel owner.

I was in Brazil some years ago and was driven down city streets lined with young girls maybe eight or ten years old. The pastor and his wife who were ministering in that area told me that these children were prostitutes, often drug-addicted and without resources. Many had run away from their homes because of incest. Many of them are trafficked through the Brazilian ports into Asian brothels. Their escape had resulted in a worse nightmare.

In a conversation with pastors in the Dominican Republic I asked about incest. They were silent for a moment or two, and then one of them finally whispered, "It is everywhere." Again many run away from sexually abusive homes to the streets where they are grabbed by brothel owners and sold for their young bodies. I sat with young women in Myanmar who were learning a skill through World Vision so they would have a way of supporting themselves other than the sex trafficking industry. The border between Myanmar and Thailand is largely jungle and not well monitored. The oppressive military regime in Myanmar leaves women with little to no opportunities for education or jobs, and so many are susceptible to being lured with the promise of jobs elsewhere in Southeast Asia.

A Canadian journalist by the name of Victor Malarek wrote a book on sex trafficking called *The Natashas*. In writing about the trafficking of girls from Eastern Europe into the rest of the world, he says that female flesh is one of the top three commodities on the world's black market. The sex industry is a big business well-entrenched in both national and international economies.

THE ECONOMICS OF TRAFFICKING

Overall the FBI says that human trafficking generates about 9.5 billion dollars in annual revenue. The United Nations has said that in the last thirty years more than thirty million people have been trafficked in Asia alone. About 14 percent of the gross domestic product of Thailand was supplied by the sex industry. In the Philippines, prostitution is the fourth largest source of the gross national product. Estimates say there are a half million involved in prostitution in that country and that at least one hundred thousand of those are children. India is said to have 2.3 million females in the sex industry, and according to a UN report 40 percent of those are under the age of eighteen. Victor Malarek and many others are calling the trafficking of females *the* human rights issue of the twenty-first century. He says, "The issue of trafficking desperately cries out for firm, committed leadership; it has to be made a global concern." Who will answer that cry?

Keeping the stories and the statistics in mind, listen to the voice of our God speaking to his people down through the centuries:

> *Learn to do good; seek justice, reprove the ruthless, defend the orphan, plead for the widow.*
>
> ISAIAH 1:17, NASB

> *Is this not the fast which I choose, to loosen the bonds of wickedness, to undo the bands of the yoke, and to let the oppressed go free and break every yoke?*
>
> ISAIAH 58:6, NASB

> *Wicked men are found among my people. . . . They know no bounds in deeds of evil; they judge not with justice the cause of the fatherless . . . they do not defend the rights of the needy.*
>
> JEREMIAH 5:26, 28, ESV

> *Pure and undefiled religion in the sight of our God and Father is this: to visit orphans and widows in their distress. . . .*
>
> JAMES 1:27, NASB

> [*The* LORD *our God*] *. . . executes justice for the oppressed; [he] gives food to the hungry. The* LORD *sets the prisoners free . . . the* LORD *raises up those who are bowed down . . . the* LORD *protects the strangers; he supports the fatherless and the widow.*
>
> PSALM 146:7–9, NASB

FOLLOWING OUR HEAD

My father was a colonel in the United States Air Force. He graduated from a military school, went on to flight school, and then headed for Europe and World War II. He returned home with medals he never displayed. When I was thirteen, the man who flew for Strategic Air Command and was a superb athlete retired because of a debilitating illness no one could diagnose. He spent the next thirty-two years becoming increasingly disabled and lived out the last years of his life in a nursing home.

As my father's disease progressed, he went from coordinated athlete to a man who could not tie his own shoes or get himself up out of a chair and was eventually unable to get his feet to walk down a hallway. I learned many lessons from my father's life. One of the primary ones was this: A body that does not follow its head is a sick body. My father was a very bright man who knew many things. He certainly knew how to tie his shoes and how to walk. However, he could not get his body to do what his head knew how to do. His body would not follow his head.

The church of Jesus Christ has a Head. Our Head has called us to follow him. When we do not, we are very sick. Listen to some descriptive words about our Head: "The Spirit of the Lord GOD is upon me, because the LORD has anointed me to bring good news to the afflicted; he has sent me to bind up the brokenhearted, to proclaim liberty to captives and freedom to prisoners . . . to comfort all who mourn" (Isaiah 61:1–2, NASB). This description of our Head simply sounds like an incarnation, a fleshing out, of the words of God we previously read.

God says to seek justice, break every yoke, defend the orphan, set the prisoner free, and care for the widow. This list is also a match for the list given previously regarding who is vulnerable to trafficking. The list of God's commands, the list describing our Head, and the list describing those vulnerable to trafficking are virtually identical. Our Head pursues those marked by the characteristics making people vulnerable to trafficking. A body that does not follow its head is a sick body.

I have been struck recently—in studying topics such as trafficking, abuse, incest, genital mutilation, suttee, female infanticide, and rape—by how the Christian community has focused for so long solely on the issues of the role and place for women. We seem far more concerned that women not overstep whatever boundaries our particular circle deems right than we are about their safety. I am not suggesting that those boundaries should not be considered in light of the Word of God. They absolutely should. But they are *not* the only issues regarding women that need to be discussed. We must also face the fact that the body of Christ has failed to lead the way in this world regarding such issues as rape, incest, violence, HIV/AIDS and sex trafficking.

Going outside the camp to rescue trashed females has not been the church's clarion call. We seem far more focused on keeping females in the so-called "right" place and concerned about anything that would take them away from the parameters we prefer. In the meantime, those in power are preying on females around the world, dragging them into positions and places *far outside* the parameters of God for *any* human being, male or female. The girls and women of this world are dying on the dung heaps.

Females make up approximately one half of the world's population. They would be more than half but for some of the statistics we heard earlier indicating that between sixty and one hundred million are missing. If we take the plagues of abuse, incest, rape, and trafficking seriously, then those females who are being so violated comprise one of the largest mission fields in the world. When you think of the phrases *mission work* or *mission field*, do you ever think of girls and women as being one of those fields? What might happen if the church worldwide caught the vision of that field and began training and sending men and women into their communities and around the world to protect, educate, nurture, and rescue women and girls in the name of Jesus? What might happen if the body of Christ followed its Head?

There is precedent for such a work. It predates our brothers and sisters in the first century. It is what lay behind their risky and sacrificial behavior. The precedent is the life of the Head that they followed. He arrived as the seeming illegitimate son of a virgin in a culture that should have stoned her because she was definitely outside the parameters. By all appearances, she had not maintained her proper place in that society. His genealogy has several trashed women in it—Tamar, Rahab, Ruth, and Bathsheba. That list brings into his history things like incest, prostitution, interracial marriage, and adultery, all of which were forbidden.

He went from there to swim upstream by saying things like simply looking on a female as a sex object was the equivalent of adultery and therefore worthy of stoning. If that is true, then what do you suppose he would say about the trafficking of girls and women? He began his ministry by blessing an unnamed bride in Cana. Women publicly traveled with him, a stunning and offensive situation in that culture. He treated one woman as a male disciple when he affirmed her presence at his feet and treated another like an apostle when he gave her the privilege of first telling others of his resurrection. He paused in his work of saving the world to raise a girl-child from the dead, return a son to a widow, and a brother to two grieving sisters. He accorded women dignity, honor, education, and privilege. If our Head did these things for women and girls, should not his body do the same?

We who are the body of Christ often pour our money into all kinds of things while women die. We work hard for fame and success in our ministries while they are trafficked. We fly around in jets and build more buildings and drive big cars while they give birth in bullock carts. We condemn them for their immorality while AIDS increases exponentially or their children die in their arms from starvation. All the while the voice of our Savior is calling us to crawl all over the dung heaps of this world, searching for the abandoned, neglected, dying, abused, and trafficked females of our century.

Our Head has called us to go the poor, the afflicted, the broken, the needy, and the imprisoned. He invites us to go where humanity is broken in pieces, violently rent, maimed, and shattered. He asks us to follow him into prisons, deserved and undeserved, places of little light and restricted movement, places without hope. He leads us into places of worthlessness and decay—places that appall and horrify us.

These are not places where you and I want to go. I fear we prefer light, freedom, beauty, comfort, and familiarity. We prefer healthy and alert minds to traumatized ones. We prefer clean bodies to dirty ones and whole bodies to crippled ones. But a body that does not follow its head is a sick body. These issues regarding the girls and women of this world are of grave concern to our God. The trauma and abuse that are devastating the females of this world are not merely the jurisdiction of psychologists and social workers. Nor is it to be left to governments and welfare institutions. The trauma and trafficking of females worldwide are the business of the body of Christ.

The abuse, prostitution, and trafficking of girls and women are not new. Many courageous souls have followed after our first-century brethren by working selflessly to rescue the females of their day. Many of us know of the work of William and Catherine Booth in the mid-1800s to set free women who were trafficked and sold. We have read of Josephine Butler's campaign, also in the mid 1800s, to end commercial sex exploitation. Amy Carmichael was in India rescuing little girls from temple prostitution.

FRONT ROW SEAT TO REDEMPTION

Gary Haugen, author of *Good News About Injustice*, founded International Justice Mission in 1997. This organization works around the globe rescuing girls and women from sex trafficking. They have rescued girls as young as five years of age. Shared Hope International works setting up homes for the aftercare of those girls rescued from brothels, helping them heal and become skilled so they are not vulnerable to the traffickers. The Salvation Army continues its work in this arena today through its Initiative Against Sex Trafficking. These ministries have web sites on the Internet. They need the active intercession and the support of the church community.

Thirty plus years ago I began my professional life as a psychologist. Little did I know where it would lead me. I have spent those years working with trauma and abuse—sexual abuse, domestic abuse, and sadly, clergy sexual abuse. God has used the broken lives of hundreds of precious people who have been battered, violated, tormented, and trafficked to take me deeper into his loving heart for this world.

Through my work I have learned something of the depth of evil in this world and in the hearts of human beings. I have seen more clearly how serious sin of any kind is, my own included, and how it damages not only individuals but the body and name of Christ as well. I have gotten glimpses of the meaning of the cross of Jesus Christ and the overwhelming nature of what he bore there. And God has given me what I often call "a front row seat to redemption" because as I have walked into the darkness of abuse and torment I have seen God's love and grace poured out and lives utterly transformed.

I know that if the body of Christ follows its Head, then he will take us places where we do not want to go, to see things we do not want to see. Such a ministry will cost us. It cost him. I also know that following our Head will result in his resurrection life being poured out on others and on us as well. It will mean that the body of Christ will look like the Son of Man in this world. It will mean that the character of God will be seen again in flesh and blood. It will mean that the name of Jesus will be exalted in the earth.

What do you suppose would happen if collectively we as Christians caught the vision? What might occur if the church around the world truly recognized the plight of females in this world today? I suspect repentance would come first. Like Daniel we would say, "O Lord, hear! O Lord, forgive! O Lord, listen and take action! For Your own sake, O my God, do not delay, because Your city and Your people are called by Your name" (Dan. 9:19, NASB).

Having repented, we would pray. We would pray for the global church to hear the cries of the largest mission field in the world. We would pray for the girls and women in our pews and in our towns and cities who are crying for help. Every country represented at this Congress has trafficked females in it. Every congregation represented here has abused and violated females in its pews. We would pray for the churches worldwide that sit side by side with the trafficked. We would pray for the girls and women who are suffering and dying without hope. We would pray asking for discernment to know what to do for the widows and orphans, the vulnerable females of this world, of *our* communities.

We would also read. We would read so as to understand the issues and thereby be able to work with our governments to be courageous in their stand against trafficking. We would challenge our leaders not to allow politics to destroy humanitarianism. As we studied we would learn that predators pick out the needy, the vulnerable, the child from a troubled home, and those girls and women whose families are poverty-stricken and barely able to exist. We would see that those the predators stake out, circle, and ensnare are the very ones the Word of God calls us to care for, protect, and defend.

And we would work. We would work in our communities to get children off the streets and to help support local law enforcement, calling them to integrity rather than corruption. We would educate our churches, our seminarians, and our pastors so they would teach others concerning the justice of our God and call the church to care for the vulnerable and speak out against incest, rape, and sexual abuse as sin. We would lift up our eyes to see the vast field and begin to actively provide resources to those in the body of Christ around the world who are ministering to a great company of women. We would learn that girls who are protected, educated, given economic alternatives, and loved are not vulnerable to traffickers. So we would actively work to offer resources to the females in our spheres of influence. We would teach parents how to provide homes that are safe for children to grow up in.

We would speak out and educate regarding issues such as domestic violence and sexual abuse. We would develop social services and safe shelters to care for those who have been abused or trafficked and for those who are vulnerable to being trafficked. We would be proactive in our churches, our schools, our seminaries, and our missions to educate and provide treatment for the men in our midst who are in bondage to pornography or sexual exploitation of any kind. The church of Jesus Christ exists in the same world as a global network of traffickers. That church has a mandate from its Master to seek justice, reprove the ruthless, and defend the helpless. Will the body of our great Head follow the one who incarnated all to which he has called us?

I would like to leave us with a glimpse of this Head that we are called to follow. "Jesus, knowing that the Father had given all things into his hands, and that he had come from God and was going back to God, rose from supper. He laid aside his outer garments, and taking a towel, tied it around his waist" (John 13:3–4, ESV). The spirit of ministration was in the blood of Jesus. We see this demonstrated over and over again throughout his life. He got it from his Father, and he followed his Head. It was the air he breathed. It was the law of his life.

The Scriptures teach us that service is a divine thing because God is the One who calls us to it. We have been called to follow our Head, to participate in the work of God by service to others. In the culture of this world, service is a step down. According to this world, to *be* served is to be honored. In the culture of our Father, those who *serve* are in the upper circle. The higher up you go, the more towels you see. The work of ministering to the vulnerable lambs, those who are weak, is a divine work, a holy work. Our Head is saying to his body, "Come up higher. Put on menial robes. Gird yourself with the instruments of servants. Dress for the road, for the dust, for the dung heap." It would seem that which men call lowly, God calls divine. Those whom men call worthless, God calls precious.

The principle of the Scriptures is this: as you leave your world, as you go out of yourself to serve others, you will return exponentially richer than before. Working with those who have been abused and trafficked has taught me many things. It has stretched my heart to love many I never knew who were living lives I could not imagine. I have been challenged to think in new ways and different categories. I have also gleaned greater insight into the heart of my Lord.

You see, he is the One who set forth the principle by leaving his world and going out of himself to give himself to others. According to the Scriptures, he returned home exponentially richer than before. How is he richer? He is richer because he has us—we who were abandoned on the dung heaps of sin to die. Wonder of wonders, his rescue of the worthless ones became his glory (Eph. 1:12), and so it will be for us if we will follow our Head. As we go to the human trash heaps of this world, seeking those who are considered worthless by this world, the glory that will be ours as his body will far exceed the inadequate substitutes we so often pursue. It will be the glory our Head has prayed for us to have: "The glory which You have given Me I have given to them . . . so that the world may know that You sent Me, and loved them, even as You have loved Me (John 17:22–23, NASB).

It is the prayer of my heart that those who follow us in future centuries will point to us as an example of the ministrant body following its ministering Head—because we have left evidence of going out to the trash heaps to rescue girls and women for whom he died and thereby eternally called precious. It is also my prayer that the Reformed community will not be known just for its bold stand for truth, but also for leading the way in protecting, defending, and nurturing the abused and violated females of this world.

The wicked hotly pursue the afflicted . . . his mouth is full of curses and deceit and oppression . . . he sits in the lurking places of the villages . . . he lurks to catch the afflicted; he catches the afflicted when he draws him into his net.

PSALM 10:2, 7–9, NASB

"The issue of trafficking desperately cries out for firm committed leadership" (Victor Malarek in *The Natashas*).

Therefore Jesus also, that He might sanctify the people through His own blood, suffered outside the gate. So, let us go to Him outside the camp, bearing His reproach.

HEBREWS 13:12–13, NASB

These are they which follow the Lamb whithersoever he goeth.

REVELATION 14:4, KJV

Note: The statistics in this paper were gleaned from the following web sites:

- www.humantrafficking.org
- www.state.gov
- www.un.org/Pubs/chronicle/2003/issue2/0203p34.html
- www.ecpat.net
- www.iast.net
- www.ijm.org
- www.chaste.org.uk
- www.ou.edu/student/amnesty/humantrafficking.htm

CHAPTER SIX

SHARING THE BURDEN OF MODERN PAGANISM

PETER JONES

The knowledge and survey of vice is in this world so necessary to the constituting of human virtue, and the scanning of error to the confirmation of truth. . . .

JOHN MILTON, *AREOPAGITICA: A SPEECH FOR THE LIBERTY OF UNLICENSED PRINTING*

Now the Spirit expressly says that in later times some will depart from the faith by devoting themselves to deceitful spirits and teachings of demons. . . . If you put these things before the brothers, you will be a good servant of Christ Jesus, being trained in the words of the faith and of the good doctrine that you have followed.

1 TIMOTHY 4:1, 6, ESV

THE GOAL OF SECULARISM

THE DECLINE OF CHRISTIANITY

If we examine carefully the history of the Christian church from A.D. 300 to the present, we will discover that the Christian church has been in decline for the last two centuries. Hugh McLeod and Werner Ustorf offer this penetrating analysis: "The decline of Christendom has been a very long, drawn-out process . . . first, there was the toleration by the state of a variety of forms of Christianity. Second, there was the open publication of anti-Christian ideas. Third was the separation of church and state. The fourth and most complex phase has been the gradual loosening of the ties between church and society."[1]

Since the sixties, the decline has been a nosedive. In the quintessential English town of Kendal in the Lake District, the home of William Wordsworth, church attendance since 1960, except in one instance, has dropped by 50 percent, while the town's population has increased by almost 50 percent. The church historian Peter Brierly states, "Britain is showing the world how religion as we know it can die." Brierly continues, "We are one generation from extinction." The demise of Christianity and the rise of pagan spirituality in Great Britain is called a "major spiritual revolution." The proof? In Great Britain only 23 percent believe in a personal God, while 44 percent believe in "some sort of spirit or life force."

You say that you are not surprised—that is godless Europe. But not so fast! These British sociologists state that there is even more evidence for the spiritual revolution in the USA than in Britain. Church attendance in the USA has fallen from 40 percent in the 1960s to 24 percent today. At the same time, there are fifteen thousand sites advertising yoga programs in New York. Further, in 2002 there were fifteen million yoga practitioners, and in 2003 35.3 million Americans said they intended to take up yoga in the future.

"U.S. Teens Involved in Their Faiths but Have Major Gaps in Religious Knowledge, Survey Says," reports Richard N. Ostling. Sociologist Christian Smith of the University of North Carolina at Chapel Hill reports the full results in the book *Soul Searching: The Religious and Spiritual Lives of American Teenagers* (Oxford University Press, 2005), written with doctoral student Melinda Lundquist Denton.[2]

Ostling makes this further comment: "The majority of American teens believe in God and worship in conventional congregations, but their religious knowledge is remarkably shallow. . . . Many were so detached from the traditions of their faith, says the report, that they're virtually following a different creed in which an undemanding God

---

[1]Hugh McLeod and Werner Ustorf, eds., *The Decline of Christendom in Western Europe, 1750–2000* (Cambridge, UK: Cambridge University Press, 2003), 5.
[2]Richard N. Ostling, The Associated Press (February 23, 2005).

exists mostly to solve problems and make people feel good. Truth in any absolute, theological sense takes a back seat. God is something like a combination 'Divine Butler and Cosmic Therapist' who's on call as needed. . . ."[3]

PREDICTIONS OF THE VICTORY OF SECULARISM

Many have predicted the demise of Christianity as a social force and have argued that, with the rise of Enlightenment rationalism, it is easy to plot the slow demise of Christianity through a series of mega-movements such as:

- 1. secularization (the world explained without reference to God who is dismissed as a *deus ex machina*)
- 2. laicization (where the welfare state takes over the tasks once provided by the church)
- 3. widespread pluralism (the child of liberal criticism [Herrick], where religious reality is dethroned as a dominant social force and relativized as the personal choice of competing religious claims)

Serious social observers and philosophers in the nineteenth and twentieth centuries predicted the demise of spirituality altogether and the final victory of secularism. Marx in the middle of the nineteenth century dismissed religion as the "opiate of the people." Auguste Comte (1857) argued that secularization was the inevitable result of human maturity. Max Weber (early twentieth century) said secularism was the process by which magic and spiritual mystery are driven from the world and the spiritual loses its "social significance." Sigmund Freud, in *The Future of an Illusion,* saw in secularism the demise of a primitive illusion in an age of scientific inquiry. So many believed in the inevitable triumph of atheistic secularism.

But did it happen? While Christianity is in retreat in the West, there seems to be a growing consensus around the globe that godlessness itself is in trouble. Wolfhart Pannenberg recently stated, "Atheism as a theoretical position is in decline worldwide."[4] Marxist regimes fell everywhere, and postmodernism undermined the self-confidence of Enlightenment rationalism.

Unfortunately, however, the place of atheism has not been taken by

---

[3]Ibid.
[4]Quoted by Uwe Siemon-Netto, "Analysis: Atheism Worldwide in Decline," UPI, March 1, 2005.

biblical theism but by a resurgence of non-Christian spirituality. In our time, spirituality has made a stunning comeback, but it is not Christian spirituality. Jean Houston, adviser to former First Lady Hillary Clinton, saw what was happening and, in 1995, said, "We are living in a state both of breakdown and breakthrough . . . a whole system transition . . . requir[ing] a new alignment that only myth can bring."[5]

This new worldview based on myth and irrationalism shares no common ground with biblical theism. It is, however, nothing less than what Christopher Partridge has called "the re-enchantment of the West."[6]

THE WITNESS OF CONTEMPORARY SOCIOLOGY

The demise of both Christianity and secularism is not a passing fad. Contemporary sociologists speak of "the subjectivist turn of modern Western culture." In their book *The Spiritual Revolution*, Paul Heelas and Linda Woodhead show that "the turn" is a turning away from life as "established roles" and "given orders of things" to states of consciousness, to the importance of the inner self as the norm of behavior and to the high priority of "subjective wellbeing."[7]

Numerous emphases within contemporary culture bear witness to the spiritual direction in which we are going. Here are a few of them:

• *personal health and fitness*: At a superficial level, the great goals are personal health and fitness and methods of stress relief. Personal well-being is the cutting-edge religion of North American culture—go to your local fitness center at 5:00 any afternoon and you will see the movers and shakers of your community.

• *self-help*: Books on self-help proliferate, and "life-trainers" are the latest fad.

• *child-centered self-esteem, outcome-based education:* Teachers no longer teach "objective," "external" facts but specialize in *child-centered outcome-based education* where the child sets the agenda. "We are teaching the child, not mathematics." The child's sense of well-being trumps the body of objective data.

---

[5]Jean Houston, *The Passion of Isis and Osiris: A Gateway to Transcendent Love* (New York: Ballantine, 1995), 2.
[6]Christopher Partridge, *The Re-enchantment of the West: Alternative Spiritualities, Sacralization, Popular Culture and Occulture* (London: T & T Clark, 2004).
[7]Paul Heelas and Linda Woodhead, *The Spiritual Revolution: Why Religion Is Giving Way to Spirituality* (Oxford, UK: Blackwell, 2005).

Here are some results of this approach to education:

A school district in Rhode Island canceled its annual spelling bee this year because administrators decided the crowning of only one violates the main principle that all children should succeed.

A local YMCA in California would not let its gifted children compete in the national swimming finals for fear that some kids would feel left out.

• *work culture of personal development*: Target stores express the *work culture of personal development* by eliminating the hierarchical command structure of old-style business and calling the checkout girl a "team member," though she still has to put in the same eight hours on her feet.

• *me-centered thinking*: The new recruitment catch phrase for military service boasts of "an army of one," whatever that could possibly mean. Some speak of the church in the same way, as "the personal church of the individual." "The phrase 'personal church' of the individual," says Kevin Miller, "must be the most mind-spinning phrase ever written about the church of Jesus Christ. Could it be that we evangelical Protestants, who have done more to fragment Christendom than any other group, are now taking that to the logical extreme: a church at the individual level, each person creating a personal 'church' experience? At any other point in church history, 'personal church' would be nonsensical. In today's America, it's the Next Big Thing."[8]

• *an ethic of subjectivity*: The general societal goal is "feeling and being comfortable with oneself," especially in the area of morals. Today we speak of an ethic of subjectivity, of "moral individualism," and of "the autonomous self," where individuals are encouraged to do "what *feels* right," to "follow your heart," because, we are assured, "Your inner You knows you." This inner You is "truthful, real, reliable, and effective."

• *sexual well-being*: A high-school-age homosexual, justifying a mass mock wedding of numerous gay couples on the school property, declared, "I am happy the way I am. What else matters?"[9]

• *philosophical roots*: This subjectivism is not a passing fad. The subjectivism of contemporary life has deep philosophical roots. It fits with the passage from the rational structures of modernity to the postmodern deconstruction of life and language and its elevation of a subjective view of truth.

Religious implications: This subjectivist "turn" has immediate religious implications. It can also be described as a turn from *religion*

---

[8]Kevin Miller, "No Church? No Problem," *Christianity Today* (January 2006).
[9]"Gay 'Weddings," *Los Angeles Times* (February 12, 2005), B5.

to *spirituality*—that is, from religion understood as giving norms of transcendent meaning to a kind of spirituality that celebrates subjective experience. According to these sociologists, this is "a tectonic shift on the sacred landscape that will prove even more significant than the Protestant Reformation."

So it is with ample justification that James A. Herrick can declare that the "new religious synthesis . . . a radical alternative to the Judeo-Christian traditions" has "already eclipsed the Judeo-Christian culture" of America's past.[10]

The Lutheran scholar Frederic Baue asks, "What comes after the postmodern?" He answers, "a phase of Western/world civilization that is innately religious but hostile to Christianity . . . or worse, a dominant but false church that brings all of its forces to bear against the truth of God's Word."[11]

THE PAGAN MOVEMENT

THE EMERGENCE OF WESTERN POLYTHEISM

Since the sixties, we in the United States have been reliving the experience of sixth-century B.C. Israel—"For your gods have become as many as your cities, O Judah, and as many as the streets of Jerusalem are the altars you have set up to shame, altars to make offerings to Baal" (Jer. 11:13, ESV).

When I arrived from Britain in the U.S. in 1964, I was immediately asked to read books by American "Death of God" theologians. We were assured this was a passing fad of a few marginal, radical scholars. Exactly one decade later, one of those scholars, David Miller, Professor of Religion at Syracuse University and for many years a member of the publication board of the Society of Biblical Literature, published a volume that he provocatively entitled *The New Polytheism: Rebirth of the Gods and Goddesses*. He stated with great foresight and unabashed glee what would happen at this liberating moment in modern history. Not only would there be a funeral for the God of the Bible, but there would also be a triumphant rebirth of the gods and goddesses of ancient Greece and Rome:

---

[10]James A. Herrick, *The Making of the New Spirituality* (Downers Grove, IL: InterVarsity Press, 2003).

[11]Frederic Baue, *The Spiritual Society: What Lurks Beyond Postmodernism?* (Wheaton, IL: Crossway, 2001), 16.

> ... the announcement of the death of God was the obituary of a useless single-minded and one-dimensional norm of a civilization that has been predominantly monotheistic, not only in its religion, but also in its politics, its history, its social order, its ethics, and its psychology. When released from the tyrannical imperialism of monotheism by the death of God, man has the opportunity of discovering new dimensions hidden in the depths of reality's history.[12]

This new polytheism—the fact that we are facing a new form of *religion*—is reflected clearly in the specific ingredients of modern paganism and in the fact that they are united in their emphasis on a kind of monism, the idea that all of reality is essentially one. This is a *theological* conviction, giving shape and substance to modern paganism just as dramatically as Christocentric theology gave shape to the church for two millennia. And the paramount symbol of this new theology is the wheel or the circle, which, in effect, carries a significance in this theology roughly parallel to the significance of the cross in Christian theology.

Carl Jung, the great psychologist of the twentieth century, was also a strong promoter of the occultic mandala, a circular picture with a sun or star usually at the center. Sun worship, as personified in the mandala, is perhaps the key to fully understanding Jung.[13] Jung taught that the mandala (Sanskrit for "circle") was "the simplest model of a concept of wholeness, and one which spontaneously arises in the mind as a representation of the struggle and reconciliation of opposites."[14]

As I expound the five points of paganism or monism, keep in mind the circle.

THE FIVE POINTS OF PAGANISM

1. All Is One and One Is All

In the Disney movie *The Lion King*, everything in the universe is a part of a single mass of energy. Obi-Wan Kenobi, the Jedi warrior in *Star Wars*, explains to young Luke Skywalker, in language like that of a pagan priest or priestess, ancient or modern, "The Force is an energy

---

[12]David Miller, *The New Polytheism: Rebirth of the Gods and Goddesses* (New York: Harper, 1974), vii–x.
[13]Richard Noll, *The Jung Cult: Origins of a Charismatic Movement* (Princeton: Princeton University Press, 1994).
[14]Carl Gustav Jung, *Memories, Dreams, Reflections* (New York: Vintage Books, 1963), 335.

field created by all living things: it surrounds us, penetrates us; it binds the galaxy together . . . it is all-powerful [and] controls everything."

In the mystical tradition from ancient times, traditions such as neo-Platonism and Hermeticism, "god" is not a divine person but "divine energy."[15] This is clearly reflected in Marie Jones's statement in her 2003 book, *Looking for God in All the Wrong Places*: "There is no single person, place or thing that is God, but every person, place or thing is God."[16] For this she uses the classic Wiccan statement: "As above, so below." There is no distinction.

Another expression of this essential universal monism comes from the pen of Isis priestess Caitlin Matthews, who argues that Sophia is the divine Savior who will lead humanity into another, more peaceful and loving civilization because She will lead us out of "the delusion of duality" and into the "marriage of humanity with Nature" and finally into marriage with the Divine."[17]

Bishop John Shelby Spong further develops this all-inclusive faith-statement: "God is not an external, supernatural being, ruling over humanity. God is rather the power of love which flows through each one of us . . . the source of life, of love, the ground of being, . . . [but] life has taught us that theism is dead. . . ."[18]

2. Humanity Is One

This second principle of monism flows naturally from the first. If all is one and one is all, then humanity is a part of God, an expression of divine oneness. Human beings are a kind of concentrated cosmic energy who create their own reality. The belief that human beings are divine, and essentially good, explains today's quest for personal spiritual discovery and the hope that we can create heaven on earth. This monistic humanism becomes a path to religious utopia.

One of the great architects of this notion was Father Pierre Teilhard de Chardin who, writing in the forties and fifties, believed that the whole universe was endowed with a collective consciousness and that by a process of "cultural convergence" would come "the union

---

[15]Herrick, *Making of the New Spirituality*, 43.
[16]Marie Jones, *Looking for God in All the Wrong Places* (New York: Paraview Press, 2003).
[17]Caitlin Matthews, *Sophia: Goddess of Wisdom* (Scranton, PA: Thorsons, 1993), 332, 327.
[18]John Shelby Spong, "The Theistic God Is Dead," in *From the Ashes: A Spiritual Response to the Attack on America* (Emmaus, PA: Rodale, 2001), 55, 58–59.

of the whole human species into a single interthinking group . . . the noosphere."[19]

Responding to the tragedy of 9/11, New Age best-selling author Neale Donald Walsch stated:

> We must create a different reality, build a new society . . . not with . . . the remembered truths of our ancestors. We must do so with new spiritual truths. We must preach a new gospel, its healing message summarized in two sentences: "We are all one. Ours is not a better, ours is merely another way."[20]

3. All Religions Are One

Think again of our circle, and now divide it like a pizza into slices. This is the way many in our pagan world think of the various religions, as pieces of the same pie. In 1993 in Chicago, delegates to the Parliament of the World's Religions held hands and danced around the room to the sound of a Native American shaman's drum. Six thousand delegates shared their experience of the divine within. If all humanity is one, then all religions are one.

Mystical oneness is at the heart of spirituality for the monist. All religions share a common, mystical experience. True believers in any religion will arrive at the same *"unio mystica"* (mystical union with God in which we become divine). All religions are pie slices that join at the center. If one believes in this oneness, one must discard rationality, for mystical union is an irrational affair. If one believes in this oneness, one must throw off doctrine. It doesn't matter if a person is a Christian, a Jew, a Hindu, or a witch; all are a part of the same whole, which is *God*. Each of us can find union with that whole—and the way to union is experience. Just bite into the pie and you will know God!

Huston Smith says that Aldous Huxley's book *The Perennial Philosophy* "converted me from naturalism to a mystical view of reality."[21] It was the "perennial philosophy" that gave him "a loose, working definition of the unity of [religions]," what can be called also "the primordial tradition," also known as "the wisdom tradition of

---

[19]Cited in Andrew J. McCauley, "Teilhard—Apostle of Death," *Latin Mass* (Fall 2002), 19.
[20]Neale Donald Walsch, "What Is the Proper Response to Hatred and Violence?," in *From the Ashes*, 21.
[21]Phil Cousineau, ed., *The Way Things Are: Conversations with Huston Smith* (Berkeley, CA: University of California Press, 2003), 80.

humankind," which is "the conceptual spine that underlies all the major religions . . . not the institutional aspects."[22] "The mystics tend to speak a universal language."[23]

And what exactly is this conceptual spine? At the deepest level, "all the attributes of the personal God melt down into an ultimate unity that we cannot imagine, though it is the only true reality."[24]

Huston Smith, who believes the Spirit of the New Age is producing a new Pentecost, bringing all the religions together, summarizes this perspective by quoting the twelfth-century Sufi master, Ibn Arabi:

> *My soul is a Mosque for Muslims,*
> *A temple for Hindus,*
> *An Altar for Zoroastrians,*
> *A Church for Christians,*
> *A Synagogue for Jews,*
> *And a Pasture for Gazelles.*[25]

4. One Problem—Wake Up

Like the ancient Christian heresy of Gnosticism, contemporary spiritual monism believes that the real problem is lack of knowledge—the knowledge of ourselves as divine. We have forgotten our true nature, lulled into metaphysical amnesia or spiritual sleep by the illusions of the external physical world. The Hindus call it *maya*—illusion. Therefore the monists point an accusing finger at structures we once considered natural, such as a father's loving authority in his home or a husband's loving leadership of his wife. These are illusions to turn us away from our true, egalitarian selves, untrammeled by any creational structures and roles.

The "Jesus" in *A Course in Miracles* states:

> Man's only sin is not remembering his own perfect sinless divine nature. The only devil is our illusion that we are separate from and not part of God . . . the lack you need to correct is the sense of separation from God.[26]

---

[22]Ibid., 88, 153.
[23]Ibid., 83.
[24]Ibid., 154.
[25]Ibid., 279.
[26]*A Course in Miracles: Combined Volume* (Glen Ellen, CA: Foundation for Inner Peace, 1975), 14.

It follows from this starting point that distinction-making/otherness is the source of all evil. God as the transcendent Other in classic Christian orthodoxy, distinct from the works of his own hand, is the deepest of all errors and thus the cause of all evil and suffering. Peacemaking will be accomplished in the twenty-first century on the basis of pagan monism. Evil will not be denounced because it is wrong according to God's holy standards, but because it does not exist.

So monism's message of hope is clear: Rid the world of distinctions, of creational structures and roles, and humanity will realize the mystical unity of all things. This is radical material, though often packaged in the righteous clothing of civil rights. Here is a partial list of distinctions that monists would like to eliminate and that, indeed, should be eliminated if their basic premise is granted:

- Creator/creature
- Christ/Satan
- God/man
- animal/human
- life/death
- Heaven/Hell
- truth/falsehood
- right/wrong
- sin/holiness
- The Bible/other scriptures
- Monotheism/Polytheism
- One woman-wife/many women
- monogamy/polygamy
- love/pornography

Since there is no ultimate good or evil, there are no saved or lost, and no one is left behind! Since everybody will be "saved" (whatever that means), good and evil are purely relative, subjective notions. Madame Blavatsky knew well how to deal with this kind of good and evil: "People with troubled consciences have only two options in life. They can repent, which means they conform their behavior to the moral law, or they can . . . conform their morals to their behavior." The latter is the option she chooses because "Man is the manifested deity in both its aspects—good and evil."[27]

---

[27]H. Blavatsky, *The Secret Doctrine: The Synthesis of Science, Religion and Philosophy*: Vol. LI—*Anthropogenesis* (Pasadena, CA: Theosophical University Press, 1970, originally 1888), 420.

5. One Solution—Go Within

With one's conscience thus appeased, one can trust the self to heal itself. In *The Lion King* the young Simba, distressed by conflict and a lack of identity, lies in a field contemplating the stars. Thanks to the deep, mystical wisdom of Rafiki, the witch doctor, Simba experiences a coming of age. He has a father/mother-earth revelation and identifies the stars, and later his own reflection in a pool, as his father—in other words, a deep experience of unity with the cosmos.

With this confidence in the self, monists tell us to complete the circle by looking into ourselves. Your self sits at the center. Spiritual understanding dawns when you eliminate distinctions and rational controls to take your place in the unity of all things.

But how does one do this? Marianne Williamson declares that we are in the midst of a "revolution that will usher in a mystical age."[28] Sixties rebels discovered themselves through drugs. Today meditation has replaced dangerous drugs as the path to the discovery of self and God. Meditation allows one to detach from his or her body's limitations and discover a connection with the whole through a mystical experience of true knowledge (*gnosis*).

This coherent system, containing the five points listed above, starts and ends with an externally contrived, cleverly manipulated experience that, in deliberately closing our distinction-making mind and thus our God-given distinction-making conscience, beguiles people into believing that they have gained absolute, incontrovertible knowledge of the way things are. They are liberated to do whatever they wish.

This is the pagan moment. How should Christians respond?

THE CHRISTIAN RESPONSE

Obviously Christians, in their attempt to respond to this nearly omnipresent paganism in contemporary culture, must move carefully and thoughtfully and, above all, humbly. First of all, because of the societal decline in traditional Christian beliefs, there is less and less of a common vocabulary for talking about what the gospel is and can offer. But even more significantly, any approach to evangelism must begin with listening and caring . . . and with being *seen* to listen and to care. Only

---

[28]Marianne Williamson, *Healing the Soul of America: Reclaiming Our Voices as Spiritual Citizens* (New York: Simon and Schuster, 2000), 254.

then, as we *show* that we believe that those with whom we are speaking were made in God's image, will we be able to achieve genuine dialogue and understanding.

Nevertheless, the powerful truths of which Archbishop Jensen reminded us at the Opening Worship Service of this General Assembly remain true. Any "mission moment" must, if it is to be biblical, have a verbal clarity that speaks truth into that moment. The confusion in today's world calls loudly for an evangelism of clarity. If paganism is wedded to oneness, biblical theism is wedded to "two-ness." That is, the Bible teaches that there are two kinds of existence: God is the unique, transcendent Creator, and everything else is creature. If one conceives of monism in terms of one circle, then Christianity draws two—one to represent the Creator and the other, below it, to represent the creation. *Keeping the circles distinct is the essence of biblical theism.*

But what exactly is entailed in keeping the circles distinct? That is what the entirety of Christian theology is about. There are many different possible starting points in discussions designed to clarify distinctions between the circles. And every one of the starting points is also a reminder to the individual Christian of an aspect of his faith that he needs to use intentionally to shape his own faith and life before God.

What follows is a list, certainly incomplete, of the points of Christian theology that must be emphasized in churches and homes if we are to be able to respond appropriately and adequately to the threat of worldwide paganism. Each of these points deserves extensive explication. They are simply listed to indicate something of the scope of possible starting points in combating paganism:

1. The biblical doctrine of God, the transcendent Creator, including his incommunicable attributes
2. The mystery and grandeur of the transcendent God
3. The holiness of God and the Creator/creature distinction
4. Divine lordship, sovereignty, and hierarchy
5. Human dignity, lordship, and stewardship
6. A creation made up of distinctions, including the male/female distinction
7. Holiness and submission
8. The twofold nature of existence making personhood possible

9. The transcendent God as the objective reference point for rationality

10. A meaningful history and eschatology

11. Ethics, the distinction between right and wrong

12. The need for divine self-revelation to the creation both in nature and in Scripture

13. The biblical notion of sin

14. Biblical divinely initiated redemption

15. The necessity and mystery of the Incarnation

16. Jesus as the only way

17. The resurrection of the body

18. The notion of covenant

19. Divine and human love

20. Prayer, not inner meditation

21. Praise, not self-praise

22. Christian experience evoked by the Word and the Spirit

So long as we understand clearly the precise differences between monism and theism, the "neo-pagan moment" in contemporary western history provides a unique, God-ordained occasion for full-orbed, biblical witness. This is not the time to panic or to withdraw to our Christian ghettos, or worse still, to gather on a mountain, dressed in white garments, waiting to be beamed up to glory.

In the past, when challenged at its core, the church has rather responded with confessions, creeds, and a deep theological understanding of the nature of the attack. Thus *now* is the moment:

1. to reengage the culture at the level of worldview—this is a new day for biblical apologetics in a postmodern world, since neo-pagans speak constantly of worldview;

2. to engage in a renaissance of full-orbed biblical theism that employs the mind in creative acts of mercy and witness and via the visual, literary, and musical arts in creative acts in celebration of the two-ness of existence that brings a crescendo of praise to God as Creator and Redeemer;

3. to seize the occasion of religious clarity that the face-off between monism and theism allows, and thus break down the gray confusion of postmodern relativism;

4. to preach the gospel of theistic grace in a world of monistic works;

5. to understand thoroughly the worldview of paganism so as better to engage the contemporary interlocutor/seeker;

6. to render the pagan worldview coherent for the laity and for our rising generation of students in order that they may be equipped for witness to a pagan world and have the courage to speak up and speak out intelligently in the mind-numbing world of politically correct newspeak;

7. to seize the occasion to bring a fully-informed restatement of gracious biblical theism and its implications for human dignity and significance to hungry people who begin to see through the ultimate hopelessness of the pagan lie and are also disillusioned with semi-paganized, halfhearted forms of Christianity.

Mark Taylor, the postmodern philosopher, sees the implications of his pagan worldview with disarming clarity: "the death of God [is] the disappearance of self [no predetermined norms] and end of history [no meaningful events] . . . [it] unleashes the aberrant levity of free play . . . purposelessness."[29] He develops the implications of this new freedom: "The lawless land of erring, which is forever beyond good and evil, is the world of Dionysus, the Antichrist, who calls every wander[er] to carnival, comedy, and carnality."[30]

Like Elijah, we need to address the church and the world with a clear message: "How long will you waver between two opinions? If the LORD is God, follow him; but if Baal is God, follow him" (1 Kings 18:21, NIV). Thus John Milton's words apply to us as we seek to understand the truth over against the lie (Rom. 1:25): "the knowledge and survey of vice is in this world so necessary to the constituting of human virtue, and the scanning of error to the confirmation of truth. . . ." May it be said of our witness in difficult, neo-pagan times that it was a responsible "scanning of error" for a compelling "confirmation of the truth." Doing so, we will be, in the words of Paul, "good ministers of Jesus Christ" (1 Tim. 4:6, NIV).

---

[29]Mark C. Taylor, *Erring: A Postmodern A/theology* (Chicago: University of Chicago Press, 1984), 158–159.
[30]Ibid., 157–158.

CHAPTER SEVEN

SHARING THE BURDEN OF DEFENDING THE GOSPEL

YUSUFU TURAKI

For the message of the cross is foolishness to those who are perishing, but to us who are being saved it is the power of God.

1 CORINTHIANS 1:18, NKJV

This presentation is divided into two major parts: (1) The first examines modern western worldviews, philosophies, and religions; and (2) the second part analyzes traditional African worldviews and religious beliefs, syncretism, and religious cults.

In the first part of the presentation, I will consider the sociopolitical context and the environment that gave rise to the modern philosophies and religions opposed to Christianity. In the second part, in which I analyze traditional African worldviews and religious beliefs and practices, a major focus will be on the ways in which African Christians often lapse into syncretism and religious cults in the expressions of their Christianity.

MODERN PHILOSOPHIES OPPOSED TO CHRISTIANITY

Many of the points mentioned here and in the section below will echo the excellent analysis of Dr. Peter Jones in his presentation on modern paganism. I believe that the points are sufficiently significant to warrant that echo, and for those who would like a fuller explication of these matters, I recommend a careful review of what Dr. Jones has said.

Here are a few crucial philosophical ingredients in the contemporary intellectual scene as we move into the twenty-first century:

> a. *Secularism*, in which man and his autonomy and freedom have been made the god of the age in place of the Almighty God of Scripture.
>
> b. *Cultural and religious pluralism and relativism*, in which the biblical presentation of the uniqueness of Jesus Christ as the only Savior and Mediator between God and men is replaced by the parity, equality, and plurality of other saviors, mediators, or intermediaries.
>
> c. *Postmodernism*, in which "Life has no point. Nothing is sacred. Reverence is an unworthy relic of the past times; everything is a potential target for mockery. There are no honored models to shape behavior. The individual is alone and there are no route maps."[1]

MODERN RELIGIONS OPPOSED TO CHRISTIANITY

Worldwide, many crucial religious and spiritual ingredients abound in the contemporary intellectual scene as we move into the twenty-first century. For this paper I will focus on the primary one that is centered in the West and the primary one that is centered in Africa. Versions of these religions appear in many countries and cultures around the world, and, therefore, understanding these can be a great help to Christian believers anywhere.

> a. *Neopaganism and New Age religions in the West*, in which the biblical belief in the Almighty God and Creator of the universe is rejected and replaced by an Earth Goddess or nature gods or many gods. As noted above, Dr. Peter Jones has provided a superb discussion of this subject.
>
> b. *Syncretism and religious cults in Africa*, in which the essential meaning of central aspects of the gospel are changed in ways that undermine and possibly even contradict essential biblical teaching. This will be discussed in some detail below.

---

[1]B. H. Son, "Cultural Relativism and the Transformation of Culture," in *Philosophia Reformata*, Vol. 66, No. 1, 2001, 12.

These are the major religious challenges to orthodox Christianity in the West and in Africa. But how exactly did they rise to their positions of prominence vis-à-vis the gospel? And that leads to a related question—what are the reasons for the decline of Christianity in the West? The places where, for almost two millennia, the Christian church was so strong and exerted so much influence seem in many ways effectively to have been de-Christianized. How and why did this happen?

SOME REASONS FOR CHANGES IN CULTURE AND WORLDVIEW IN THE WEST

The emergence of modern philosophies and religions in the West is due to the radical historical change of worldviews and culture. New social forces have generated new worldviews radically opposed to Christian worldviews. They have enforced a way of seeing, understanding, interpreting, and applying biblical truths and the Christian faith that dramatically differ from what had been the norm in the Christian church for centuries.

The Bible and the Christian faith have been reinterpreted to accommodate modern practices and beliefs such as homosexuality, feminism, materialism, hedonism, and neopaganism. In the West, it is now possible for an individual to claim to be both a Christian and a homosexual, or a racist, or a feminist, or a hedonist, or a materialist. And the reason for this incredible possibility is that there has been a historical shift of worldviews in the West.

Worldview as a concept needs to be defined. Worldviews are guides to life. Elsewhere I defined worldview as "a people's total way of seeing, of understanding, of interpreting, and of constructing the reality of existence (life) out of their historically transmitted and ordered systems of meanings, of symbols, of conceptions of nature, of self, and of society."[2]

Christianity itself constitutes a worldview, a way of looking at and understanding and responding to the world in which we have been placed. The Christian worldview places all of human experience into a specific framework, a specific context. Just so, secularism, pluralism, relativism, and postmodernism are worldviews that offer frameworks

---

[2]Yusufu Turaki, "Christian Worldview Foundations: A Methodological Approach," in *Orientation,* 1993, 86.

and contexts that are, at best, inconsistent with a Christian worldview and, at worst, that flatly contradict a Christian worldview.

A number of crucial historical events have contributed to this change of worldviews in the West. I will outline a few of the most significant. Obviously, these outlines are extremely sketchy, but they are also, I am convinced, accurate and in keeping with most historical analyses of these periods.

THE RENAISSANCE (FOURTEENTH AND FIFTEENTH CENTURIES)

The Renaissance, as historians have presented it, means primarily the rebirth of classical scholarship, mainly the study of Greek and Latin writers of the ancient times. This revival of scholarship was directed at those disciplines called the "humanities," especially languages, literature, poetry, history, and moral philosophy. Because of the preoccupation of medieval scholars with logic, metaphysics, law, and systematic theology, the humanities were neglected until the fourteenth and fifteenth centuries, when they again attracted the scholarly attention of the great centers of learning.

Correlative to this focus on the humanities was an emphasis on the significance of the creators of humanistic writings—human beings— and this quickly led study of the humanities into the movement that has been called "humanism." Moving from eternal truths (such as those dealt with in metaphysics and theology), Renaissance humanism focused its attention on temporal realities, and in doing so, it subtly but decisively shifted ultimate values from the divine to the human realm.

For example, in a humanistic environment, man is not defined in terms of his divine Creator or, indeed, in terms of any reality beyond himself. The result was

> . . . the belief that human beings are *autonomous*. This means that human beings are their own source of meaning and authority . . . the authority of human beings is the final arbiter . . . human beings are regarded as actually creating their own nature. Man has the power to determine the very essence of his own being. . . . In secular humanism, man is his own creator.[3]

---

[3]Jon Chapin, et al., *An Introduction to Christian Worldview* (London: The Open Christian College, 1986), 131.

Correlative to the notion that man is autonomous is the conviction that the *individual* human being, not societal or cultural or religious groups, defines his own identity and destiny. It is not just that humanity is autonomous; each individual man and woman is also autonomous. And the result of this conviction is what might be called the cult of individualism, in which the desires and the rights of the individual take precedence over everything and everyone else.

And, of course, the church would count as a "someone else." Immediately we see the intrinsic linkage between what those in the West often regard as a political blessing and what is, in fact, a religious curse. At least it is a curse if we regard the rise of anti-Christian philosophies and religions as a negative phenomenon!

But the Renaissance exalted not only autonomous, individualistic human nature in and of itself; it also exalted man in his relationship to the rest of nature. In place of the biblical concept of man's stewardship role in relation to the rest of creation, the Renaissance emphasized human mastery and manipulation of nature. As other scholars have pointed out, "the claim of human autonomy" led inexorably to "the idea of human domination of nature" through science and technology.[4]

These three themes—humanism, individualism, and naturalism—were, therefore, among the most significant of the contributions of the Renaissance to modern thought. They are the essential roots of neo-paganism and New Age religions in the West.

THE SCIENTIFIC REVOLUTION (SEVENTEENTH CENTURY)

The Scientific Revolution of the seventeenth century was built largely on the intellectual foundation of the Renaissance, and especially on that part of the foundation that advocated man's mastery of nature through science. Of course, not all seventeenth-century scientists or philosophers of science exercised faith in science itself. Yet, overall we see in this century the development of a powerful and influential scientific humanism. The period has been characterized as follows: "Human horizons were expanding, and modern science was on the

---

[4]Ibid., 134.

upsurge. Indeed, science was to take the leading cultural role in the early development of the West."[5]

Intrinsic to the understanding of science that emerged in the seventeenth century was a radical emphasis on the empirical method. Science dealt with things that could be "tested" and "proven," and gradually through the century the idea took hold that only conclusions reached in this manner had any true validity. Again, the Wikipedia Internet encyclopedia provides an excellent simple definition:

> Empiricism is, therefore, the *philosophical* doctrine (-ism) of "testing" or "experimentation," and has taken on the more specific meaning that all human knowledge ultimately comes from the senses and from experience. Empiricism denies that humans have innate ideas or that anything is knowable without reference to experience. It is generally regarded as the heart of the modern scientific method, that present theories should be based on our observations of the world rather than on intuition or faith; that is, empirical research and a posteriori inductive reasoning rather than purely deductive logic.

Faith in science, therefore, often meant nothing more or less than faith in the empirical method. But, as is obvious, faith in the empirical method is as much an aspect of worldview as is the Christian doctrine of biblical revelation, which that method slowly seemed to supplant in the Western mind. The fact of faith did not change. Only its object did.

THE ENLIGHTENMENT (EIGHTEENTH CENTURY)

The Enlightenment is usually referred to as the "Age of Reason," and its central ideological components arose directly out of the emphases of the Renaissance and the Scientific Revolution. If man is self-defining and autonomous, and if trustworthy knowledge comes only through human exploration of the empirical world, then it is clear that the human mind is ultimately the arbiter of truth.

Here is one summary of the essence of the Enlightenment:

> . . . the view of human reason as the source of all real knowledge became widespread. . . . Autonomous human reason came increas-

---

[5]Ibid., 136.

ingly to be seen as ushering in a new end of illumination. Vast hopes came to be vested in the power of reason to unlock the hidden truths of the world. To be fully human was to be "rational" in all fields of human life. By following the dictates of a reason unspoiled by faith, tradition, and dogma, true human fulfillment and happiness could be realized.[6]

"Enlightenment" as a personal attribute thus came to be defined in terms of the degree to which an individual placed his intellectual confidence in himself. More and more, as should be obvious, man, rather than God, was becoming "the measure of all things." And more and more, as the Enlightenment continues its extraordinary influence on modern thought, are secularism, relativism, and postmodernism characteristic of contemporary western culture.

THE ROMANTIC REACTION (NINETEENTH AND TWENTIETH CENTURIES)

There was, of course, a strong negative reaction to the conclusions of the Scientific Revolution and the Enlightenment, and that reaction has continued into the present even as the implications of the Scientific Revolution and the Enlightenment continue to dominate western culture. Surely, many have argued, there is more to man than his reason and more to life than empirical inquiry. There is the sheer beauty of poetry and music. There is the power of artistic creativity. There are joy and love and hope. With such arguments, Christians have—and should have—agreed. But the definition of the "more than" has often been as firmly established on the foundation of the Renaissance as were the Scientific Revolution and the Enlightenment, and often the church has not seen this.

When the Renaissance assumption of human autonomy is left unchallenged, when the worldview of individualism remains intact, the results of any reaction will be as anti-Christian as that against which the reaction has been raised. And so it has been in the Romantic reaction.

In its modern forms, this Romantic reaction has produced a variety of "counterculture" movements that are at least as fundamentally

---

[6]Ibid., 140–142.

opposed to biblical Christianity as were the Enlightenment and the Scientific Revolution. The abandoning of traditional morality and values, the rejection of established authority and institutions, the emergence of the hippie culture, rock music, and the experimentation with alternative lifestyles and drugs were all forms of protest against the modern scientific humanist worldview.[7] These modern cultural protests have not, however, led to a return to the Christian and biblical worldviews. These protests have led instead to further alienation and lostness, the celebration of the age of human freedom and humanism, and the emergence of neopaganism, New Age religions, cults and occult organizations, hedonism, and postmodernism.

In this very brief survey, we have looked at a few of the historical periods that have contributed to the dramatic shift in worldviews in the West during the past five hundred years. The results of the shift are many, and all of those results have made a major impact upon the church and its mission. But the most devastating of those impacts has been the development of religious and cultural pluralism and relativism.

When man becomes "the measure of all things," whether the perspective is that of Enlightenment Rationalism or of Romantic emotionalism, the results are always the same—the claims of all religions, and especially Christianity, are made into the private preferences of the individual, with no objective force or standing in the lives of those who simply prefer a different direction. This is the aspect of the modern western worldview that challenges in the most profound way the essence of the Christian worldview.

Let us turn to examining the devastating effects of religious and cultural pluralism and relativism upon Christianity.

RELIGIOUS AND CULTURAL PLURALISM AND RELATIVISM IN THE WEST

In the West, relativism and pluralism of cultures and religions have forced a paradigm shift in Christian evangelization of cultures and religions. The result is that the teachings of Christianity, the Bible, the prophets, the apostles and the Christian tradition, and especially the uniqueness of Jesus Christ are being challenged or rejected. Lesslie

---

[7]Ibid., 144.

Newbigin, in his book *The Gospel in a Pluralist Society* (1989), and Ken Gnanakan, in *The Pluralistic Predicament* (1992), have both offered penetrating analyses of the impact of pluralism and relativism on the contemporary Christian church.

In short, the relativist questions the place and authority of biblical and apostolic Christianity with its "absolute" claims of the unique necessity of faith in Christ for salvation. The argument is often put this way: in our "modern" society there are (and should be) many religions and cultures living side by side. These are all assumed to have equal standing in terms of their truth claims. Here are Gnanakan's words:

> Some propose that what is needed is for all religions to come together forgetting their differences. After all, they would claim, Christianity is not really unique. We may have rightly claimed uniqueness at one time, but today's situation is totally hostile to such claims. What we have learnt in recent times about religions and of their own "truth claims" compel us, we are told, to cast aside all the unique claims that we make about Christ and accept on equal terms similar claims of all other religions.[8]

According to Ken Gnanakan, the main challenge presented by the pluralist to the Christian church has to do with the One who gives his very name to that church. Who exactly is Jesus? Is he one among many ways to God? Or is he the *only* way? Here is Gnanakan's answer to those questions:

> We have made it quite clear that salvation is through Jesus alone. In this sense, we would unashamedly be Christocentric. The pluralist, we have shown, is wanting to be theocentric, soteriocentric, even reality-centric and has consequently surrendered any certainty to much needed foundations. Even the inclusivist, we have noted, will claim to be Christocentric, but is willing to allow for salvation to be experienced in other religions only claiming the normativity of Jesus Christ. This falls short of what the Bible is saying. Jesus Christ is not merely the norm, he is the name through which men and women are saved.[9]

This must be the consistent and vigorously defended position of the Christian church, especially in an age of pluralism. We must not

---

[8]Ken Gnanakan, *The Pluralistic Predicament* (Bangalore, India: Theological Book Trust, 1992), 3.
[9]Ibid., 211.

allow this essential aspect of the Christian worldview to be eroded by constant cultural pressures. We must stand firm.

But, many would (correctly) point out, most of us actually live in a culturally pluralistic environment. Even countries where a majority would claim commitment to Christian values allow and encourage religious diversity. How do we deal appropriately with that reality without allowing the pluralistic worldview to shape our own lives?

In his excellent article "Being a Christian in a Pluralistic Society," Dallas Willard makes these points:

> Pluralism does *not* mean that everyone is equally right in what they think and do. It does not mean that we must agree with the views or adopt the practices of those of other persuasions. It does not mean that we must *like* those views or practices. It does not mean that we will not appropriately express our disagreement or dislike for other viewpoints. Pluralism also does not mean that we will not try, in respectful ways, to change the views or practices of others, by all appropriate means of persuasion, where we believe them to be mistaken. In fact, pluralism should, precisely, secure a social context in which full and free interchange of different views on life and reality can be conducted to the greatest advantage of all.[10]

Lesslie Newbigin presents a perspective that matches that of Gnanakan. What is pluralism, and how does it find cultural expression? "In a pluralist society such as ours, any confident statement of ultimate belief, any claim to announce the truth about God and his purpose for the world, is liable to be dismissed as ignorant, arrogant, dogmatic."[11]

Newbigin presents these challenges to the church, in the context of this pluralism:

> 1. There is a need for understanding "afresh the nature and the role of the church's mission in today's pluralistic world."
> 2. There is a need "for an authentic expression of the meaning of the gospel and the mission of the church in the midst of a plurality of cultures and religions."
> 3. There is a need to identify and expose the dangers of pluralism, relativism and humanism as modern worldviews and ideologies held

---

[10]Dallas Willard, "Being a Christian in a Pluralistic Society," in *The Student*, 1992.
[11]Lesslie Newbigin, *The Gospel in a Pluralist Society* (Grand Rapids, MI: Eerdmans, 1989), 10.

out against Christianity, which in themselves have no credibility, or basis of denying Christianity a place in a modern pluralist society.

4. There is a need for a strong call and return to the "renowned confidence in the gospel of Jesus Christ" and "how as Christians we can more confidently affirm our faith in the mind and intellectual climate" of a pluralist society.

5. There is a need for analyzing "the roots of the present crisis of Christian confidence" in a pluralist society.[12]

There is no way in which the Christian church in the West can defend the gospel without taking on the kinds of challenges Newbigin has laid down. And there are no better resources to use in this effort than Newbigin's own works.

But the church in the West is not the only church, and I turn now to examine the syncretism and religious cults in Africa. As I do so, some striking points of similarity between the western church and the African church will be discovered.

AFRICAN TRADITIONAL RELIGION

Any meaningful and effective approach to the theology of African traditional religion and its accompanying worldview must begin with the fundamental religious beliefs within that religion. These beliefs are found throughout Africa, even though they may be expressed differently from region to region or from people to people. My objective here is not to state in detail how these beliefs find expressions in different places. It is, instead, to present certain fundamental and basic tenets that are common to all forms of African traditional religion. There are five of these tenets.

BELIEF IN IMPERSONAL (MYSTICAL) POWER(S)

At the root of Africa's traditional religious beliefs, feelings, practices, and behavior is a belief in mystical and mysterious powers. This belief is pervasive in traditional African religious thought. Creation, nature, and everything that exists is infused with this impersonal power, which has been given various names. Edwin Smith called it the *mysterium tremendum* and stated that this phenomenon was "played upon, defined,

---

[12]Ibid.

and rationalized by myths and creeds and put to use through control and conciliation."[13] This power has also been referred to as mana, the life force, vital force, the life essence, and dynamism.

Medicine men and women, diviners, and seers use the impersonal power associated with natural objects, plants, and animals for medicine, magic, charms, and amulets. Some believe that the mysterious powers embedded in things or objects can be extracted for specific uses. Mysterious powers can also be transmitted through certain objects or by purely spiritual means. They can be sent to specific destinations to accomplish good or evil. They can also be contagious by contact with objects carrying or mediating such powers.

The impersonal powers can be used for both good and evil. The existence of wicked human beings and wicked spirit beings, who also have access to the mysterious powers, makes life full of uncertainties—rife with unpredictable wickedness and evil, and dangerous to human beings. Therefore, traditional Africans who believe in the impersonal powers feel that they are at the mercy of benevolent or wicked users of these powers.

BELIEF IN SPIRIT BEINGS

Mystical power is not the only mysterious force in traditional African belief. The religious world of African people is very densely populated with spirit beings, spirits, and the living dead or the spirits of the ancestors.[14] These are "psychic beings that are intelligent, purposive, and personal as opposed to the impersonal potency at work in dynamism."[15] There is a very close relationship between spirit beings and the mystical or impersonal powers and forces described in the previous section. Like those powers, spirits are believed to inhabit certain trees, rocks or mountains, caves, rivers, lakes, forests, burial grounds, animals, human beings, the skies, the ground and other sites, carved or molded objects, charms, amulets—the list is endless.

Spirits are ranked hierarchically in accordance with their power and the role they play in the ontological order in the spirit world.[16] First

---

[13]V. B. Cole, "The Christian and African Traditional Religion and Culture: Some Basic Principles of Understanding and Approach" (unpublished manuscript, 1989), 3.

[14]J. S. Mbiti, *African Religions and Philosophy* (London: Heinemann, 1969), 75.

[15]Cole, "Christian and African Traditional Religion and Culture," 3.

[16]E. D. Oji, "Ikpu Alu (Atonement) in Igbo Traditional Religion" (Jos, Nigeria: ECWA Theological Seminary, B.A. thesis, 1988), 17.

in the hierarchy is the Creator, then the deities, object-embodied spirits, ancestors' spirits and other miscellaneous spirits that are nonhuman, comprising both good and harmless spirits and evil spirits. Human beings stand between this host of spirits and the world of nature.

Spirit beings are usually categorized as either the spirits of the dead elders (the ancestors, who are close to human beings and serve as their custodians) or nonhuman spirit beings. They can also be classified as good or evil, depending on whether they use the powers with which they are endowed to achieve positive or negative goals, to bring blessings or curses. B. H. Kato argues that evil spirits are always associated with Satan.[17] The spirit world or the realm of the supernatural is, in a sense, a battleground of spirits and powers that use their mystical and spiritual powers to influence the course of human life.

Spirit beings can be malicious and capricious, and so one must be wise and tactful in one's dealings with them to avoid angering, provoking, or injuring them. If human beings only knew how to master and control the realm of the supernatural, the world would be a much happier place. Consequently if one wishes to be successful, or merely to enjoy well-being, it is important to consult those human specialists with experience of and access to mystical powers. These specialists include medicine men, rainmakers, mediums, diviners, sorcerers, magicians, witches, and all others who have the ability to manipulate spirit beings so that they serve humans, or vice versa.

Other sources of safety and protection in a world dominated by the spirit beings and powers include religious rites, reverence for ancestors, symbolic totems, and adherence to taboos, rituals, superstitions, and customs. Some, if not all, of these are needed for guidance and protection.

BELIEF IN MANY DIVINITIES

Some African scholars no longer accept the term "polytheism" (worship of many gods) as applied to African traditional religion and prefer the term "divinities" or "deities" to "gods." There has been indeed much inconclusive debate on whether African divinities were worshiped as gods or whether they were only intermediaries or mediators. Some have argued that Africans do not worship either their divinities

---

[17]B. H. Kato, *Theological Pitfalls in Africa* (Nairobi: Evangel Press, 1975), 36–41.

or their ancestors, but only God. In terms of this argument, sacrifices, offerings, and prayers are not directed to the divinities or the ancestors as ends in themselves but are directed ultimately to God.

African traditional religions in some parts of Africa have an elaborate pantheon of divinities. The Yoruba of Nigeria, for example, are known to have several hundred divinities. But this is not the case in Southern Africa and some parts of West Africa. Some African ethnic groups do not seem to have any divinities, while others are known to have no special shrines or places of worship associated with divinities or a Supreme Being.

In those places in Africa that have divinities, these are many, and each has its specific area of influence and control. Some were originally mythological figures in African legends and primordial histories and cosmologies, while some were tribal heroes or heroines. Divinities are usually associated with different aspects of life, society, and community; there are, for example, divinities of the sea or the waters, rain, thunder, fertility, health or sickness, planting or harvest, and tribal, clan, or family deities. African divinities take the forms of mountains, rivers, forests, the mother earth, the sun, the moon, the stars, and ancestors.

The plurality of divinities with their varying powers, influence, hierarchy and territoriality, even within one ethnic group or community, clearly indicates that traditional religious thought is open to religious accommodation, tolerance, assimilation, and adaptation.

The introduction of Christianity and other monotheistic religions, such as Islam, may have added what is called henotheism to the African worldview—that is, the worship of one god without denying the existence of other gods. Traditional beliefs can accommodate the worship of the Christian God along with other gods without creating any serious theological crisis for the believer. A plurality of gods or divinities permits plurality of beliefs, practices, feelings, and behavior in one religion. This belief also gives room for accommodation, adaptation, and domestication of new gods or divinities into the old religion.

BELIEF IN A SUPREME BEING (GOD)

Some of the pioneering anthropologists and missionaries denied that Africans had any awareness of God. They were wrong. It is now firmly established that Africans do have a concept of a universal God and Creator.[18] It is, however, also generally agreed that traditional Africans do not actively worship this Supreme Being who is above the lesser divinities and the hierarchy of beings. This, of course, gives rise to additional questions as to why the Supreme Being is not worshiped directly and who or what takes the role that other religions ascribe to such a Supreme Being in daily affairs.

E. B. Idowu calls the Yoruba religion "diffused monotheism."[19] This means that the Yoruba were originally monotheistic, but over the centuries a proliferation of divinities overshadowed the earlier monotheistic beliefs and practices. Similar ideas of diffused monotheism are scattered across the continent of Africa. However, the overwhelming burden of evidence suggests that even though Africans generally have an awareness and belief in a Supreme Being, this Being was not worshiped exclusively. Instead, African divinities and the ancestors, who are lesser beings, have dominated the everyday religious life of traditional Africans. They are the ones who most often directly receive the sacrifices, offerings, and prayers offered by traditional Africans.

The attitude of traditional Africans to this Supreme Being exerts a profound theological influence. The God who is above the lesser gods seems "not to be intimately involved or concerned with man's world. Instead, men seek out the lesser powers to meet their desires."[20] This leads people to turn to impersonal powers, divinities, ancestors, and spirit beings for help. God (the Supreme Being) is only occasionally mentioned, remembered, or approached.

BELIEF IN A HIERARCHY OF SPIRITUAL BEINGS AND POWERS

One component in the apparent disregard for the Supreme Being is the fundamental belief that all spiritual beings and powers form part of a hierarchical order. The Supreme Being enjoys the highest and greatest position. Gods (or divinities) occupy a lesser position. Next come spirit beings, whose authority, power, influence, and legitimacy depend upon

---

[18]E. B. Idowu, *Olódùmarè: God in Yoruba Belief* (London: Longman Press, 1962). See also J. S. Mbiti, *Introduction to African Religion* (London: Heinemann, 1975).
[19]Ibid.
[20]Philip M. Steyne, *Gods of Power: A Study of the Beliefs and Practices of Animists* (Houston: Touch, 1989), 35.

their position within the ontological order of being. However, it is important to note that this hierarchy is a fluid one, where the distinction between spirits may be vague and their powers diffuse.

Spirit beings dispense and control the effects of spiritual and mystical powers and forces and influence the morality and ethics of human societies.[21] Traditional Africans respond to these spirit beings according to each spirit's place in the spiritual hierarchy, its power and influence, territoriality, legitimacy, and role.

SUMMARY

The influence of the first two components of African traditional religious thought—namely, the belief in impersonal powers and spirit beings—is pervasive throughout the continent. The third component is not as pervasive, for not every ethnic group in traditional Africa has well-defined divinities or gods. While belief in a Supreme Being is also pervasive, it differs from the other three components in that it is a belief that does not generate any religious fervor or encourage any intimate relationship with the Supreme Being. The Supreme Being seems to be remote from traditional African everyday life. The religious activities of the traditional Africans revolve mainly around the first three entities. The ranking of spirit beings in a traditional religious worldview has important consequences for traditional concepts of morality and ethics.

Right away we can see the similarities between some aspects of traditional African religious thought and the pluralism and relativism that have come to dominate western culture. More such comparisons will appear as we move to consider African philosophical systems.

AFRICAN PHILOSOPHICAL BELIEFS

As in the previous section, so here I do not intend to provide in-depth analyses. Rather, I will suggest some of the common tenets that permeate much of African philosophy. The combination of the religious (discussed in the previous section) and the philosophical (presented in this section) creates a worldview that dominates traditional African thought.

---

[21]Emefie Ikenga-Metuh, *Comparative Studies of African Traditional Religions* (Onitsha, Nigeria: IMICO, 1987), 243–259.

HOLISM

Holism refers to a state of complex interdependency, in which each part of an organism has a function. Philosophically, holism is the term for the view that life is more than the sum of its parts. Steyne defines the concept in the following way:

> The world interacts with itself. The sky, the spirits, the earth, the physical world, the living, and the deceased all act, interact, and react in consort. One works on the other and one part can't exist nor be explained without the other. The universe, the spirit world and man are all part of the same fabric. Each needs the other to activate it.[22]

This view of the world means that there are no clear boundaries between the physical and the spiritual dimensions of life. There is no sharp distinction between secular and religious activities, between one's work and one's community responsibilities—they are "all knit together in a whole [so that man] feels at one with his world."[23] Kwame Bediako expresses it this way: "Man lives in a sacramental universe where there is no sharp dichotomy between the physical and the spiritual. The physical acts as a vehicle for spiritual power, while the physical realm is held to be patterned on the model of the spiritual world beyond."[24]

Because nature, humanity, and the spirit world constitute one fluid coherent unit, there are clearly pantheistic elements in African holism. In fact, nature is defined as

> . . . this visible material world or universe, comprising both living and non-living things, visible and invisible powers, plants and animals, the inanimate and the natural phenomena, like lightning and thunder, all centered around man. The spirit world is all the same tacitly understood as inclusive in nature.[25]

Thus nature includes both the impersonal or mysterious powers and spirit beings. Bediako shows how this leads to pantheism:

---

[22]Steyne, *Gods of Power,* 58.
[23]Ibid., 59.
[24]Kwame Bediako, *Christianity in Africa: The Renewal of a Non–Western Religion* (Edinburgh: Edinburgh University Press, 1995), 95.
[25]Oji, "Ikpu Alu," 15.

> [Man had] a sense of kinship with nature, in which animals and plants, no less than human beings, had their own spiritual existence and place in the universe, as interdependent parts of a whole. . . . Any object of the natural environment may enter into a totemic spiritual relationship with human beings or become tutelary and guardian spirits whilst the environment itself is used realistically and unsentimentally but with profound respect and reverence and without exploitation.[26]

Africans do not live in a confused world of non-integrated parts. Life is mysterious, but it is part of a whole. And that whole is governed by a law of harmony, the goal of which is to maintain a state of agreement or peacefulness. The traditional African seeks to live in harmony and to balance his life in a harmonious and peaceful existence with his entire world and especially with the spirit world.

SPIRITUALISM

In the previous section we stated that traditional beliefs do not distinguish between the material and the spiritual worlds. But that was actually an inadequate way of formulating the traditional African philosophy. It might be truer to say that this world in essence is spiritual rather than material and that life is saturated with supernatural possibilities. Steyne puts it this way:

> The whole universe is interconnected through the will and the power contained in both animate and inanimate objects. Everything man is, does, handles, projects, and interacts with is interpenetrated with the spiritual. His sociocultural structures, down to their finest details, are under the control of the spiritual powers or forces. Nothing in man's environment escapes the influence or the manipulation of the spirit world. The world is more spiritual than it is physical, and it is spiritually upheld.[27]

The whole of creation is replete with the dominant and pervasive presence of the impersonal powers and forces, spirit beings, many divinities, and gods. Consequently "it is of utmost importance to maintain good relations with the spirits and secure their favor."[28]

---

[26]Bediako, *Christianity in Africa*, 85.
[27]Steyne, *Gods of Power*, 37.
[28]Ibid.

> Whatever happens in the physical realm has a spiritual coordinate and, likewise, whatever transpires in the spiritual realm has direct bearing on the physical world. Man is related to and dependent upon the unseen. For this reason all of life is to be understood spiritually. The correct response to any situation is spiritual, whether the matter is a family affair, sickness, or ceremonial practice.[29]

Thus in African traditional philosophy, answers to questions of meaning in life (the "Why?" questions) are always dominated by the spiritual emphasis. When trouble comes in the form of disease, natural disasters, or untimely deaths, traditional Africans look beyond the obvious physical causes and consult religious specialists to find the ultimate spiritual cause.

This philosophy both draws on and supports the pantheistic, polytheistic theology described in the previous section. The law of the spirit is a universal principle that governs and controls universal events and unseen powers and mysteries. It affects the destiny, the well-being, and the general life of individual human beings as well as the lives of people-groups or families, clans, communities, and tribes; it manifests itself in and through the spirits, human beings, and inanimate objects; it defines the reality of African worldview; and it is pervasive, hidden, unexplainable, unpredictable, powerful, dreadful, and awesome. This law is reflected in moral laws and religious practices that govern the interrelationship and integration of spirit beings and humans in the traditional spirit world.

DYNAMISM

Given the convictions regarding holism and spiritualism just discussed, the natural response is to look for ways to establish communication with the spirit world. Because that spirit world is impersonal, unseen, and unpredictable, there is a desire for power that will bring security in a dangerous world. Steyne describes this power-consciousness in the following words:

> Life's essential quest is to secure power and use it. Not to have power or access to it produces great anxiety in the face of spirit caprice and the rigors of life. A life without power is not worth living. . . . Power

---

[29]Ibid., 59.

offers man control of his uncertain world. The search for and acquisition of power supersedes any commitment to ethics or morality. Whatever is empowering is right.[30]

Power can be obtained in a variety of ways, some of which Steyne lists:

> . . . ritual manipulation . . . in the form of sacrifices, offerings, taboos, charms, fetishes, ceremonies, even witchcraft and sorcery. . . . The power may also be secured by the laying on of hands or by encountering a spirit being, either directly or through ritual means. The power may be transmitted through contact with persons of superior religious status or by using clothing or something previously associated with such a person. How it is secured is a secondary concern. It must be acquired whatever the cost.[31]

This all-consuming need for power exerts an enormous influence on morality and ethics and on the relationship between human beings and spirit beings and forces. It also affects how traditional Africans assess the potency or efficacy of a new religion or ritual practice. This view of the world as governed by a law of power creates a need for a theology of power if we are to address the traditional theological conception of power and also how this law of power operates in traditional Africa.

FATALISM

The concepts of destiny and fate in the traditional worldview are closely related to the belief in spirits and mysterious powers. Destiny is the belief that some external, supernatural force has predetermined the position, place, and status of individuals or groups. Fate is similar to destiny in that it means that certain events are predetermined to happen. The end result of a strong belief in destiny and fate is fatalism, the doctrine that events are fixed in advance for all time in such a manner that human beings are powerless to change them.

The traditional worldview considers that one is either born with or given at birth a destiny or a guardian spirit. Thus destiny is both a gift and a decree from the Creator. Individuals, families, and groups

---

[30]Ibid., 60.
[31]Ibid.

each have their own unique destiny decreed by the Creator and are accompanied throughout life by their destiny spirits. Their destiny may be known or it can remain hidden. If one wishes to know one's destiny, one can consult diviners and other spiritual resources.

One's destiny is fixed. It cannot be changed and should be accepted with gratitude. Any attempt to change it will have devastating consequences. However, one can be hindered from fulfilling one's destiny by others or by spiritual powers. This is where the concept of fate comes in. Spirits and mysterious powers control the world of fate, and God does not seem to be active in protecting man against evil activities by these spirits and powers. One has to find one's own protection and security.

The apparent lack of active protection from God has great theological implications for the traditional Africans, especially in their search for spiritual powers that will offer them protection and security. What is the traditional African reaction to the fact that someone or some spirit powers can hinder them from realizing their destiny? The obvious answer is to pursue power that can be used to counteract such attacks. Where other people are thought to be thwarting achievement of one's destiny, there can be serious social conflict between individuals or people groups.

Individuals or groups attempting to determine their own destiny or that of others can also manipulate the concept of destiny. They usually ascribe themselves a superior destiny or status and consign others to an inferior role. Both roles are then assumed to be fixed and unchangeable. This attitude sometimes develops into castes and social classes. Even though these distinctions are man-made, they may obtain religious and social sanction. When this occurs, there is great potential for social conflict. Humans have usurped the role and function of God and the spirit powers in determining destiny or fate.

In modern Africa, certain ethnic groups claim that they are from a superior human stock and are thus destined to rule over and control others. The designation of some ethnic groups as "natural rulers" by their colonial masters or by self-proclamation has created serious political crises in post-colonial Africa. Identifying caste systems with destiny in modern Africa has also had devastating consequences, with some groups being denied political participation and representation.

The status quo and the principles governing succession and leadership have been interpreted in terms of decreed destiny. Where such beliefs have been challenged, there have been tension, violence, and conflict.

COMMUNALISM

If everything that exists is in an organic relation to everything else that exists, as discussed in the earlier section on holism, then the same applies to how human beings interact. People are not individuals, living in a state of independence, but part of a community, living in relationships and interdependence.

In contrast to the western approach, one does not claim personal rights and freedoms but rather fulfills one's communal obligations and duties. B. J. Van der Walt lists some forty characteristics of African communalism that contrast with western individualism.[32] These characteristics can be summarized in terms of communal self-respect, interdependence, survival of the community, group assurance, cooperation and harmony, affiliation, and shared duties.

This concept of community is not restricted to the community of human beings alone but embraces a communal attitude to the world of the spirits and ancestors as well as to the world of nature.

Communalism in Relation to Fellow Human Beings

A traditional African community consisted of clans with different histories, emblems, and taboos and also their subclans and kindred (lineage system). Villages were occupied by fairly well localized kindred, although some might include people who did not belong to the principal group in the village. At the next level of organization was the household, which consisted of a small social group of parents and children.

The fact that African traditional societies were organized around the basic social unit of kinship or lineage is very important in understanding African concepts of community, religious beliefs, behavior, practices, morality, ethics, and ethnicity. The integration of tribal groups into modern African states did not eradicate kinship but incorporated it. At the root of kinship is a belief in a shared common

---

[32]B. J. Van der Walt, ed., *Cultural Diversity in Africa: Embarrassment or Opportunity* (Potchefstroom, South Africa: IRS, 1997), 29–44.

progenitor or ancestor. Genealogical relationships and the legend or tradition of the founding ancestor provide the philosophical basis of unity in a clan or lineage or even for a whole tribe. Stories of heroes and their great exploits add pride and prestige to the members of a lineage, clan, or tribe.

Each clan or lineage has its own name, identity, and social function in a community. Each lineage is differentiated from others by certain symbolic means (totems) and is assigned a corporate function or social role. For example, one lineage or clan may be the custodian of religious affairs, while another is responsible for warfare and another for hunting. Each lineage comprises a number of families or households that may consist of children, parents, grandparents, uncles, aunts, brothers and sisters, and other immediate relatives. The most powerful principle of social organization is the concept of brotherhood, and all members have affinity, loyalty, and obligations to the blood-community.

The kinship system provides the principles of social differentiation and social organization that guide communal life. It regulates social behavior and attitudes and structures social interaction. Religious and social norms and codes of behavior govern interactions among kinsfolk and also how kinsfolk relate to outsiders and to strangers.

The fragmenting effects of this social differentiation are countered by social institutions that unite and coordinate the various sectors of kinship-based communities. These institutions include communal festivals and feasts, hunting expeditions, wars, and religious rites that accompanied births, initiations, marriages, deaths, and sickness. Much eating and drinking, dancing, and singing usually accompany the festivals, feasts, and ceremonies, and these social activities create and strengthen social ties. Working together in such corporate contexts inculcates social responsibility and accountability. The exogamous marriage system also creates a network of kinsfolk with binding ties.

This system of relationships has been seriously disrupted by the introduction of universal religions such as Christianity and Islam and of modernity. It has also been affected by the realignment of tribal units in the new modern states. The changes have resulted in many social and political problems, including fears, suspicions, rivalry, tensions, and conflicts among the various ethnic and tribal groups.

Communalism in Relation to Ancestors and the Spirit World

The human community is not only intimately related to its living members but also to the spirit world, the community of the ancestors who now live in the past, and to those still to be born. The life of the community of the living is controlled, maintained, and protected by the community of the ancestors. Communal life in this kinship system can be described as ancestrally chartered. Steyne observes that outside this ancestral kinship "there lies no possibility of life" and that "personhood is meaningless" apart from these ancestral kinships and relationships.[33]

The belief in the continuity of community life has important implications for the traditional view of marriage:

> Man is only man in relationship, as he participates in family and community life. . . . . Marriage is more than a physical relationship. It has eternal consequences. Not to marry is to cease living now and in the hereafter. Marriage establishes essentials in life and in death. Begetting children guarantees eternal life. Not only do children provide for the reincarnation of the ancestors, they also sustain the ancestors through prescribed rituals such as sacrifices and offerings.[34]

The communal perspective also has important implications in regard to the spirit world that permeates everyday existence. If human beings are part of a holistic community with the spirit world, it is as important to avoid offending the spirits as it is to avoid offending one's human community. However, should one offend either community, the responsibility is not solely one's own but is shared by the community to which one belongs, for one is the product of one's family, clan, and tribe and of the spirits. This traditional belief results in a denial of responsibility for one's own actions that has serious consequences for morality and ethics in Africa.

Communalism in Relation to Nature

The law of holism, which was presented earlier, stresses that everything is part of an organic whole. Thus people seek to understand the mysterious forces that lie behind natural phenomena. Any natural object may carry a message that needs to be deciphered.

---

[33]Steyne, *Gods of Power,* 64–65.
[34]Ibid., 66.

Totemism is one expression of this relationship to nature:

> In totemism certain taboos apply to the totem animal(s) and/or plant(s). Totem objects are not to be killed, spoken of by name, eaten, or even looked at in some cases. They elicit feelings of brotherliness. They are believed to have souls similar in nature to man's. They may be emblematic of abstract and emotional attitudes claimed by a group of people.[35]

The belief in totemism sets apart some animals or plants for certain kinship affinity and religious or medicinal purposes. The potency, value, and efficacy of each are determined by its nature, which can be enhanced or reduced by other objects in its proximity. Animals and birds for sacrifices, objects for offerings, and ritual or ceremonial sites or groves are carefully selected on the basis of their religious value and efficacy. Nature provides a vast array of contact points with the world of the spirit.

SUMMARY

Given the traditional African worldview and beliefs as defined in the previous sections, it should occasion no surprise to learn that the traditional African may act in the following ways and that these behaviors often become syncretized into various expressions of Christianity in Africa. The traditional African . . .

> 1. May seek to control, conciliate, acquire, and use spiritual and mystical powers and forces to meet his personal, communal needs and purposes.
> 2. May develop types of rituals and ceremonies as means of controlling, conciliating, and acquiring these spiritual and mystical powers and forces.
> 3. May develop mystical means of exercising control over the spirit world.
> 4. May develop mystical means of communicating with the spirit world.

Specific examples may be found of all of these behaviors, even within otherwise orthodox African Christian churches. Just as in the West, in Africa philosophical and cultural values have had and con-

---

[35]Ibid., 70.

tinue to have an impact on the Christian church. Those who would care for that church must be alert to such impact in whatever forms it appears.

CONCLUSION

This paper has emphasized that neopaganism and New Age religions in western society must be understood from the twin perspectives of (1) the powerful and pervasive influence of modern philosophies on the church; and (2) the dominance of western colonialism and ethnocentrism in much of the theologizing of the western church. Western Christianity must repent of the influence and power that it has allowed secularism, pluralism, relativism, postmodernism, humanism, materialism, and hedonism to exercise. And western Christianity must return to the simple apostolic presentation and proclamation of the gospel of Christ.

The African church faces a similar challenge. Syncretism and religious cults plague the church in Africa. These two phenomena cannot be fully understood and combated unless we understand thoroughly (1) the traditional African religions and their religious beliefs, practices, and worldviews, and (2) such African philosophical issues as holism, spiritualism, dynamism, fatalism, and communalism. African Christianity has repentance issues of its own, and it, too, is called to return to the apostolic gospel.

Perhaps, in this work, African Christians and western Christians can share the burden of defending the gospel to the honor and glory of the Savior, Jesus Christ.

CHAPTER EIGHT

SHARING THE BURDEN OF HIV/AIDS

DAVID R. HABURCHAK

Jesus replied, "A man was going down from Jerusalem to Jericho, and he fell among robbers, who stripped him and beat him and departed, leaving him half dead. Now by chance a priest was going down that road, and when he saw him he passed by on the other side. So likewise a Levite, when he came to the place and saw him, passed by on the other side. But a Samaritan, as he journeyed, came to where he was, and when he saw him, he had compassion. He went to him and bound up his wounds, pouring on oil and wine. . . . Which of these three, do you think, proved to be a neighbor to the man who fell among the robbers?" He said, "The one who showed him mercy." And Jesus said to him, "You go, and do likewise."

LUKE 10:30–37, ESV

Jesus, the master teacher, used the parable of the Good Samaritan to answer the question, "Who is my neighbor?" There is no doubt that this story has captured the imagination of all mankind. More hospitals and clinics are named for this unnamed Samaritan than any other. Today I want to shift the focus of attention somewhat to the others in the story, particularly the victim. The time is at hand for the church to have a major impact on the burden of AIDS to the glory of Christ.

My life's journey first encountered AIDS in December 1981. Then, as an Army infectious disease physician in Georgia, I first read reports of unusual infections occurring in homosexual men in New York, Los Angeles, and San Francisco. To look back now, people ask, "What did you do before AIDS?" and I can hardly remember. It started slowly, more of a curiosity, and prompted me to give a lecture on the disease to my students in early 1982.

In May of that year, Providence transferred my family and me to San Francisco, an epicenter of the syndrome. At the time it had the strange name of GRID—Gay Related Infectious Disease. Less than two weeks after arriving, I came upon my first case, a twenty-nine-year-old Puerto Rican soldier admitted to the intensive care unit with severe pneumocystis pneumonia. Within two weeks, despite the best medical care available, this man was dead. He was just the first of what would be thousands of patients I and now all mankind have met on our road from Jericho to Jerusalem.

The early years of the epidemic were terrifically "exciting" and "terrifying." Each scientific meeting had "late breaking discoveries" in both the epidemiology and clinical manifestations of the disease. It seemed to be spreading in two groups of people, homosexual men and intravenous drug abusers. Clinicians devised methods to treat the complex infections resulting from suppressed immunity. But the outcome was inevitable: ghoulish wasting and a feverish death within months of apparent onset. It seemed like a satanic curse cast upon victims, victims easily blamed by many in the church for their sinful behavior.

Modern-day priests and Levites, coming upon the scene, thundered sternly from Scripture. Meanwhile, health authorities staggered between homosexual demands for continued free love and the public's denial that the health problems of drug abusers mattered to anyone. Early on, however, some churches in San Francisco, such as ultra-liberal Glide Memorial Church, and others in major cities reached out to provide supportive care for patients and their families. Almost all of them continue to do so today.

As an Army infectious disease physician in a city that had a large number of so-called "at risk" people, I participated in citywide planning to develop a response to the disease. By late 1982, the city hospital had set up a model ward to care for acutely ill patients. The sick and dying multiplied ferociously according to the mathematics of sexual promiscuity and promptly filled the ward. Little did we imagine the worldwide number of such crowded death wards in the most remote hospitals in just a few short years.

By 1984, when I left San Francisco for Denver, two things had happened. (1) In somewhat unbiblical but American fashion, the "victims" of the epidemic ignored the stares and mutterings of priests and Levites. They didn't wait for Good Samaritans but organized themselves for care and prevention of the disease. (2) Scientists in France and America discovered the virus causing the plague, a discovery still sadly denied by some in positions of authority more than twenty years later.

Initially, the major benefit of the discovery of the HIV virus was a reasonably quick and reliable blood test to identify those infected. The U.S. Army ordered compulsory testing for all recruits as well as periodic screening of all soldiers every two years. This led to what has been the singular public health success in the epidemic: the early identification of those infected, especially those with few, if any, symptoms. This permitted cautioning individuals about their risk of infecting others and, even more remarkably, starting therapies to prevent opportunistic infections. Simply speaking, it was now possible to find infected travelers on the Jericho road before they tumbled into the ditch or caused others to fall.

This opportunity for early diagnosis caused secondary dilemmas, of course. The first was stigma, and the second was shame. Concerns for privacy and personal rights weighed heavily against the sad truth of infection. The medical benefit from knowing the diagnosis earlier rather than waiting for symptoms seemed marginal, especially when testing positive for the virus meant being shunned, slandered, or worse. Even many health care workers refused to care for patients out of ignorance or fear. Unfortunately, all of this conflict between personal and public knowledge had to be worked out in each country, culture, society, and community when AIDS arrived. In every instance people had to get used to the idea that AIDS patients were not lepers, not really contagious, but they did need compassion and care.

Shame and guilt were ignored by the medical profession. The attitude of many in the church to blame the victim didn't help. Chaplains and Christian friends tried to present the good news of the cross: Christ taking our guilt and shame. Some HIV/AIDS victims heard, and a few responded to his call. But many hardened their hearts.

The sovereignty of God in salvation is an awesome mystery. I presented the gospel too seldom, but God always blessed in some way when I did. A young woman in my examining room had dangling earrings shaped as crosses. I asked her if she went to a church. "No." Had she accepted Christ? "No." The earrings were just for fashion. Would she like to put her faith in Christ? "Yes." So we prayed together.

Except for special circumstances like the military where mandatory testing was possible, voluntary testing was recommended. Tests today are simple and may give results on the same day. For medical professionals, and especially Christian medical professionals, it is frustrating to know that a positive test still often carries fear, stigma, and reprisal to the point of murder in many parts of the world.

Voluntary counseling and testing programs (VCT) are strongly advocated in many countries but to date are underutilized. A recent exception is Botswana, where routine testing is offered at any medical encounter. There as many as 35 percent of individuals now know whether they are infected, whether they are sexually infectious, and whether they should seek newly available therapy. The Anglo-American Mining Company of South Africa hoped to enroll at least half of its 145,000 employees in VCT by the end of 2005 and is successfully using VCT with great benefit to preserve its work force.

VCT works. A controlled study of VCT in Kenya and Tanzania reported significant reduction in unprotected sex with non-primary partners (38 percent reduction compared to 16 percent reduction in controls). VCT is more effective when couples are tested together than as individuals. It also works best when applied through church-like social networks and when coupled with anti-viral drug therapy. A major burden for the church will be to endorse, facilitate, and even implement widespread VCT. This must be more than righteous exposition of the Seventh Commandment. The church must provide Christ's love and protection for those found positive, like the woman caught in adultery in John 8.

Testing provides much more than a diagnosis. It identifies the victim in the ditch. One of the most striking things about my journey along the Jericho Road has been the variety of victims I have encountered over time. Epidemics have a life course of their own. They behave through social networks and affect different people at different times. For a predominantly sexually transmitted disease like HIV, the earliest cases will be the most promiscuous and most recently infected or the contacts of these "hot" cases. After enough people are infected, the epidemic becomes "generalized," and transmission is more a matter of *whom* you meet rather than how many.

This is exactly what happened with syphilis beginning in the sixteenth century in Europe and extending to the present. Today the single biggest risk for being HIV positive in Africa is whether your spouse is positive. Working husbands brought syphilis home to their wives in New York in 1906; they bring home HIV all over the world today. Inflammatory venereal diseases like herpes, chlamydia, chancroid, syphilis, LGV, and trichomoniasis all enhance the likelihood that a single sexual encounter will transmit HIV. Adequate medical care and treatment controls these infections and lowers rates of HIV.

The discovery of the virus and of how it killed mandated massive education. This was education performed on a scale without historical precedence. Collectively, we wrote and spoke about HIV and AIDS to anyone and everyone. After all, conventional wisdom is that "knowledge is power." We told everyone that there were robbers on the Road to Jericho, how travelers were vulnerable, and what kinds of fatal injuries occurred. We taught through clinics, posters, schools, newspapers, television, advertisements, books, magazines, word of mouth, and even Sunday school lessons to giggling teenagers.

To this day, after a slow start, especially in the church in Africa, teaching continues and must continue everywhere. Teaching is an absolute necessity, but unfortunately insufficient to change the behavior of most people. This was recognized early, and the problem was attributed to "failure to make the teaching culturally appropriate." Supposedly those "most in need" of the message were not receiving it. With some exceptions the epidemic continues its relentless spread. There are still robbers along the road, and travelers are still susceptible to mugging. It will take preaching rather than mere teaching truly to change people . . . preaching infused by the power of the Holy Spirit rather than by the inadequate power of knowledge. There is, we must affirm, power in the gospel message to change boys and girls, women and men, communities and entire cultures from the vices of this age to the moral law of the kingdom of God.

The role of the church in teaching and preaching in the age of AIDS was thoughtfully proclaimed more than twelve years ago in the Declaration of Kampala: "We are watchmen standing in the gap and stewards of the hope of Good offered in Christ. The pain and alienation of AIDS compel us to show and offer the fullness and wholeness that is found in him alone. In this, our time of weakness, may the rule of Christ's love in us bring healing to the nations."

Since I arrived in Augusta, Georgia in 1987 and left the Army in 1994, my new patients are increasingly poor, uneducated young women, mentally disturbed and drug-addicted men, ex-convicts, and depressed unwed mothers, all reared without effective fathers. It became clear that the problem was more than just the virus. Rather, the virus *exploited* families and societies that operated contrary to the laws of Almighty God. The virus pummeled the spirit, soul, and bodies of the poor, the confused, the uneducated, and especially women who had no purpose or power to control their own lives. It was not just the individual or the family that suffered the bruises and fatal injuries, but the whole landscape along the roadbed was polluted. What kind of a burden was this to become?

In the first half of the 1990s we learned from our patients about life and death, what mattered and what didn't. They were articulate and taught us through their suffering. Both medicine and the church learned much: palliative care, hospice programs, home visits, giving comfort for the inevitable wasting, death, and separation. Somehow people even got *used* to the idea of young people dying of a sexually transmitted disease. Novelists and playwrights even romanticized it.

All too slowly churches began to develop AIDS ministries geared specifically for the terminal care of patients. And the love of Christ continues to be expressed in countless ways by volunteers, nurses, physicians, social workers, and public health officials working in city clinics, hospitals, nursing care centers, and patient homes.

The experience of three visits to Africa and the accounts of missionary friends have overwhelmed me. God is wonderfully at work in the midst of it all! The compassion and love of Christ shines in the dark slums of Nairobi, the mission hospitals, church-based ministries to the dying, schools for orphans, and every conceivable kind of ministry developed to meet the needs of people and families with AIDS. Among the extraordinary AIDS ministries are those of Dr. Flip Buys (flip@mukhanyo.co.za) and Mrs. Melanie Prinsloo (melanie@lambano.org.za) in South Africa and the Rev. Peterson Sozi (sozip@lycos.com) in Uganda. They are carrying the burden with joy and are an inspiration to the church and the world.

It will take courage to continue carrying the burden. It is fitting that the Second General Assembly of the World Reformed Fellowship (for which this paper was originally prepared) take place in God's "Beloved Country," South Africa. Surely we all cry tears of sorrow, yet also tears of joy at this land's struggles and blessings from God. We celebrate the courage of its leaders of all races who have brought freedom to this beautiful land, and we recognize the courage displayed in its activists for scientific, as well as just, care for patients with AIDS. We admire the courage of the millions and their families who have lived and continue to live with HIV, and we praise the Lord for the ministries here of Dr. Buys and Mrs. Prinsloo.

AIDS, which has always been a political issue, by the early 1990s became a financial and fiscal issue as well. Governments began to expend extraordinary amounts of money in two areas: direct patient care and research for therapy and a vaccine. In the past fifteen years more tax money has been spent per HIV patient in the United States than for any other disease. This cash outpouring accomplished a breakthrough in drug therapy, but much more important, it has bolstered the hope of the patients and their families and, indeed, of the entire world. What was a brief, almost poetic, and tragic fatal illness became a chronic, expensive, and often interminably exasperating ordeal.

Unfortunately, the *source* of hope seemed to have changed with the advent of highly active drugs. Patients previously expected to die. Their hope was set on heavenly or existential realities. Hope now suddenly became pills, and lots of them, for an indefinitely long time. A hope for a prolonged life: a few more weeks, months, or years. For the past century medicine's alchemy has deceived us: It depicts the illusion that hope is in the potion, that death delayed will never come. Medicine entices man's desire to deny that he is but dust and to dust he must return.

Today Africa and much of the developing world are at the same place where America and Europe were in 1997. AIDS has changed for those who can afford it and who take their medications without fail. There is no doubt that it is better to live than die prematurely. There is no doubt that many have benefited and that the kingdom of God has advanced through secular and church-based treatment centers, perinatal drug therapy to prevent children getting the disease, and projects to upscale treatment opportunities for millions around the world. What some governments did for their people certainly should and probably will be attempted for all the peoples of the world. This will be accomplished through the generosity and leadership of the United Nations, Bono and the Gates family, and many of the rich and famous.

There is also good news that educational programs are bearing fruit in changed behaviors and lower rates of infection. First in Uganda (under the Rev. Sozi's leadership) and Thailand and now in Zimbabwe, rates of HIV in young men and women have fallen 25 to 49 percent. Young people are responding to government and church education to abstain, delay sexual activity, be faithful, and use condoms. Epidemiologists believe that knowledge, access to condoms, and especially fear of disease are lowering the rates. Perhaps the epidemic's fury has begun to burn out in some societies. We can only hope so.

As a member of Christ's church, I have a nagging feeling of unease about all of the new excitement, now twenty-five years after my journey with AIDS began. In some respects I feel like Jonah after the demonstration of the Lord's compassion at Nineveh: The sovereign Lord is providing a reprieve, another chance at life for millions fallen along the Jericho Road. He has used many individual Samaritans who have given many silver coins to accomplish it. Maybe what I feel is that we, the priests and Levites, should have done more, been more organized, acted more quickly and with more compassion. I know, however, that this is pride speaking, but nevertheless it points out that, as followers of Christ, anything less than our very best is too little for him. Maybe this will be the saddest and longest burden of the church—the regret that we did not do enough in the time of AIDS.

Because HIV infection is slow, with an incubation period of ten years or more, because it continues to spread around the world in the absence of either immunization or the spiritual vaccine of revival, because it remains an expensive and incurable disease, there will be many, many more fallen along the road for decades to come. All of us will need to carry more patients than we can imagine.

Most of these victims will leave behind orphans and widows that have in a special way the ear of God (Exod. 22:23). Surely, these millions of orphans will be the greatest and most important burden for the church as their grandmothers and great-aunts pass away. *The church must rear and love them as it has orphans throughout its history.* The church must do this because the future of these orphans is the future of the societies in which they live. They will embody either the kingdom of God or the kingdom of this world for the next few generations. How the church loves them will determine whether they are to be the next generation of robbers along the Jericho Road.

When the Samaritan deposited the broken body of the victim at the inn, he left him in the care of the innkeeper. Jesus ended the narrative there. But, of course, he implied the rest of the story: the innkeeper assumed the burden of the victim and restored him to health. How could it be otherwise or the whole exercise would be futile, and the priest and Levite would be justified in their behavior.

But who is this innkeeper and what is this inn astride the road between wicked Jericho and the Temple in Jerusalem? This inn contains a healer and restores people who are lost, hurt, and alone—people who are fallen, as we all are in some way on our journey of life. I like to think that perhaps the innkeeper is Jesus himself, making new the mangled lives brought to him.

AIDS is but the latest of burdens carried to Jesus by Samaritans and Christians. As the church of Jesus Christ, we have special knowledge of this wonderful innkeeper. There are five parts to our burden that we lift up to him: First, to inform and to seek to modify the behaviors and the cultures that put people at risk of being mugged; second, to promote widespread voluntary HIV testing in order to identify those already infected and to try to prevent others from suffering the same fate; third, to substitute the love of Christ for the fear, stigma, and reprisal of being diagnosed with HIV/AIDS; fourth, to seek to bring healing to the sick (even those who we believe have sinned) with all the oils and compassion at our disposal, especially at the end of life; and fifth, to nurture the widows and the orphans left behind.

The Good Samaritan had tools to do the job. So do we. We have the wonderful provision of prayer to access God, to call for his awesome power to heal both individuals and our societies. How little have we passionately prayed for the healing of body, mind, soul, and culture! How little have we prayed for the conversion and salvation of those transmitting the infection, whether they do so in innocence and ignorance or as the vilest rapist!

Of course, we must earnestly but humbly teach God's moral laws, which are as obvious as the law of gravity and literally have life-or-death implications. If we are to live out the lesson of the Parable of the Good Samaritan, we must, confronting the burden of HIV/AIDS, preach God's love and forgiveness, not his wrath and condemnation. The gospel is eternal and universal. The age of AIDS is, more than ever, an era needing good news. This gospel must be lived out in love of neighbor both by individual Christians and by formal church bodies. The church is the Father's plan for community, *ubuntu*, that aspect of life so precious and uniquely cherished in Africa.

We do all these things because we know the innkeeper. We know this is what he wants done. He said so by his words and by his actions. One day soon this innkeeper will decide that enough victims have fallen along the road and will use his power to stop the beatings and bring all robbers to justice. He will create a new landscape: a gentle road with fragrant caressing breezes and flowering vistas; safe, holy, and without fear or stigmatizing wounds. We will rejoice to abide with our innkeeper, Jesus, forever.

As we travel our Jericho road anticipating that imminent and wonderful day, we carry our most important burden, in comparison with which all the others are secondary: to declare by our words and actions the glory of the innkeeper. We trudge up the mountain way, weary with our own needs, laden with the sickness and injuries of our own souls, but with deepening faith and hope in the One waiting at our destination. We tell both AIDS victims and fellow travelers along the road about the love and wisdom of this innkeeper. We carry humanity's sick and injured up the rubble-strewn path toward him. As we look up, our steps quicken and our load strangely lightens. When we see his smile, every one of our questions is answered and every one of our hopes is realized.

The burden of HIV/AIDS is now twenty-five years old. It may, in fact, have just begun. I encourage *every* Christian to help to pick up the victims of HIV/AIDS and carry them to Jesus:

As our Lord himself has said:

> *Come to me, all you who are weary and burdened, and I will give you rest. Take my yoke upon you and learn from me, for I am gentle and humble in heart, and you will find rest for your souls. For my yoke is easy and my burden is light.*
>
> **MATT. 11:28-30,** NIV

PART THREE

PRACTICAL APPLICATIONS—SHARING OPPORTUNITIES

CHAPTER NINE

SHARING THE OPPORTUNITY OF MISSIONS

JOHN NICHOLLS

The prophet Elijah once famously complained, " I, even I only, am left" (1 Kings 18:22; 19:10, 14, esv). Of course, he was wrong, but not so wrong as any Elijah-like pastor or mission worker would be today were they to complain of being a solitary witness for the truth. The most recent statistics on global missions include these[1]:

	1900	**mid-2006**
Christian Denominations	1,900	38,000
Christian Service Agencies	1,500	26,000
Foreign-mission Sending Agencies	600	4,410

These figures reflect in part the great advances that Christianity has made in Africa, Asia, and South America during the twentieth century. Allowance must also be made for geographical, linguistic, and political factors that make separate groupings of churches and separate

---

[1]David B. Barrett, *International Bulletin of Missionary Research,* Vol. 30, No. 1, January 2006, 27–30.

organizations appropriate or unavoidable. But there is another aspect that cannot be ignored. Sociologists say that "the denomination is precisely the visible form that the church takes when a secularized society privatizes religion."[2]

Some of the proliferation of denominations, agencies, and societies, in the western world at least, is the result of the theological liberalism that devastated the churches in the twentieth century. But a not insignificant part of that fragmentation may also be evidence of the corrosive effect of an individualistic culture, even on theologically conservative churches.

Whatever the underlying reasons may be, anyone who engages in mission today is likely to be faced, not with a virgin territory where no gospel messenger has yet ventured, but with a field more or less crowded by the presence of other churches, church-planters, and agencies, all confident that God has called them to work in that location. Many will share much of our missionary's theology. Most will nonetheless differ from him or her in some points of doctrine and practice.

Standing as we do in the Evangelical/Reformed[3] tradition that has given birth to a considerable (perhaps the major) proportion of those denominations and agencies, we cannot engage in missions without addressing the resultant question of cooperation. Can we simply ignore all others who are working in the same mission field? Is it possible to work together with those whose confessions, liturgies, and polities differ from our own?

"Sharing the Opportunity of Missions" is the theme of this paper, and it will be covered in two parts. In the first we shall look at the London City Mission as a model of cooperation in mission. Founded in 1835 to evangelize the burgeoning population of a city that was then bigger than Paris, Berlin, and Moscow combined, the London City Mission (LCM) was the first significant organization to unite English Christians of different denominations in directly evangelistic work. It continues its work today, still committed to the biblical gospel, and still based on its original template. Of course, the LCM is far from perfect and has made many mistakes in its long history. It is not being consid-

---

[2]Cited by Lesslie Newbigin, *A Word in Season* (Grand Rapids, MI: Eerdmans, 1994), 64.
[3]I use the word Evangelical in the Anglo-Saxon sense that includes Reformed, rather than in the European sense that sets the terms over against each other.

ered as an ideal response to mission in a multi-denominational world, but as an experiment whose long continuance suggests either that the English are very slow to recognize their mistakes or that even the English can get some things right! In the second part we shall underline some of the issues raised by this case study.

WORKING TOGETHER IN LONDON—AN OVERVIEW OF THE LONDON CITY MISSION

Speaking in London in the 1880s, a Methodist preacher accounted for the great improvement in social conditions that had been achieved in the previous fifty years. "There have been at work among us," he said, "three great social agencies: the London City Mission, the novels of Mr. Dickens, and the cholera."[4] Its days as a prime agent of systemic social change were in the nineteenth century, but the LCM's team today continues to pursue its main and original aim—going to the people of London (especially the poor) "for the purpose of bringing them to an acquaintance with salvation, through our Lord Jesus Christ, and of doing them good by every means in your power."[5]

THE LCM TODAY

As of 2006, the team numbers 397, about half of whom are regular volunteers. The LCM has ministries to homeless people and to refugees and asylum-seekers. But it is by no means restricted to working among the socially marginalized. Its prime target group includes what in Britain may still be termed "the working class"—a group largely untouched by most evangelical churches. So LCM has workplace ministries, visiting the staff of bus depots, the major London Markets, the ambulance service, the Post Office, several of London's Police Forces, the London Underground, and the capital's railway companies. Many of these were heavily involved in ministry to workers and members of the public caught up in the suicide bombings in the city in July 2005.

Over sixty LCM staff have regular ministries in the city's state

---

[4]Cited in Irene Howat and John Nicholls, *Streets Paved with Gold* (Fearn, Scotland: Christian Focus, 2003), 81.
[5]London City Mission, "Instructions to Agents, Committee Minute Book" (unpublished, 1835). The London City Mission archives are available for study. For contact details, see the LCM web site, www.lcm.org.uk.

schools, taking the gatherings we know as "Assemblies," teaching classes in Religious Education, and running lunchtime Christian clubs. Others have specialized ministries to some of the ethnic minorities who together make up more than one third of London's seven million residents (ministries that are increasingly global in their links) or to particular "faith groups" such as Jews and New Age devotees.

The largest section of the Mission's staff serve as "district missionaries," aiming to make contact with the residents and workers within a defined geographical area, earn their respect, and develop appropriate opportunities for meaningfully communicating the gospel. Door-to-door visiting is still an effective way of doing this in many of the city's poorer areas, but many other methods are pursued as well. Initial contacts are reinforced by invitations to a wide range of activities, from Internet cafés to summer camps, which give staff the chance to express Christian love and to build friendships. Some such district ministries are based in buildings owned and staffed by the LCM, while others are developed by City Mission staff directly loaned to local churches and operating as part of the church's staff.

FUNDING AND RECRUITMENT—HOW THE CHURCHES SUPPORT THE LCM

LCM staff are drawn from a wide range of evangelical churches. None is recruited without a recommendation from his or her church leaders. On completion of their initial training, recruits return to the home church for a service of commissioning to the ministry of evangelism in London. Donations from Christian congregations and individuals of many different denominations fund all the LCM's activity. In 2003, donations came from 20,630 individuals and 2,109 churches. No regular funding is received from the government or from secular sources. All LCM staff (other than volunteers) are salaried and do not need to raise their own support. Evangelistic staff are housed by the Mission, and retirement housing is also provided for those who have served for twenty years.

A regular program of visits to churches across the UK and a free quarterly magazine sent to 28,000 people are the main means of fundraising.

STEPPING-STONES—HOW THE LCM SUPPORTS THE CHURCHES

Obviously, the evangelists who are loaned to churches are directly contributing to the growth of the church. But *all* of LCM's ministries have that as their aim. The Mission's 2005 Strategic Plan identified one of the challenges facing it as follows: "To work with London's Churches, or live in its own world?"

In a period when the Christian church is very weak (representing less than 10 percent of London's population) there is more need than ever for Christians to "share the opportunity of missions."

To ignore existing churches and ministries leads to a diversion of time and energy away from evangelism. It also undermines the claims of the gospel in the minds of non-Christians. Yet it is not easy to overcome the suspicion and parochialism that often stand in the way of genuine cooperation, at both a London-wide and a local level.

LCM's core method of "district evangelism" requires that both individual missionaries and LCM's Christian Centres work with their local churches (including appropriate church-planting ventures), not duplicating their ministries, but channeling contacts and converts into them. Recent developments, especially in the Church of England, involving the replanting of inner-city churches, provide new opportunities for LCM to work closely with the churches.[6]

The LCM insists that it is not a church but exists to enable churches and Christians to go to the unchurched people of London and to bring them into the city's churches. It sees its ministries as "stepping-stones," laid down in the broad "river" that separates the worshiping church from the unbelieving community, and sees its workers as being sent in dependence on the Holy Spirit to persuade and enable unbelievers to cross over.

In this context, *church* is to be understood as an evangelical congregation, of whatever denomination. Such mission work may be described as interdenominational or nondenominational, but a better (if little-known) term is "pan-evangelical,"[7] with the precise implication that the LCM exists to build up any and every evangelical church. LCM also cooperates with a number of parachurch organizations,

---

[6]London City Mission, "Strategic Plan" (unpublished, 2005), 8.
[7]See, for example, Donald M. Lewis, *Lighten Their Darkness: The Evangelical Mission to Working-Class London, 1828–1860* (Carlisle, UK: Paternoster, 2001), 177ff.

forming partnerships for special events and for ongoing ministry. This cooperation is reflected in the LCM's magazine, which features work by other organizations and carries a regular interview with church leaders. Today there may seem to be little that is revolutionary about such an organization as the LCM. But in 1835, when the LCM was founded, it was controversial in the extreme.

THE ORIGINS OF THE LCM

London of 1835 was, to those who witnessed it, an appalling sight. Its population had virtually doubled since 1800, to some two million—a phenomenon totally unprecedented in post-classical Europe. Cartoonists depicted the city as a voracious monster, spewing out bricks and chimneys, and swallowing up the countryside and its villages. "Its problems of growth—crime, destitution, epidemic disease, overcrowding—seemed to be on the verge of overwhelming the city."[8] In 1835 Charles Dickens was visiting some of the slums, preparing to write a novel entitled *Oliver Twist*. Elsewhere in London, the capital's leading evangelical Anglican, the Rev. Baptist Noel, was writing an open letter to his bishop, entitled "The State of the Metropolis Considered," leading one commentator to remark that "a more appalling or melancholy statement has seldom issued from the press of a civilized country." Noel's letter began, "There is something, my Lord, unspeakably painful, in the contemplation of this mass of immortal beings . . . living, as we have reason to fear, without God and without hope. . . ."[9] In his opinion, the poorer classes would never, of themselves, take the initiative to come to the churches. The churches must take the initiative and go to them.

But the churches were terribly divided. Indeed, in 1834 relations between the Church of England and dissenters (or nonconformists) reached a bitterness without precedent in English history.[10] Evangelicals were as vocal as any others in the disputes, which centered on the establishment of the Church of England. To rally the churches for any sort of combined missionary initiative seemed a hopeless cause.

But into that situation came one very determined Scotsman, David

---

[8]Peter Hall, *Cities in Civilisation* (London: Weidenfeldt & Nicolson, 1998).
[9]Lewis, *Lighten Their Darkness*, 49.
[10]See Owen Chadwick, *The Victorian Church,* Part 1 (London: SCM, 1987), 61.

Nasmith, a layman from Glasgow. He had a blueprint for systematic outreach that involved sending evangelists to the homes of the unchurched, with each evangelist allocated to a specific district. The basic idea was borrowed from Thomas Chalmers, the great Scottish Reformed preacher and church leader, who developed it during his ministry in Glasgow from 1815 to 1821. But Nasmith's scheme had two significant improvements: The evangelists were to be full-time, paid workers rather than the sometimes unreliable volunteers used by Chalmers; and the scheme was to be applied and funded, not by an individual congregation of one particular denomination, but by as many churches as would join in, whatever their denominations. Nasmith's term for this was "catholicity." The City Mission was to be a "catholic," or pan-evangelical, mission. Its evangelists were told to "avoid all unnecessary controversy upon religious subjects," but to urge people to regularly attend church, and "if they attend no place of worship . . . name those places in which the gospel is proclaimed, in your district or neighborhood; and beware directly or indirectly of seeking to promote the interests of a party, the sole object of the Mission being to bring sinners to the Savior. . . ."[11]

The LCM was to have a "scripturally-constructed platform for Christian union and cooperation—so scripturally narrow as to exclude those who are not sound in the faith of God's Word—so scripturally broad as to admit all those who hold the Head, who revere the Spirit, who take God's inspired Word as their one sole and sufficient rule of faith and practice."[12] The essential truths held and proclaimed by LCM were listed by way of a series of Bible verses: Romans 3:23; John 1:1; John 3:3; 1 John 1:7; Romans 5:1; Acts 4:12; Hebrews 12:14; 1 Corinthians 6:11.[13]

DEFENDING THE LCM'S "CATHOLICITY"

After some delay, Nasmith's scheme was launched, and within thirteen years the LCM had 197 "agents" at work in London's worst slum districts. However, that progress had not been achieved painlessly. Some attacked the LCM for its use of lay workers. But far more serious was

---

[11]London City Mission, "Instructions to Agents," 1835.
[12]*London City Mission Magazine*, 1864, 63.
[13]Today the LCM uses a summary of essential doctrine based on that of the Universities and Colleges Christian Fellowship (UCCF).

the hostility aroused by its "catholicity." Many Anglicans viewed it as a "Trojan horse for Nonconformity" that would use Anglican resources to build Baptist congregations. Others said that it was essentially unworkable and would inevitably be torn apart by internal disputes on such matters as church government and the sacraments. The Bishop of London wrote to his clergy forbidding them to have anything to do with the new Mission. Many evangelical Anglicans, anxious to defend their credentials as loyal Anglicans so they could win the Church of England from within, joined in the criticism and in ostracizing the LCM. The followers of the Clapham Sect were among these. But a significant group of Anglican evangelical clergy, joined by a larger number of lay Anglicans, risked the wrath of their bishop and worked with and for the LCM. The willingness of this group to work with other denominations "was probably due to the strong influence . . . of non-Anglican, reformed theology from Scotland and the Continent."[14]

Supporters of the LCM argued the case for cooperation, or catholicity, on a number of grounds. Naturally, they turned to biblical passages such as John 17:20-23 to show that "God's purpose and desire is for unity" and that cooperation in evangelism was at least a part of such visible unity.[15] They also used more pragmatic arguments, some of which probably reflected street-level insights:

• Having evangelists who advocated attendance at *any* evangelical church did away with the suspicions of the poor that any minister who evangelized the poor was really aiming to boost the financial income of his own church.

• Forbidding evangelists to get involved in discussions about church government and other denominational peculiarities kept their minds focused on the main points of the gospel and enabled them to avoid many of the "distractions" that their hearers threw at them.

• Working together with people from other denominations gave evangelists the stimulus of fellowship beyond their own, familiar party.

• Catholicity provided the LCM with a larger pool from which to draw recruits and a wider financial support base.

• Catholicity drew together the financial strength of many Anglicans and the manpower strength of the Nonconformists in a body-like ministry that neither could have achieved without the other.

---

[14]Lewis, *Lighten Their Darkness,* 53.
[15]See John Garwood, "The Importance of City and Town Missions Preserving a Catholic Character," in *The London City Mission Magazine,* 1859, 91–103.

• Catholicity opened doors for ministry in workhouses, the military, prisons, and workplaces that would have been barred to a narrowly denominational mission.

• "Catholic" evangelists found advantages in going to Roman Catholics and Jews without the handicap of Protestant divisiveness.

One final, and perhaps surprising, term should be mentioned: the LCM's approach was sometimes described as "catholic and *unfettered.*" Far from being held back by arguments within its ranks, the supporters of the LCM turned the objection around, claiming that it was denominationally-based ministries that were, in practice, struggling to find recruits and being held back by arguments on where workers should be placed and what resources they might use. By 1859 an Anglican mission society that had been in existence for nearly as long as the LCM had still not managed to agree on which tracts were suitable for use by its evangelists.

As the years passed, the LCM could also appeal to its effectiveness. Gaining well-known lay and clerical supporters such as Lord Shaftesbury, Charles Haddon Spurgeon, and John Charles Ryle, the Mission could point to a constantly growing team (there were 362 evangelists by 1859 and 499 by 1891) and to a large number of new communicants resulting from the Mission's outreach (some fifty thousand between 1880 and 1905) spread proportionately across the churches of all denominations that supported the Mission. The LCM could claim that cooperation in mission, by congregations and clergy from across the evangelical spectrum, could and did work.

That success was jealously defended. Great care was taken to ensure that all positions within the Mission were equally staffed by Anglicans and Nonconformists, from the governing committee, through the "clerical examiners" who approved applicants, to the general secretaries who ran the Mission's day-to day affairs. Local ministers of all denominations provided regular supervision for individual missionaries, in line with the Mission's ethos. Any transgression of the "principle of catholicity" was treated as a *moral* offense and was likely to result in dismissal. The only area where equality could not be enforced was in the ranks of the missionaries themselves, which always contained more Nonconformists than Anglicans.

THE LCM'S IMPACT AND RELEVANCE

In its approach to cooperation in mission, the LCM cut a path that many followed. It made such cooperation respectable in at least a large section of British Evangelicalism. Its influence can be traced, directly or indirectly, in the founding of many of the societies for evangelism and Christian social activity that abounded in Victorian Britain. While the Mission was in favor of catholicity, it was certainly not lax in its commitment to core gospel doctrine. Roman Catholicism, Ritualism, Infidelism, Socialism, and the emerging German theological liberalism were all roundly condemned.

A century and a half later, much of the context had changed. In 1835 evangelicals were largely agreed on all but church government and the sacraments. (The Arminian Methodists do not feature strongly in the LCM's early days.) In 2006 evangelicalism contained a far wider spectrum, with new differences on such issues as the inerrancy of Scripture, women's role in ministry, healing and prosperity, the nature of the atonement, and the significance of unfulfilled prophecy.

In 1835 the LCM could cooperate only with the evangelical churches and with a tiny number of societies such as the Bible Society and the Religious Tract Society. In 2006 a vast array of parachurch organizations and specialist ministries were operating within the city. Cooperative actions and partnerships are more complex—as, for instance, in the current discussions on Christian outreach to the Olympic Games, scheduled in London in 2012. No model from the distant past can be simplistically applied to a different time or to different places. But for Reformed Christians grappling with the challenge of mission in an increasingly urbanized world, a case study of the LCM, derived as it was from the Reformed ministry of Thomas Chalmers and largely led by ministers with Reformed views, at least provides a starting point for reflection on cooperation in mission.

WORKING TOGETHER IN MISSION—REFLECTIONS AND ISSUES

The pioneering work of the LCM (at least within the British context) and its long continuance as an evangelical and evangelistic missions organization provide a backdrop for reconsideration of some of the recurring elements of any discussion of cooperation in mission. Four particular elements may be put in propositional form:

- Cooperation in missions is mandatory, not optional.
- Cooperation in missions has significant practical benefits.
- Cooperation in missions challenges us at a variety of levels.
- Cooperation in missions is essential in a globalizing urban world.

COOPERATION IN MISSIONS IS MANDATORY, NOT OPTIONAL

This is not the place to enter into an exhaustive exposition of the biblical data on Christian unity, but several key texts and biblical themes should be noted as having a special relevance to our theme of working together in mission. Proponents of the early LCM frequently referred to some or all of the following, arguing that cooperation was not just permissible but essential, not optional but mandatory:

> **John 17:22–23**—*The glory that you have given me I have given them, so that they may be one, as we are one, I in them and you in me, that they may become completely one, so that the world may know that you have sent me and have loved them even as you have loved me.* (NRSV)

This is not so much a prayer for unity as a statement of unity in mission. It is a statement of what Christ has done for his followers as part of being "sent" by the Father. It is an assertion that he indwells them and is working within them to bring about the desired goal of unity and to make the world know his divine credentials. Christ's having been "sent" by the Father to be the Savior of the world is the very basis of Christian mission (John 20:21), and the indwelling Christ is never passive but is actively pursuing the goal for which he was sent. So the unifying work of Christ, which lies at the heart of this verse, is not some ecclesiastical activity focusing on organizational unity as an end in itself—an end that, incidentally, may have the desirable side effect of making mission to an unbelieving world more successful.

Nor is this an invisible spiritual unity that exists in the shared piety and fellowship of individual Christians. Rather, the unity that Christ brings into and works out within his followers is unity *in* mission, a sharing in the mission that the Father has given the Son, and in which the Father indwells and cooperates with the Son. Working together in missions and true Christian unity are inseparable.

> **Luke 9:49–50**—*"Master, we saw someone casting out demons in your name, and we tried to stop him, because he does not follow with us." But Jesus said to him, "Do not stop him; for whoever is not against you is for you."* (NRSV)

Jesus' sayings to his disciples are often deliberately enigmatic and not by themselves intended to be rule-making. But at the very least, Jesus' reply to John on this occasion was intended to make John see that the work he and the rest of the Twelve had been given to do must not be regarded with jealousy, as if it were somehow theirs alone. Of course, that might raise troubling questions about apostolicity, but perhaps that is just the point! Mission may overflow the boundaries of our knowledge, logic, and church order. There may be what one Victorian writer delightfully called "auspicious inconsistencies,"[16] or what some Presbyterians term "irregular but not invalid" actions. Mission cannot wait until church order is perfected.

> **Ezekiel 33:7–9**—*So you, mortal, I have made a sentinel for the house of Israel; whenever you hear a word from my mouth, you shall give them warning from me. If I say to the wicked, "O wicked ones, you shall surely die," and you do not speak to warn the wicked to turn from their ways, the wicked shall die in their iniquity, but their blood I will require at your hand. But if you warn the wicked to turn from their ways, and they do not turn from their ways, the wicked shall die in their iniquity, but you will have saved your life.* (NRSV)

Another frequently used argument of the early advocates of the LCM implies a biblical case for *mandatory* cooperation. Early issues of the *LCM Magazine* often gave precise figures on "Mortality"—i.e., the number of people who had died in London in a given period.[17] In 1840, in a period of four weeks, 3,155 people died. From January 1 until June 13 of that year, 20,112 people died in the city. Why this statistical exactness? Because those running the Mission felt an awe-

---

[16]Isaac Taylor, *A New Model of Christian Missions*, cited in *The London City Mission Magazine*, 1840, 115.
[17]*The London City Mission Magazine*, 1840, 112.

some responsibility toward all of their fellow-citizens and considered it a terrible and shameful thing if anyone in their city should die without having heard the gospel of Jesus Christ. Though they may not have spelled it out in the exact terms, is not this the spirit of the "watchman" (NIV) of Ezekiel 33, conscious that the blood of the wicked may be required at his hands if they are not warned of the coming judgment? The sheer size of the city rendered it impossible that any one church or denomination could hope to warn the whole population. London's Christians had no option but to cooperate in sending into and supporting evangelists in every unreached area of the city, if they were not to have the blood of their fellow citizens required at their hands.[18]

COOPERATION IN MISSIONS HAS SIGNIFICANT PRACTICAL BENEFITS

The early supporters of the LCM did not hesitate to use biblical arguments. But as we have seen, they did not hesitate to assert that cooperation, or catholicity, in the work of mission had practical advantages as well as biblical support. Pulling those together and looking at them in a wider context might yield the following list:

Working together in missions:

- refreshes our own theology and piety,
- focuses our evangelistic encounters more sharply on the heart of the gospel,
- avoids many of the barriers to the acceptance of the gospel created by the divisions among Christians,
- makes better use of the manpower, gifts, and resources of the various churches, and
- avoids some of the restraints on mission that come from our traditional and imperfect denominational structures.

In the practice of the LCM, anecdotal and organizational evidence could be adduced for each of these. The following extra note on the first of these must suffice here.

Working together in missions, by limiting attention to the core gospel itself, may well *refresh our own theology and piety*. Too often

---

[18]See an article in *The London City Mission Magazine* for October 1849 during an outbreak of cholera: "a near view of death would soon reconcile men of good principles one to another . . . it is chiefly owing to our easy situation in life, and our putting these things far from us, that our [divisions] are fomented . . . ," 226.

that core gospel is taken for granted by orthodox churches, while disproportionate attention is given to the denomination's own distinctives. Especially the doctrines of the Trinity and the Incarnation have suffered neglect in many evangelical/Reformed circles, while even the atonement and justification have been studied more in relation to the inadequate views of other Christians than to the need to proclaim them meaningfully to a non-Christian population. When churches do missions on their own, there is a constant danger that a desire to replicate themselves in every detail may overshadow centrality of the gospel. Cooperative missions ought to bring key doctrines back to center stage.

It can be a healthy exercise, also, to operate outside the familiar patterns that our own churches believe and practice. Our distinctive practices and beliefs may be seen to be of less importance than we imagined. But they may also be seen as more valuable than we had previously appreciated when seen from the perspective of other churches and Christians who may never have encountered them before.

Working with Christians from other backgrounds may enrich our piety and worship by introducing us to new concepts in prayer and sung praise, new styles of preaching, and new examples of profound piety and ministry. Of course, such influence can be harmful, but those of the Reformed faith should be the last to be instinctively negative, remembering the sovereignty of a God who can reveal his truth, or parts of it, in the most unlikely places.

Finally, working together with other Christians frequently enriches our whole faith and assurance through a very real experience of active fellowship within the body of Christ—a body that, we now realize, is much larger and more strongly united than we had previously known. In this, cooperation satisfies a very real and profound Christian instinct.

COOPERATION IN MISSIONS CHALLENGES US AT A VARIETY OF LEVELS

This heading might well have been subsumed under the previous one, for it is undoubtedly a very practical benefit to be challenged and called to self-examination, whether as individuals or as churches and organizations. Left to themselves, those involved in missions have a tendency to work within a comfort zone of their own. An essentially middle-class urban church will tend to develop ministries that are good at reaching other middle-class people. A missionary with a passionate interest in youth culture may well end up planting a "youth church." Cooperative missions work can and should take us outside such comfort zones in several specific areas.

Theologically and ecclesiastically, as we have seen under the previous point, cooperation challenges our priorities. Reformed churches that have come into being through a separation or secession on theological grounds are prone, as Francis Schaeffer analyzed in his *The Church Before the Watching World*, to multiply distinctives and to split again on such issues. A distinction has frequently been made between "primary" and "secondary" issues, but agreement on what comes under each of the headings has been consistently elusive, with a temptation to consider that all of our own distinctives are primary matters! If cooperation is to be seriously and theologically grounded, a developed theological framework covering this principle is essential if we are to avoid both the scandal of doctrinal laxity on the one hand and that of unbiblical schism on the other. Perhaps it will be a framework that draws on the insights of "symphonic theology."

Culturally, working together may challenge us in different ways, depending on which particular culture is the dominant context of our church life. For example, some of us have spent our whole lives in a western culture that is dominated by values established in the economic marketplace. Free market economics ascribe almost unlimited powers to competition, and the trend has been for competition to be applied far beyond the economic sphere. Where competition is idolized, cooperation may be especially difficult. Such marketing economics also tend to thrive on short-term success, with "key performance indicators" and "outcomes" dominating planning and evaluation. But the ministry of missions is more complex—and on a different timescale—than most marketing campaigns. Cooperation may take longer to bear fruit and thus be less attractive to an impatient constituency.

Marketing theory is also contributing to the increasing replacement of the parachurch (including colleges as well as mission societies) by the megachurch, franchising its outlets worldwide, claiming to have the successful product that is applicable in every setting, building its own self-enclosed world of training courses and colleges, publications, and conferences. While this may have some of the appearances of cooperation, from other perspectives it looks uncommonly like empire building. True cooperation is not a matter of pursuing the latest technique.

Non-western cultures have their own characteristics that may be inimical to the practice of genuine cooperation. These might include styles of leadership, attitudes toward those of another caste or clan, or attitudes toward financial and employment matters. It is not for me to pontificate on other cultures, except to emphasize the point I am making—namely, that working together in mission with those from different cultural backgrounds will challenge our own inevitably enculturated attitudes.

Pastorally, working together may intrude upon the comfort zones of our members. In Reformed churches, especially those originating in a recent separation, many of the members may have strongly negative views toward other churches because of their past experiences or because of an exaggerated loyalty to their present church. In that situation leaders may find that initiating cooperation with other churches hurts or even antagonizes their own flock. There is nothing new about this (it was analyzed in great detail as long ago as the 1650s by the Scottish writer James Durham[19]), but it is nonetheless challenging for all that.

Psychologically, the individual church leader may be challenged in all the above ways and in others that spring from our own imperfectly sanctified personalities. As a Christian leader, I am *never* immune to insecurity, to ambition, to a dogmatism that makes me eager to preach and teach but reluctant to listen and swallow, to the empire-building instinct, to the "big fish in a small pond" syndrome, to individual prejudices on the grounds of race, class, education, and such like things, or to the greed that clings to the wealth of an uncooperative ministry. If I move into the realm of working together, I may well be liable to new levels of scrutiny and disclosure that are not applied to me on my home turf. Am I ready to accept this scrutiny for the sake of the gospel? This is a hard but critical question.

COOPERATION IS ESSENTIAL IN A GLOBALIZING URBAN WORLD

The sheer and increasing diversity of our cities demands that we work together. Today's world cities contain a vast array of ethnic and linguis-

---

[19]See James Durham, *Concerning Scandal* (reprinted Dallas: Naphtali Press, 1990), especially Part 4, "Concerning Scandalous Divisions."

tic communities, devotees of all the world's major religions and many of its minor ones, and social, psychological, and medical situations of great complexity. Ease of travel and the globalization of the economy and popular culture produce vast and constant movements (London has some twenty-six million visitors in a typical year).

Today's evangelistic contacts and converts in London may tomorrow be living and working in Durban, Dubai, or Detroit. In such a setting there is no way that an organization can exist and operate completely on its own—even one as large and as diverse as the LCM, which, as we have seen, is itself a cooperative venture, having staff from twenty-six different countries, including converts from Islam, Hinduism, and the New Age and others with experience of all manner of addictions, imprisonment, and theological training! Any missions organization *must* draw on the expertise and experience of others and *must* network with many churches in order to be able to find the most appropriate context for Christian caring and growth for its contacts and converts.

Globalization is seen most dramatically in world cities. But other cities and towns share in at least some of their characteristics. A world city is not on another planet. Rather, it is a portent and a shaper of the future. In London we cannot, and we dare not, work alone. We are learning to apply to ourselves the exhortation of John Calvin to William Farel—urgent and realistic as it is, and it is with this exhortation that I conclude my discussion of "sharing the opportunity of missions":

> I entreat you, my dear brother, in so great iniquity of the time in which we live, that you will do your utmost endeavor to keep together all who are in any way bearable.[20]

TEN QUESTIONS FOR DISCUSSION AND FURTHER REFLECTION

1. What does the unity of a church or a congregation mean if it is not related to mission? What biblical passages are relevant to the question of cooperation?

2. How openly and persistently have you worked through the distinction between "essentials" and "secondaries" and discussed your

---

[20]John Calvin, *Letters of John Calvin*, Vol. 1 (reprinted New York: Lennox Hill, 1972), 103.

conclusions with your brothers and sisters in Christ who might disagree with you?

3. What other pragmatic arguments for working together in missions might you adduce from your own experience?

4. What problems does cooperating in missions bring—and how can they be guarded against without abandoning the work?

5. Why do some church leaders relish cooperation, while others in the same denomination find it deeply disconcerting and threatening?

6. What opportunities and challenges of globalization have appeared in your ministry setting, and how are you going about dealing with them?

7. In what ways has working together in missions enriched your own piety and that of your church fellowship?

8. Regarding cooperation in missions, what are the implications of the widespread practice of individuals raising their own financial support?

9. What other models of working together in missions have you come across, besides that of the LCM? Assess their strengths and weaknesses.

10. Think of three initiatives you could take in your ministry context to develop new ways of working together in missions with other evangelical/Reformed Christians.

CHAPTER TEN

SHARING THE OPPORTUNITY OF MINISTRY TO THE GLOBAL URBAN POOR

MANUEL ORTIZ

The danger of globalization for Christians today comes from its power to shape not only how we live but also how we think and how we place ultimate value on things. It seems to me that Bob Goudzwaard is trying to tell us in his book not to demonize globalization but to think much more missiologically about global issues.[1] We must engage globalization as a missiological challenge. In other words, no matter how bad things look, we must not ignore what God has given us. How can we be good stewards of God's economy, God's world? "The earth is the LORD's and the fullness thereof" (Ps. 24:1).[2]

We are all trying to understand globalization and its implications for world missions. Globalization is a recent major world phenomenon beginning after the end of the Cold War. We must realize that from the start the body of Christ was meant to become a global community. While some of Jesus' disciples wanted to restrict the gospel message to the Jewish people, the Holy Spirit made it clear that all nations of the

---

[1]Bob Goudzwaard, *Globalization and the Kingdom of God* (Grand Rapids, MI: Baker Books, 2001).
[2]Scripture references in this chapter are from the English Standard Version, except as indicated otherwise.

world should hear the good news and participate in the new life. Thus, long before the present process of globalization began, God's message of global good news went forth and began its work.

The idea of globalization, therefore, is not foreign to the Bible. In fact, Paul uses a Greek word that is very close in meaning to globalization. In his letter to the Ephesians, Paul writes about the last mystery that God is unveiling, namely, "to bring all things in heaven and on earth together under one head, even Christ" (Eph. 1:10, NIV). The question for us is, what kind of globalization should we be supporting?[3]

DEFINITION OF GLOBALIZATION

So what is globalization? "*Globalization* refers to increasing global interconnectedness, so that events and developments in one part of the world are affected by, have to take account of, and also influence, in turn, other parts of the world. It also refers to an increasing sense of a single global whole."[4]

Another way to think of globalization is to recognize that the world is compressing. Local phenomena are spreading throughout the world. For example, world travelers can find a McDonald's almost everyplace they go. We also find English idiomatic expressions in the daily life of people whose first language is not English, primarily due to the use of computers. Another aspect of globalization is that people around the world are becoming more conscious of being inhabitants of the world as opposed to just a country, a state, or a city. In summary we see that the political, economic, and social lives of the people throughout the world are dramatically interconnected.

EXPLANATION OF GLOBALIZATION AND ITS CAUSES

Globalization lies at the heart of modern culture—and cultural practices lie at the heart of globalization. This is a reciprocal relationship.[5] Thomas Friedman, in his book *The World Is Flat*, indicates that globalization is caused by three revolutions: (1) the computer revolution, (2)

---

[3]Goudzwaard, *Globalization*.
[4]Richard Tiplady, "Introduction," in Richard Tiplady, ed., *One World or Many? The Impact of Globalisation on Mission* (Pasadena, CA: William Carey Library, 2003), 2.
[5]John Tomlinson, *Globalization and Culture* (Chicago: University of Chicago Press, 1999), 1.

the Internet revolution, and (3) the software revolution.[6] Another cause is widely acknowledged: the breaking down of the dominant two-world power structure (East and West) politically and economically after the Cold War led to significant migration and other movement throughout the world. Mobility of ideas and information through technology has altered any possible control over what people know.

Many cultures are challenged because their identity comes from their local context, family, and tribe. In some ways their identity now comes from what they want to be and what they want to do. The breakdown of traditional ties and the growth of individualism promote the mobility of people.

GLOBALIZATION AS A MISSIOLOGICAL CHALLENGE

Globalization entails movements that, in turn, provide opportunities for world evangelization, church planting, leadership development, and contextual theology. Let us look at four of these movements.

We have already alluded to the first movement. *We are going from having two dominant world powers to being a multi-centered world.* The old paradigm of East or West, Communism or democracy has changed. Alignments that had previously been established along East or West lines are now different and multiple. In other words, movement and loyalties are being redefined. Nations can align with different nations and countries. There are profound complexities about these alignments.

Second, *the world's economy is mobile and is moving through global cities.* Trillions of dollars now move around the world.

Third, *we are moving from nationalism to classism.* For example, the rich, educated people in New York, Sao Paulo, Paris, and Tokyo are more like each other than the poor in their own country. Mexican youth may be more like youth in Philadelphia. The major reason for this has to do with the idea that modernity emphasizes appearance, individualism, and consumerism. Let's review several features of this.

Government loses control of their money power. Capitalism and a competitive market promote the private sector and minimize the public

---

[6]Thomas L. Friedman, *The World Is Flat: A Brief History of the 21st Century* (New York: Farrar, Straus & Giroux, 2005).

sector. Local government has less and less control over what we learn and see; therefore, they cannot control people and what they are learning. And finally, globalization lifts up individual rights and undermines family/tribe and local culture.[7]

Our fourth movement is that *cities are becoming national powerhouses and brokers*. Globalization merges global cities such as New York, London, and Tokyo. Who really runs this nation? Is it London? Tokyo? We have gone from global village to global cities to world-class cities. City-states are becoming so powerful that we will have to redefine our mission and local concerns. Because of technology and the media, for over a half-century we have been urbanized and have embraced a city culture that is being spread over the world. Immigration exploits the poor. The poor are to be used at will, and children are pawns for the rich. What we have in our cities are the very rich and the very poor. There is a growing classism, and the disparity between rich and poor is expanding.

MANIFESTATIONS OF GLOBALIZATION

Globalization is manifested in many areas of life. We will look at just a few of these. First, there is the phenomenon of people moving around the world. There are hundreds of thousands of foreign-born residents in New York City from twenty-four foreign countries plus Puerto Rico. The Dominican Republic has almost 370,000 foreign-born living in New York, and China has over 260,000.

A more unusual immigration pattern can be seen in Ireland. There is a large group of Nigerians in Ireland, with most of them living in the capital of Dublin. They have brought with them African churches, African shops, and African services. This immigration is happening in a country that is more used to mass *emigration*. Ireland has witnessed significant immigration only relatively recently because it has recently achieved economic success, which draws people to the country. The influx of Nigerians grew in the late 1990s due to political turmoil back home but has since leveled out.

A second manifestation of globalization is the movement of *religions* around the world. Philip Jenkins says:

---

[7]Mark Gornik, "Globalization and Urban Missions: Some Brief Reflections," unpublished paper, 1999.

Most of the global population growth in the coming decades will be urban. . . . The result will be a steadily growing number of huge metropolitan complexes that could by 2050 or so be counting their populations in the tens of millions. . . . Rich pickings await any religious groups who can meet the needs of these new urbanites, anyone who can at once feed the body and nourish the soul. Will the harvest fall to Christians or Muslims? And if to Christians, will the winners be Catholics or Pentecostals?[8]

Operation World has researched the growth rates of various religions in the world (see graph below).[9] The growth of Christianity is just barely keeping even with the growth of the population in general (represented by the dotted line in the graph below). However, the growth rates of Islam, traditional religions, and Sikh are all exceeding that of the world's population.

Table 1:
Annual Growth Rates of Religions in the World

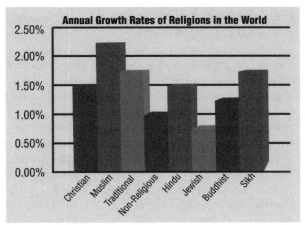

Source: Operation World, 21st Century Edition

As one might expect from this graph, Islam is growing in the United States. Chicago now has over four hundred thousand Muslims and, since 2002, has had a Muslim city comptroller. Black Muslims

---

[8]Philip Jenkins, *The Next Christendom: The Coming of Global Christianity* (New York: Oxford University Press, 2002), 93–94.
[9]Patrick Johnstone and Jason Mandryk, *Operation World, 21st Century Edition,* CD-ROM.

tend to worship in urban centers. "There are over 25 mosques in Philadelphia, and approximately half of them are in West Philadelphia. This estimate does not include the basement or storefront makeshift mosques that spring up in people's houses or businesses five times a day for the required prayers. These informal mosques are a nationwide urban phenomenon in cities with high concentrations of Muslims."[10]

Not only are numerous religions spreading around the world, but Christians from numerous nations are also making an impact around the world. One example of this is the fact that the African Christian church is said to be the fastest growing evangelical church in New York City. But not only is African Christianity spreading to the world, the world in turn is affecting African Christianity.

Wanyeki Mahiaini, in writing about globalization and Africa, says:

> We are living in an age in which, increasingly, African Christianity is becoming representative of the Christian church. This trend is related to a shift in the centre of gravity of Christianity from the North to the South. Because of this shift, we cannot afford to ignore what is happening in Africa. Globalization is all the time increasing the integration of national economies into the global economy through trade, investment rules, and privatization, aided by technological advancement. These trends are affecting the church in Africa in very profound ways. Not surprisingly, TV is making its own mark. . . .
>
> The last time I was in Nairobi, I was, as always, interested to see what was on the TV "family channel." This channel normally carries Christian programs. The programs I saw fell into two groups— Kenyan preachers copying American televangelists and American televangelists. Perhaps there is nothing wrong with these groups, except that as the effects of globalization bite harder into the African church, we are beginning to see more and more African speakers holding entrenched and inflexible positions, which reflect the obstinacy and the narrow-mindedness of their Western financial and theological backers. If you ask our televangelists why they agree with T. D. Jakes, for example, or Benny Hinn, and why they disagree with John Stott or, for that matter, the Proclamation Trust stable of Bible teachers, you will find that the conclusions they have reached are not actually their own. They are merely repeating the biases and the prejudices that are common in the West. One such prejudice is the apparent divide

[10]Tabassam Shah and Jeffrey Diamond, "A Research Paper on the Sunni Muslim Community in West Philadelphia" (Department of History, University of Pennsylvania, 1995), http://www.upenn.edu/ccp/ Ford/WPhila_Muslims. html).

between charismatic and non-charismatic churches in the UK. In my experience, there is less suspicion between the two church traditions in many parts of Africa. I fear that with the help of globally available TV programs, we are already seeing the early signs of the two camps building a mental caricature of each other in Africa.[11]

A third area affected by globalization is economics and, more specifically, poverty. Economic disparities both within and between countries have grown over the past decade, and incomes are lower in real terms in about one hundred countries. Outsourcing labor-intensive jobs to countries with low wage structures has contributed to this gap. One fact that Christians must consider is that around 1.3 billion people live in grinding poverty with incomes of less than a dollar per day (see graph below).

Table 2

Source: World Relief power point presentation, Spring 2005.

The population of the developing world numbers 4.4 billion, and significant proportions of this population lack sanitation, clean water, health care, and enough dietary energy and protein.[12]

---

[11]Wanyeki Mahiaini, "A View from Africa," in Richard Tiplady, ed., *One World or Many? The Impact of Globalisation on Mission* (Pasadena, CA: William Carey Library, 2003), 160–161.
[12]Steven Fouch, "Globalisation and Healthcare Mission," in Richard Tiplady, ed., *One World or Many? The Impact of Globalisation on Mission*, 125.

Health care is an important area on which to focus. Globalization has had both negative and positive effects on the health of the world. Negatively, the easy mobilization of people has also led to the mobilization of diseases. AIDS is perhaps a good model for the way that modern globalization is shaping not only disease and socio-medical responses, but also cultural and religious ideas. We can see the enormity of how quickly AIDS spreads, but also how quickly it brings an activism at a global level.

Some forty million people have been infected with HIV/AIDS in the last twenty years. Half of these have died, and new infections occur at a rate of fifteen thousand per day worldwide. In some countries as many as 40 percent of the population may be infected in the next few years, almost all of whom will suffer periods of debilitating illness before they die, effectively wiping out the twenty to forty-five age group in some nations.[13]

But globalization has also had *positive* effects on health care. "One example of how Western medicine and globalized technology and communications can come together beneficially is in the whole area of *telemedicine*. New technologies, from digital cameras to the Internet, allow the sharing of complex medical knowledge between centers of excellence in major cities in the developing world or the West, with smaller district hospitals and clinics."[14]

How does this work? One way in which telemedicine can be helpful is that pictures and statistical data can be e-mailed to other healthcare facilities, which can allow for suggested diagnosis, treatment, or further lines of inquiry from doctors thousands of miles apart. This gives patients the ability to have specialist consultations they would not otherwise receive. Also, health professionals from both the North and the South are traveling to share training and input, models of practice, and expert consultation. "Healthcare mission, like all mission work, is increasingly from everywhere to everywhere."[15]

From this we can see that ability to travel widely, advancements in technology, and the globalization of the economy have in some cases contributed to the spread of health problems. In other situations they have provided medical access to confront these same problems.

---

[13]Ibid., 135.
[14]Ibid., 137.
[15]Ibid.

Another way in which globalization is manifested is through its effect on culture and, beyond that, its actual *production* of new emerging cultures. This is readily seen if we look at youth. Sam George says, "Globalization and the emerging culture are deeply intertwined subjects and have a reciprocal relationship. The emerging generation will shape the future of both."[16] This is a new form of culture that knows no boundaries and is spreading globally.

There are two facets to this youth culture. The first facet is what George terms TechnoCulture. "Tech savvy-ness is a chief character of the emerging generation around the world. . . . The inclination of youth toward technology and their capacity to acquire techno-skills and knowledge are universal."[17] Essentially every country in the world is now connected to the Internet, and the youth of the world are skilled at maneuvering through web sites, chat rooms, and blogs.

A second facet of youth culture George terms TerrorCulture. "Since the events of September 11, 2001, the culture of terrorism has been etched in the minds of people worldwide. The ongoing war on terrorism and the growing militancy around the world have a youthful face. Young people comprise the army of terrorist networks globally, and there is a growing propensity toward violence."[18]

George concludes by stating, "Both TechnoCulture and TerrorCulture are representative of the global youth. They are not 'either/or' features but a *concurrent* reality of the global youth populace."[19]

IMPLICATIONS FOR MISSION

Some evangelicals believe that mission movements will have to rethink their approach to church planting from a quantitative to a qualitative analysis. We must begin asking, how does the kingdom of God have an impact on community and society for renewal? Ecclesiology will have to engage the subject of globalization missiologically. In other words, we need to reintroduce in our mission movements the discussion of what the church is and what its role is in the face of globalization. Just

---

[16]Sam George, "Emerging Youth Cultures in the Era of Globalization: TechnoCulture and TerrorCulture," in Richard Tiplady, ed., *One World or Many? The Impact of Globalisation on Mission*, 33.

[17]Ibid., 34.

[18]Ibid., 35.

[19]Ibid.

as Jesus broke into human history through his birth, we must incarnate Christ into this age of terror and technology. The incarnational Christian realizes that the gospel travels through time, not in some ideal form, but from one acculturated form to another.

Now let's look at some specific implications for missions. First, *missions must be city-centered.* Our strategies must be urban. Our leadership must have both theological and sociological preparedness. "Cities will be the most important site for church planting. This calls into being a diverse church planting movement. We will have to be especially attentive to multi-ethnic and multi-faith realities, especially at the neighborhood level."[20] Incarnational ministry will have to take precedence over a regional model. The urbanization of the world is real and growing, and we need to prepare for it. Church planting strategies have to focus on the cities.

There is a strong trend for people to come to cities. Cities are welcoming to new immigrants for various reasons. A person's identity in the city becomes much more complex. When groups go to cities, they have overlapping relationships. Classes mingle across cultural lines. Hispanic, Korean, and Chinese language churches are planting English-speaking churches. African-Americans are planting multiethnic churches. Africans are planting African-American churches. Center-city churches are being Asianized because of the overlapping cultural effects and also because of the concentration of universities in cities. In the city we have identities that are interacting and changing. We must think cities, vocations, and neighborhoods.

A second implication is that *missions must be globalized.* The church will have to be *intentionally* the church in matters of impact. How does the gospel penetrate this culture and its particular worldview? How does the church transform a community? We must think of reaching cities in their totality. The old paradigm of foreign or home mission is challenged. Globalization shifts mission to urban centers, and the idea of foreign and home missions will die, especially in the U.S. Cities are linked to cities. Churches in Philadelphia will reach cities like Hong Kong or those in the 10/40 window or in Central America through natural connections. In Chicago they will reach Liberians

---
[20]Gornik, "Globalization and Urban Missions," 1.

because of the natural connection with those in Liberia. Cities are bridges to other global cities.

Third, *theological training should be globalized*. Our churches must become serious about training. They should become Bible institutes with theological and missiological courses. Our Sunday classes need new wineskins. Seminaries and church institutes must globalize their curricula. Curriculum must be aimed at *shalom*. Scripture does not necessarily make a distinction between Beethoven and John Coltrane, but it must make a distinction between wealth accumulation and the cry of the poor. God hears the cry of the poor, the oppressed, and the victimized. These touch the heart of God. This is right and orthodox.

What we have before us is a need not to dichotomize or compartmentalize, but rather to be integrative and missiological. For example, in seminaries, apologetics and elenctics should be taught in conjunction with each other. The same should be true with courses on the church in the modern age and on mission movements. We must teach not only *about* justice but also *for* justice. Preaching should be done in context and not in a vacuum. How would you preach in a Hispanic low-income community? How would you communicate in a multi-ethnic community that has non-book people?

If we reach the cities, we reach the world. Ministry that is effective in world-class cities has wide application, especially with the emerging generation. Learn to minister in the city, and it will help you to minister in the whole of the world. Urban training should be in urban centers where the students learn the city and influence their surroundings. There is a great need for many local seminaries. The old and classical model will continue but must be supplemented. It is often far too costly to send students away to study.

Another issue that traditional seminaries must face is the danger of the enculturation of international students. Frequently when students study in a culture different from their own, they become "conformed" to that new culture, and this makes many of them ineffective in their homelands when their studies are done. While this does not always occur, traditional ministerial training institutions that welcome large numbers of international students must be alert to the danger and must have processes in place to identify and to deal with the problem.

Otherwise they are not appropriately measuring the actual effectiveness of the training they are providing.

A fourth implication of globalization on missions is *that missions must be done in partnerships*. Missions agencies must seek serious partnership with Two-thirds World evangelical leaders without syncretism or paternalism. The challenge is doing theology contextually with biblical integrity.

The fifth implication of globalization on missions is that *missions must be intentional about reaching youth*. For our youth, death means more than life. The obsession with death causes young people to take risks and dare death to come and get them. Suicide rates are three times higher among Xers than among boomers.[21] Martyrdom is popular. Globalization and the emerging culture are deeply intertwined subjects and have a reciprocal relationship. The emerging generation will shape the future of both. George says, "A cross-cultural missiological paradigm to engage these emerging cultures [TechnoCulture and TerrorCulture] is key to doing ministry in the 21st century."[22]

Sixth, *missions must choose the global-local poor*. James 2:5 asks, "Has not God chosen those who are poor in the eyes of the world to be rich in faith and to inherit the kingdom he promised those who love him?" (NIV). Missions must become increasingly committed to the poor. Wolterstoff's notion of shalom propels us toward a world-systems analysis of global development.[23] He suggests that at least some pain and suffering around the world occurs precisely *because* we in the West form the center or core of the economic system, and developing countries form the periphery.[24]

In this era of globalization, how do we know we are fulfilling our kingdom responsibilities *as God has described them*? What are some of the specific marks that we are living in a way that brings honor and glory to our Creator/Redeemer God? The Word of God identifies several necessary indicators, one of which (and, some would say, the *primary* one of which) is that, *globally*, the poor, orphans, widows,

---

[21]Sam George, "TerrorCulture: Worth Living for or Worth Dying for," in Richard Tiplady, ed., *One World or Many? The Impact of Globalisation on Mission*, 64.
[22]George, "Emerging Youth Cultures," 36.
[23]Nicholas Wolterstorff, *Educating for Shalom: Essays on Christian Higher Education* (Grand Rapids, MI: Eerdmans, 2004).
[24]Ibid., xiv.

and oppressed are being cared for. Listen again to these *inspired and inerrant* words from the prophet Isaiah:

> *Is not this the fast that I choose: to loose the bonds of wickedness, to undo the straps of the yoke, to let the oppressed go free, and to break every yoke? Is it not to share your bread with the hungry and bring the homeless poor into your house; when you see the naked, to cover him, and not to hide yourself from your own flesh?* Then *shall your light break forth like the dawn, and your healing shall spring up speedily; your righteousness shall go before you; the glory of the* LORD *shall be your rear guard.* Then *you shall call, and the* LORD *will answer; you shall cry, and he will say, 'Here I am.' If you take away the yoke from your midst, the pointing of the finger and speaking wickedness, if you pour yourself out for the hungry and satisfy the desire of the afflicted, then shall your light rise in the darkness and your gloom be as the noonday.*

> ISA. 58:6–10, EMPHASIS ADDED

And our Savior reaffirms and strengthens Isaiah's challenge in that familiar but still-marvelous passage at the end of his Olivet discourse, just before his arrest and crucifixion:

> *When the Son of Man comes in his glory, and all the angels with him, then he will sit on his glorious throne. Before him will be gathered all the nations, and he will separate people one from another as a shepherd separates the sheep from the goats. And he will place the sheep on his right, but the goats on the left. Then the King will say to those on his right, "Come, you who are blessed by my Father, inherit the kingdom prepared for you from the foundation of the world. For I was hungry and you gave me food, I was thirsty and you gave me drink, I was a stranger and you welcomed me, I was naked and you clothed me, I was sick and you visited me, I was in prison and you came to me." Then the righteous will answer him saying, "Lord, when did we see you hungry and feed you, or thirsty and give you drink? And when did we see you a stranger and welcome you, or naked and clothe you? And when did we see you sick or in prison and visit you?" And the King will answer them, "Truly, I say to you, as you did it to one of the least of these my brothers, you did it to me."*

> MATT. 25:31–40

Of course, complexities abound when we seek to implement what Jesus and Isaiah have said. And these descriptions of kingdom living cannot be considered in isolation from other passages that describe doctrinal faithfulness or personal holiness. But we must never forget that where the actions described by Isaiah and Jesus are *missing*, our Creator/Redeemer God is not receiving the honor and glory that is his due. It is a simple biblical truth that those who would live in *full* obedience to the inspired and inerrant Word of God must be *active* in "sharing the burden of ministry to the global urban poor."

The phenomenon we have been discussing, globalization, makes such obedience both more difficult and more important. As we have noted, globalization tends to increase the disparity between rich and poor (look again at Table 2 above). As this reality is recognized, those Christians and churches concerned to *live by* as well as to *believe in* "every word that comes from the mouth of God" (Matt. 4:4) must correspondingly increase their commitment to "ministry to the global urban poor." According to Matthew 25, Jesus may just regard those who do as "sheep" and those who do not as "goats."

Finally, of course, *missions must be confessional.* Jesus is Lord. And Jesus must become Lord. Every system, every power, and every city must be brought under the lordship of Christ. We do not minister to global youth for the sake of global youth. We do not minister to global urban poor for the sake of global urban poor. We do not even perform such ministries in order to achieve the status of sheep rather than goats. We do ministry/missions for the sake of Jesus. We do them in order to bring *him* honor and glory. We do them as a way of seeking to move the cosmos toward that day when "at the name of Jesus every knee should bow, in heaven and on earth and under the earth, and every tongue confess that Jesus Christ is Lord, to the glory of God the Father" (Phil. 2:10–11). We do them because that will be the best expression of globalization of all!

CHAPTER ELEVEN

SHARING THE OPPORTUNITY OF MINISTERIAL SPIRITUAL FORMATION

VICTOR COLE

The challenges facing theological education include the need for balance between academic, spiritual, and practical dimensions—or the need to balance head, heart, and hands issues. However, in the usual discussion of theological education, focus is too often given to *formal* theological education to the neglect of vitally complementary aspects of the *non-formal* and *informal*. For a holistic approach, all three modes must be considered in a discussion of theological education and spiritual formation. It is just such a holistic approach that this paper addresses.

CHALLENGES FACING FORMAL THEOLOGICAL EDUCATION

Edward Farley set the stage for an intense discussion of this subject when, in 1983, he alleged that the era of enlightenment had resulted in theology's loss of its unifying purpose as it became fragmented into discrete academic disciplines. The twentieth century witnessed emphasis on the practical aspects of ministerial tasks, or the trend toward "clerical paradigm."[1]

But even earlier, in 1956, Richard Niebuhr had observed that in the mid-twentieth century a dual challenge faced theological education. In his extensive studies Niebuhr concluded that seminaries in North America were "in quandary," torn between "proximate and ultimate" goals,[2] and together with his associates in another report noted that the theological curriculum was overloaded in an attempt to satisfy the call to infuse more "practical courses" into the curriculum.[3]

Niebuhr, in explaining the nature of this "quandary" in North American seminaries, claimed that uncertainties existed about the nature, the purpose, and the functions of the church for which the seminaries are expected to prepare ministers. Clark Gilpin also talks of a "perplexity" that confronts seminaries because (western) societies have now resorted to naturalistic explanations of state, economy, school, and family.[4]

This outlook has affected the church, as it accepts naturalistic instead of religious explanations of the changing social institutions. In short, it is a perplexity about irreligion, an irreligion with respect to church, nation, and school. I suggest that this naturalistic trend is largely responsible for the struggle to know how to appropriate spiritual formation in theological education. Even seminaries in non-western societies have not gone unscathed, as the face of irreligious religion is seen all over.

If the theological academy is plagued by a crisis of *credibility* in the many calls within and without it for reform, the church is plagued by a crisis of *identity*, not knowing clearly what it is and exactly why it exists—as the central forum in which God is at work today. All of the factors contribute to making direction of formation quite uncertain, as Niebuhr and others have noted. It is no wonder that spirituality is endangered, shunted aside, sometimes eclipsed, and occasionally even lost completely.

---

[1]Edward Farley, *Theologia: The Fragmentation and Unity of Theological Education* (Philadelphia: Fortress Press, 1983).
[2]Richard H. Niebuhr, *The Purpose of the Church and Its Ministry* (New York: Harper & Row, 1956).
[3]Richard H. Niebuhr, R. Williams, and J. M. Gustafson, *The Advancement of Theological Education* (New York: Harper & Brothers, 1957).
[4]Clark W. Gilpin, *A Preface to Theology* (Chicago: University of Chicago Press, 1996), xxiff.

The trend of the past two hundred years to look at ministry and its training from the perspective of post-Enlightenment professionalism (discussed below) constitutes at least two challenges. The first is the tendency and temptation to devalue the priesthood of all believers. The second is the wholesale adoption of the formal mode of training, not mindful of its limitations, particularly in the area of formation having to do with the affect, which is the primary realm of spiritual formation.[5] Thus a real challenge facing formal theological education is not just plurality of the field that is dispersed and lacks material unity in its various disciplines, but there is also the underlying need to integrate head, hands, and heart into a holistic process of formation.[6]

CHALLENGES FACING NON-FORMAL THEOLOGICAL EDUCATION

Most organized out-of-school (or out-of-classroom) theological education endeavors qualify as *non-formal*. The best known is Theological Education by Extension (TEE), although other non-formal forms may exist in out-of-school contexts. TEE goes back to the early 1970s beginning in Guatemala. Robert Banks notes that TEE, designed for and adopted in the non-western world, has done well in an attempt to keep a balance between "*being, knowing,* and *doing*," or the balance in matters of head, heart, and hands, a critically important balance if spiritual formation is, in fact, one of the essential components of effective theological education.[7]

TEE is sometimes misperceived as "inferior" to the formal mode of theological education. To counter this misperception, some educators who adopt it feel obliged to make it conform to and even to look more like a formal residential mode. But in so doing, the original design in the "technology" of the "split-rail fence" tends to be lost.[8] That "technology" requires active combination of study, ministry, and

---

[5]In his discussion of spirituality, Robert Roberts places the subject in the framework of the emotive, and rightly so (see Robert C. Roberts, *Spirituality and Human Emotion* [Grand Rapids, MI: Eerdmans, 1982]).
[6]See Francis Schüssler Fiorenza, "Thinking Theologically about Theological Education," in *Theological Perspectives on Christian Formation: A Reader on Theology and Christian Education,* ed. Jeff Astley, Leslie J. Francis, and Colin Crowder (Grand Rapids, MI: Eerdmans, 1996), 318–341.
[7]Robert Banks, *Reenvisioning Theological Education: Exploring a Missional Alternative to Current Models* (Grand Rapids, MI: Eerdmans, 1999), 135.
[8]Ted Ward, "The Split-Rail Fence: Analogy for Professional Education," *Extension Seminary* 2 (1976).

intermittent seminars that bring together otherwise individual learners into a temporary community of learners who share personal, ministry, and Christian-life experiences while engaging in ongoing ministry. Thus the non-formal mode's value for a holistic approach is clear, *if* adopted appropriately.

A non-formal mode of theological education is, of course, subject to its own set of limitations. Non-formal theological education tends to be short-term, hands-on, practical-oriented, and less focused on theory and reflection. It may, therefore, provide less traditional theological *content* than formal theological education. But this possible "limitation" must be considered in the context of the exact training objectives for any specific program of theological study, and the natural strengths of formal theological education must not be the only criteria considered. In other words, non-formal theological education must not be required to demonstrate its equivalency with formal theological education any more than the formal theological education should be required to demonstrate its equivalency with non-formal theological education. What is needed is the mode of theological education appropriate to the desired educational outcomes, and this frequently will mean a combination of both formal and non-formal modes.

CHALLENGES FACING CHURCH-BASED THEOLOGICAL EDUCATION

The matter of definition is one of the challenges facing church-based theological education. There is, for example, a widespread perception that education within the church is *less than theological*.[9] This underscores the tension between the intellectual and the other legitimate functions of theological education. A balanced and biblical approach would see theological equipping of the saints in the "whole will of God" as part of the educational task of the church. The divorce

---

[9]For example, Robert Ferris once took issue with William Dyrness, who reserved "theological education" for intellectual functions and used the term "ministry education" to describe what is regarded as the less prestigious task of clergy preparation. See Robert Ferris, "The Role of Theology in Theological Education," in *With an Eye on the Future: Development and Mission in the 21st Century,* ed. Duane Elmer and Lois McKinney (Monrovia, CA: MARC, 1996), 105. Others reserve the use of "theological education" and "theology" for what is termed clergy education (Farley) or "specialized leadership training" (Wagner), and the use of "Christian education" to mean education of the larger community of faith (Farley) or "edification of the entire body of Christ" (Wagner). See Farley, *Theologia,* 134, and Ralph R. Covell and Peter C. Wagner, *An Extension Seminary Primer* (Pasadena, CA: William Carey Library, 1971), 29.

between church and academy in the course of theological education, therefore, comes to a head with this dichotomy between education that is or is not church-based. As with non-formal theological education, however, even church-based theological education faces challenges.

Perhaps the most important challenge is for the church to accept its own educational responsibilities. It simply is not biblical for the church to outsource all ministerial training to other institutions or agencies. It is, in the final analysis, *the church's* responsibility to provide ministers for its pulpits. It may, of course, delegate some aspects of ministerial training to seminaries, but it must closely supervise and wisely supplement the training that it does delegate. So the first challenge for the church is to recognize and embrace the educational aspect of its own identity.

As a direct corollary, the church must actively seek to forge formal bonds of cooperation with any agency or institution to which it delegates any part of ministerial training. This is especially critical in the area of spiritual formation.[10] This is toward the noble end of declaring to the local church the whole will of God and equipping her to engage the world. But it is a challenge because it requires the church to devote significant resources (time, energy, and money) to a task that in the recent past the church often has delegated completely.

WHAT IS SPIRITUAL FORMATION?

Spirituality is a term to which the contemporary world seems recently to have awakened. There are, of course, many different forms of spirituality—African spirituality, Buddhist spirituality, feminist spirituality, Hindu spirituality, Islamic spirituality, and so forth.[11] My discussion, however, is limited to Christian spirituality, and it deals with this subject in a general sense rather than with respect to any particular tradition. It is about the practical Christian life, the habit of personal existential knowledge of God motivated by deep love for God.

---

[10]I do not hereby imply that spiritual formation should take place only within the context of the local church, for it is realized that even in the context of the theological school, there are ample opportunities for informality that could enhance spirituality in the formation process.

[11]For examples of the different non-Christian approaches see Cline Erricker and Jane Erricker, eds., *Contemporary Spiritualities: Social and Religious Contexts* (London: Continuum, 2001). See also Jacob K. Olupona, ed., *African Spirituality: Forms, Meanings and Expressions* (New York: Crossroad, 2000).

GENERAL PERSPECTIVES ON SPIRITUALITY

Spirituality is sometimes defined as the development of virtue and character. Broadly described, it is the human quest for depth and values.[12] Specifically applied to Christianity, Sheldrake says it is "how people relate their beliefs about God in Jesus Christ to their core values and then express these beliefs and values in spiritual practices and also in how they form social and religious communities and relate to social and cultural realities."[13]

In addition, however, it is crucial to recognize that *spirituality is vitally about developing a relationship*. This is why discipleship is a vital aspect of spiritual formation.[14] James E. Loder therefore underscores the conscious and intentional appropriation of "transformational" experiences in the process.[15] For his part, Lindbeck first defines spiritual formation non-theologically, to accommodate different religious traditions, saying it is "deep and personally committed appropriation of a comprehensive and coherent outlook on life and the world." Then he specifies its Christian form as dispositions and capacities for speech, feeling, and action, which are distinctive of Christianity and also shaped deeply by culture, personal history, and genetic constitution.[16]

In all the different perspectives, it is noteworthy that spirituality is defined in terms of dimensions of human experience as well as a reference to the discipline concerned with that experience.[17]

A CHRISTIAN PERSPECTIVE ON SPIRITUALITY

While it is important to be aware of these general perspectives on spirituality, we in the World Reformed Fellowship are most concerned about what Scripture says.

---

[12]Fiorenza, "Thinking Theologically," 323.

[13]Ibid., 53.

[14]By discipleship I mean the lifelong process of following Jesus Christ and becoming like him (i.e., transformation) as a result. Thus the making of a man or woman of God (being) precedes service (doing) and not vice versa.

[15]James E. Loder, "Transformation in Christian Education," in *Theological Perspectives on Christian Formation*, ed. Jeff Astley and Leslie J. Francis (Grand Rapids, MI: Eerdmans, 1996), 271–283.

[16]George Lindbeck, "Spiritual Formation and Theological Education," in *Theological Perspectives on Christian Formation*, 287–288.

[17]Spirituality is first "fundamental dimensions of the human being"; second, it is the "lived experience that actualizes that dimension"; and third, it is "the academic discipline that studies that experience." See Sandra M. Schneiders, "Spirituality in the Academy," in *Modern Christian Spirituality: Methodological and Historical Essays*, ed. Bradley C. Hanson (Atlanta: Scholars Press, 1990), 17.

We begin by noting the Pauline injunctions, where spirituality is likened to an exercise. Spirituality has to do with "godliness" (*eusebeia*) or reverence for God. Paul's admonition to Timothy is clear and specific: "Train yourself to be godly" (1 Tim. 4:7, NIV). Quoting Trench, John Stott says that this injunction refers to a personal experience of "mingled fear and love, which together constitute the piety of man toward God."[18] Stott then goes on to describe biblical spirituality as the experience of a "Copernican revolution of Christian conversion from self-centeredness to God-centeredness."[19]

It is instructive that Paul, in his admonition to Timothy, employs the term "train" (*gymnaze*). Thus godliness requires training or exercise! And if this is the case, it is inexcusable if theological education is ever conducted in a way that neglects training in *godliness*!

Such godliness or spirituality, again according to the Word of God, has at least two dimensions—the *relational*, which has to do with love for God and love for one's neighbor (see 1 John 4:20) and the communal or *ecclesial*, because we are created and re-created to function in community, in this case as new creation in the community of faith. Later in this paper I will consider both of these dimensions as I explore how spirituality should be an integral part in theological education. But first I will provide a context for this consideration by offering a perspective on theological education as a professional field.

THE ESSENCE OF MINISTERIAL TRAINING IN LIGHT OF THE PROFESSIONS

The direct application of theory (learned in school) to practice (in the form of cases encountered in real-life settings) is said to be unusual in the professional fields. Professionals are not usually concerned firsthand with basic research; instead they simply are expected to transfer knowledge gained by experts in basic research to problem-solving situations. Common to modern professionals however is "esoteric knowledge systematically formulated and applied to problems of a client"

---

[18]John R. W. Stott, *Guard the Truth: The Message of 1 Timothy & Titus*, The Bible Speaks Today (Leicester, UK: Inter-Varsity Press, 1997), 117.
[19]I do not think Stott here implies that this "godliness" has to do simply with the conversion experience; rather conversion is the starting point from which the journey of a lifetime begins. See Loder, who aptly points out that "Spiritual formation involves, but is not the same as, conversion or personal commitment." ("Transformation in Christian Education," 287).

as well as exclusive "right to practice."[20] But in reality, professionals are known to generate theory on their own in the course of practice and to apply the same as situations arise. For this reason, professional ministers are often advised to become "Reflective Practitioners" and "Practical Theologians."[21]

But for my purpose, it is vitally important for us to understand exactly what "practice" entails in Christian ministry as a profession. In the other professions, "way of life" is not a criterion for determining qualification as a professional.[22] In Christian ministry as a profession, however, "practice" is inseparable from lifestyle. If professionals "profess to *know* better than others the nature of certain matters," the Christian minister, as a professional, professes in both knowledge *and life*. Thus, any dichotomy between *knowing* and *being* is unwarranted—both in the ministerial profession and in training for the ministerial profession.

The aspects of experiential knowledge of life in and outside the faith community and the bringing to bear of critical and informed reflection on these require extension of training beyond the four walls of the classroom. This is why I propose church-school linkage in the formation process. If action-reflection can occur in the process of professional practice after school training, it can even be richer during school training when the tools of reflection tend to be sharper. The dialectic of reflection-action, while in school, should allow the integration of the areas of factual knowledge, spiritual formation, and hands-on practical ministry skills through formal, non-formal, and informal processes, thus enabling holistic formation.

What is taught or learned during professional training of the ministry must be related to life and must in turn be communicated by life to others. This is a particularly marked distinction of Christian ministry as a profession, by comparison with other fields of profession. In most other professions, the professional is required to be "objective" in ways he or she would find painful personally to apply back to self! "This is why it is unfair to ask the physician to heal himself"![23] Of particular interest is that in other fields, professionals are allowed to deviate

---

[20]Everett C. Hughes, "Professions," *Daedalus* 92 (1963), 655–666.
[21]Joseph C. Hough and John B. Cobb, *Christian Identity and Theological Education* (Chico, CA: Scholars Press, 1985), 81ff.
[22]Bernard Barber, "Some Problems in the Sociology of the Professions," *Daedalus* 92 (1963), 671.
[23]Hughes, "Professions," 656.

from lay conduct in matters that they profess! This sort of deviation is, however, not credible in the Christian ministry as a profession. The Christian professional is required to be empathetic and is often required to swallow his or her own "bitter pill" also! This is patterned after Jesus, the sympathizing High Priest (Heb. 4:15).

Authentic theological education must involve holistic teaching and holistic learning, which are not simply the communication of ideas to minds. As touching the ministry and its training, holistic teaching and learning concern communication of heads (or minds), hearts, and hands.

HOW SPIRITUALITY IS TAUGHT: CASE STUDIES

There are different approaches that may be broadly categorized into two: teaching spirituality as an academic discipline and teaching spirituality as a practical discipline. While the former is cognitive, rationalistic, claims objectivity, and tries to maintain a detached posture, the latter is affective, personal, subjective, and overtly engaging.

David Wells, in a disturbing report concerning the landscape of North American theological education in the early 1990s, reveals that seminarians, while *cognitively* holding dear to theological beliefs, do not allow those beliefs to "intersect very cogently with the world they inhabit mentally and practically."[24] This finding suggests a critical disconnect between learning and living. This is an issue that should disturb theological educators everywhere and should serve as a wake-up call on the need to reconcile piety and intellect in theological education. Sandra Schneiders is absolutely correct when she says, "Only a theology that is rooted in the spiritual commitment of the theologian and oriented toward praxis will be meaningful in the Church of the future."[25]

However, the teaching of spirituality in the context of the school is no easy task and is beset by many challenges, one of which is the manner in which theologizing is often done—from a detached, purely cognitive perspective. In that manner, spirituality is taught as an academic subject, which addresses more of the mind than the heart. This approach is much more prevalent in those educational circles whose public is

---

[24]David F. Wells, *God in the Wasteland: The Reality of Truth in a World of Fading Dreams* (Grand Rapids, MI: Eerdmans, 1994), 186–213.
[25]Schneiders, "Spirituality in the Academy," 17.

limited to the academic guild, even though those who claim the church public struggle as much in this regard. Now let us consider some specific case studies, which employ various aspects of formal, quasi non-formal, and informal modes within the context of the academy.

Formal Approaches

Spirituality can be taught either as an academic discipline or as a practical discipline within the context of the school. Here is an example of each.

As an academic discipline: case of an M.A. in Christian spirituality. This is a freestanding degree course of study from two centers, the Heythrop College at London University and Sarum College in association with the University of Wales, Lampeter.[26] From the outset, students are warned that this is not "a form of personal spiritual formation."[27] The program of study is from a purely academic perspective, based on an inductive *process* of reflecting on experiences and practices from a variety of different contexts in light of Christian history and tradition that are recognized as "radically plural."[28]

The focus of study is on content and method of spirituality, problems of historical context, and textual interpretation from reading primary texts. The *methodology* adopted by the teacher, in seminar settings, is interactive, starting off with an introduction of text materials and posing critical questions. Students then lead sessions in which they take turns presenting sections of a pre-assigned text guided by questions such as, "What understanding of self is found in this text?" Group discussions are also student-led. Each session concludes with the module teacher giving a brief summary of the discussions, while highlighting significant points and calling attention to issues that might have been left out during discussion.

The curriculum is comprised of two core modules and four optional modules, capped by a twenty-thousand-word dissertation. The core modules are designed to challenge students to "question many assumptions and values that lie behind so much of the spirituality they have inherited . . . also invite students to step out of the religious boundaries that are familiar to them. Evangelicals learn to study sympathetically a

---

[26]A full description of this model may be found in Philip F. Sheldrake, "Teaching Spirituality," *BJTE* 12:1 (2001), 53–64.
[27]Ibid., 61.
[28]Ibid., 60.

text of the Catholic Reformation . . . Catholics seek to understand the birth of a distinctive 'Anglican' spiritual tradition. . . ."[29]

The modules examine spirituality in relation to a variety of texts and spiritual traditions from diverse times and places. The *core* modules feature two key areas: 1) "Foundations of Christian Spirituality," concentrating on selected classic spiritual texts ranging from the patristic period to contemporary liberation spirituality, and 2) "Theology of Spirituality," which examines theologies of the human person, while adopting an interdisciplinary approach to spirituality and to theology.

Students also select as many as four *optional* modules that are wide-ranging in nature. Among the options are: 1) "Spirituality in Christian Traditions" (such as western mysticism, Celtic, and early English spiritual traditions), 2) spirituality and social processes of human existence (such as ecological spirituality, literature and gender, liberation, and "political" spiritualities), 3) "Dialogue between Spirituality and Pastoral Theology," which includes liturgy, spirituality and ministry, and Christian spiritual direction, and 4) "Personal Research on the Study of Spirituality" (which, of course, must not be based on introspection or individual spiritual experience).

The whole learning experience is thought to create in students "strangeness, otherness, and discomfort," because, according to Sheldrake, spirituality is a "self-implicating field."[30] In the belief that the search for knowledge through a process of critical analysis implies inevitably some form of transformation, according to Sheldrake, "an academic course in spirituality, perhaps in a more immediate way than other elements of theology, tends to bring students face to face with questions of personal faith and appropriate spiritual practice."[31] But then it should be realized that transformation involves personal and subjective encounters with the "truth" of whatever knowledge students encounter. So how should the teacher handle it in the contexts of the classroom or in tutorials? Sheldrake answers as follows:

> As long as critical analysis is not set aside and rigorous study is not subverted . . . it is artificial as well as unhelpful to the learning process to exclude all reference in class to questions of personal appro-

---

[29]Ibid.
[30]Ibid., 61.
[31]Ibid.

priation. This would be to confine "knowledge" purely to "objective information about something" based on distance and detached reasoning—a reductionist understanding of knowledge that I reject as inadequate.[32]

All well and good, but in the same breath Sheldrake clarifies his position, stating:

> I hasten to add that "reference to personal appropriation" should be distinguished from allowing lengthy testimonies or from encouraging students to use introspective individual spiritual experience/practice as the central subject matter or as the basis for research. Likewise, I do not think it appropriate to allow classes to become forms of group spiritual direction, let alone individual spiritual guidance! However, reference to personal experience or pastoral practice may be one tool among many, alongside historical, theological, and other intellectual ones, to enable us to come to grips with a spiritual tradition. Overall, I have found that students quickly come to understand the boundaries and that this has enhanced rather than diluted the learning process.[33]

The above is an example of attempts to teach spirituality purely as an *academic discipline* within a strictly formal context of the academy. I now examine another formal approach, but this one exemplifies teaching spirituality as a *practical discipline*.

As a practical discipline: case of spiritual formation as a subject. This is an illustration from the Theological College of Zimbabwe, Bulawayo. Up front, this approach is unpretentious about attempting to promote personal spiritual formation in learners within the context of the school, attempting to infuse spiritual formation into the "Practical Theology" component of studies.[34] This component comprises a range of subjects, including two first-year subjects in Spiritual Formation.

Spiritual Formation as a subject is divided into two introductory subjects: First-year students are offered, in the first term, an introductory course (Spiritual Formation I) which focuses on "inner disciplines" of personal growth and helping others with the same. This subject was

---

[32]Ibid., 62.
[33]Ibid.
[34]A full description of this model may be found in Robert Heaton, "Teaching Spirituality from an African Perspective," *JACT* 6:2 (December 2003), 44–49.

designed in response to the realization that the church has not been able to help incoming students with the discipline of personal growth. This introductory course covers such basics as fellowship, prayer, Bible study, personal devotions, worship, knowing God's will, and developing a Christian mind. The main assignment requires the student to keep a daily spiritual journal, describing his or her spiritual journey as far back as the student can recall. This touches key events, people, and places that God may have used to bring the student to faith. Also there is a character quality assessment project, as well as a short and a long personal evangelistic testimony. The projects are done over the course of the term, during which the student meets with a lecturer three times to assess progress and to assist with any difficulties.

In the second term, the course (Spiritual Formation II) focuses on "outward disciplines" having to do mainly with discipleship. This subject was designed because it was thought that very few incoming students have been discipled in any meaningful way. This course covers the philosophical foundation and the practice of discipleship. The main assignment of the course requires each student to disciple someone for several weeks while employing principles taught in class. Other topics covered are: the biblical ethic of work, the biblical perspective on the spirit world, conflict and interpersonal relationships, and spiritual gifts.

Both subjects are examinable, featuring not just projects and assignments but exams. An approach of this nature that tends to be more personal and introspective also comes with its challenges when adopted within the context of formal school setting. Heaton reports that while the goal is for personal long-term growth and benefits of students, some of them simply go along just to fulfill all righteousness or just to make the grade!

Quasi Nonformal/Informal Approaches

This was the approach adopted at the ECWA Theological Seminary, Jos, Nigeria, in the 1980s while I served as the Academic Dean there. The curriculum attempted integration of classroom subjects with a program of field education, small-group meetings with faculty, and personal discipleship.[35] The spiritual formation component of the pro-

---

[35] Allusion to this model is found in Robert W. Ferris, *Renewal in Theological Education: Strategies for Change* (Wheaton, IL: The Billy Graham Center, 1990), 79–89.

gram, as it concerned students preparing for the pastorate, was quasi non-formal/informal. It took place largely out-of-classroom within the contexts of a chaplain/pastor's study and a local congregation and other informal settings to which students accompanied the chaplain.[36] The program hinged very much on the person of the seminary chaplain, "an older pastor, highly respected among the ECWA churches . . . providing pastoral care for all students and systematic discipling for students in the pastoral ministries program . . . (as) an on-campus model for students preparing for pastoral ministry."[37]

The seminary had intentionally recruited the chaplain from a prominent and successful pastorate. He was reputed to demonstrate deep spirituality as a man of prayer, integrity, and one who maintained a clear Christian witness in private and public life. The idea was for him to serve as a *model* on-site, in a situation where local church and school met in such a unique arrangement. The pastor/chaplain would take on three or four students at a time, for a period of three months, in an apprenticeship of observation. In the process he opened them to his prayer life, personal life, and ministry; he invited them to observe elders' meetings, and they assisted him with pastoral duties such as preparation of the elements for the Communion service, etc.

This approach is probably more informal than non-formal. The exposure of the students to a model, within the context of a learning and worshiping community, provided a mentoring relationship between the pastor/chaplain and learners. The proximity of the classroom with practice of the Christian life and ministry had the potential to enable learners to reflect on practice vis-à-vis classroom learning in a more holistic way. This is yet another approach to spiritual formation, but one that attempts integration of head, heart, and hands.

TOWARD A CURRICULUM FOR MINISTERIAL TRAINING AS HOLISTIC FORMATION

If theological education extends to the whole people of faith, as I have argued, and if it is best accomplished by means of reflection-action, there should be different levels of those means.

---

[36]The seminary chaplain was also pastor of a local congregation meeting on the campus of the seminary. By a special arrangement, the congregation and the seminary shared the same physical facilities for worship.

[37]Ferris, *Renewal*, 80.

THE TRIPARTITE LEVELS OF TRAINING

Three vital levels are discernible when ministerial training is conceptualized in terms of an inverted pyramid. However, this pyramid is designed to convey qualitative rather than quantitative difference. It is for that reason that the pyramid is inverted, to symbolize the Christian ideal of servanthood required of those who serve as leaders.[38] Equally important is the realization that there are any numbers of cadres within a level.

The Grassroots Level

This is the broadest end of the inverted pyramid because this is where most members of the community of faith are. Whereas the level itself is broad-based, there might be different cadres represented. These are those who need basic nurturing in the faith; others are at a higher degree of Christian maturity and are able to assume greater responsibilities. Some might function in various leadership roles, providing nurture and care to some others; and others might be able to function in pastoral and administrative roles. Different forms of training appropriate to each cadre are therefore needed.

The education appropriate to each cadre at the grassroots level must be characterized by the practical Christian life, that personal existential knowledge of God motivated by deep love for God. The biblical and theological understanding that this habit of the Christian life produces would have both *relational* (inner and outer) and *ecclesial* elements. Both of these correspond to the vital aspect of *being* or the making of the man or woman of God.[39] This habit provides the common level ground for all cadres, not only at this, but at all three levels of the inverted pyramid, as I will explain shortly.

Following this common core just described, there is the need to provide knowledge and practical skill acquisition appropriate for each cadre. For example, the cadre needing nurture in the faith will require basic *knowledge* in Bible, Christian doctrines, and a level of knowledge of church history. In addition to this knowledge base, various *practical skills* would be taught. Some of these may relate to worship and

---

[38]That is to say, the levels are distinct only in terms of role differentiation and not intended to be in terms of superior-inferior relationships.

[39]See note 16 above.

liturgy—personal and corporate—and how to testify as a witness to the faith, including the area of the Christian's conduct in society. The last example could conceivably involve the *relational* aspect of the *practical Christian life*, and rightly so. This then goes on to show how that habit could permeate the other areas dealing with pure knowledge (or information) and practical hands-on skills, for a holistic or integrated approach.

The curriculum for theological education at the grassroots level as suggested here is, in significant ways, similar to that found in the formal school setting. The similarity is in terms of the broad areas of the divisions of the course of studies, so that most things in the school curriculum may conceivably be covered at the grassroots level.

Vital to the promotion of grassroots theological education is the leadership of the church—both lay and professional. This leadership must be so trained as to facilitate at the grassroots level an education that is similar to what this leadership itself has received. That is, education that promotes development of both inner and outer life; the ability to engage in the dialectic of action-reflection; education that empowers believers within life situations to respond to those situations. That way, believers at the grassroots level won't have to sit back as mere observers in the church or remain aloof to situations in society. In the same manner, there should be in evidence greater initiative at the grassroots level to respond to situations and needs—spiritual, social, material—within the church and the larger society.

Only pedagogy of leadership training that moves from mere *telling* others to *facilitation*, as catalysts of the massive potentials at the grassroots level, can bring about the sort of transformation here envisaged. However, what is proposed here for the grassroots is not the extension of school into the local church or the transfer of the schooling approach to the local church setting. Rather, this is theological education in, for, and by the local church.

The church leadership must, however, serve as catalyst and facilitator of the whole process. The part played by the school in equipping this sort of leadership is discussed next under the middle level of the inverted pyramid. The context of training at the grassroots level is already within a real-life setting. That context must be fully employed through a combination of the formal, non-formal, and informal modes.

Believers must be trained in action-reflection as they respond to situations-in-life. The part the church could play in facilitating holistic theological education with the school will also be mentioned when treating education at the middle or professional level.

The Middle (Professional) Level

This is the level that historically has catered to training of the professional clergy. However, since William R. Harper's earlier call, seminaries have tried to cater to the training of other Christian workers and not just those training to be preachers.[40] The school has traditionally been the locus of training at this level. The school should serve a double function: first as a place for the movement of the mind toward God, "that place where the church exercises its intellectual love for God" (Niebuhr); second it should serve as a center that provides service for the church's other activities, such as bringing criticism to bear on those activities. Only a church-school linkage could make this a reality.

The first function has to do primarily with reflection, while the second has to do primarily with the *practical Christian life*. It is, however, too well known that the school's strength traditionally lies more with reflection than with practice, as theory-practice dichotomy has long plagued the school.[41] It is, however, in that tendency to separate action from reflection that the theory-practice dichotomy promotes both the loss of the practical Christian life and the dispersion of the field in theological education.

There is yet another important function of the school—as that center through which the church retains access to its intellectual heritage. The school has functioned as a center that has kept alive that intellectual heritage. In so doing, the potential for an authentic Christian renewal remains.[42] But part of that intellectual heritage has been to regard the school, that center which has also functioned primarily to train the church's leadership, as purely a center for reflection. Accordingly, much of the traditional curriculum, as represented by the fourfold divisions,[43] has concentrated purely on reflection, even in

---

[40]William R. Harper, "Shall the Theological Curriculum Be Modified, and How?" *American Journal of Theology* Vol. 3, 1899, 56–59.
[41]"Practice" here concerns both the practical habits of the new life in Christ and practice of ministry skills.
[42]Hough and Cobb, *Christian Identity,* 17.
[43]The divisions are Biblical, Theological, Historical, and Practical Studies.

the so-called "practical disciplines."[44] This is the usual way seminary professors have been trained, and that is how they, in turn, train their students.

No doubt the context of school training is artificial in its form vis-à-vis practical Christian life. It is little wonder, then, that so long as theological education majors primarily on reflection, the practical life of faith remains elusive in the curriculum, even sometimes intimidating. My argument is that theological education, in its essence, requires not just reflection or just action. In fact, there probably is no pure reflection or pure action because engaging in the one may actually make the other inevitable. The critical issue, therefore, is whether both are *consciously* and *intentionally* directed toward appropriate ends.

For example, the practical Christian life and the practical skills of ministry should both be guided by informed reflection. In the same manner, reflection should be balanced at every level with informed action. To concentrate only on reflection, especially in a field that is so practical to life, is fraught with dangers. The paralysis of analysis only is too well known!

In addition, trying to offer reflection only, even with the understanding that action will follow later (perhaps when the individual graduates and enters into ministry), creates an unwarranted artificiality. It is imperative that school training break out of any such artificiality in the formation process. This is because action-reflection actually functions best when it is seen and utilized as dialectic.

Crucial to training at the middle level, then, is the need to train the professional cadre as facilitators at the grassroots level. To these two vital points I now direct attention.

Training at the middle level is both strategic and pivotal. Those trained at this level must be able to facilitate in the faith community a level of biblical and theological understanding necessary for the faith life and for the role and functions of the church in the world. This is one reason why those who are trained at this level must themselves know firsthand what they are called upon to facilitate in others. The requirement, however, strictly does not have to do with just *knowledge* and information. It has to do vitally with experiential knowledge of

---

[44]See Robert Heaton, "Teaching Spirituality from an African Perspective," *JACT* 2 (December 2003), 44–49.

the *Christian life* and existence, and so does it have to do with *skills* required for ministry. This again underscores why training *only* within the four walls of the classroom cannot be adequate. To this end, the call was made at the close of the nineteenth century for "theological clinics."[45]

The Specialist/Technical Level

The apex of the inverted pyramid concerns those who function in technical and specialist areas, a very tiny proportion of the community of faith. This group possesses skills in carrying out high-level, pure research. The community of faith requires at this level those who can uncover the past and delve into areas that require specialist skills in linguistics, historiography, archaeology, etc. These individuals deal with "the mode of understanding that attends the life of inquiry and scholarship," described in the Middle Ages as "the doctors of the church."[46]

The direction of the fourfold pattern within the modern university and in advanced seminary studies has focused on training specialists. Requiring middle-level professional training for ministry *primarily* to take the same direction is, in my view, largely responsible for the prevailing discord between the school's theory and the church's practice.

Certain crucial questions arise with the acknowledgment of this specialist and technical level of training. What level, for instance, must those intending to go into specialist training achieve? Obviously, the answer is the middle level! If so, is the kind of training proposed for professionals at the middle level likely to prepare one for entering into specialist training thereafter? Can the middle level cater both to those who are intending to enter pastoral ministry and to those seeking a scholarly career? Should specialist training be engaged in isolation from the development of the practical Christian life? Should the erudite Christian scholar be excused from the need to develop and to cultivate the inner and outer life or be aloof to the ecclesial dimension of the Christian life in the course of duty? These are all critically important questions, which I will try to answer briefly.

While specialist concern is about "self conscious inquiry under

---

[45]Harper, "Shall the Theological Curriculum Be Modified," 61.
[46]Farley, *Theologia*, 158.

scholarly and scientific requirements" (Farley), for such specialist concern to be genuinely Christian in character, it must be carried on at the same time as the scholar personally develops in his/her Christian life and in his/her personal relationship to God. Just as the Christian professional, in the name of objectivity, may not function as such without also getting *personally* involved in the life he or she professes to others, the Christian specialist may not, in the name of scholarly detachment, claim to be functioning as a *Christian* specialist without also *personally* being captivated in the quest for truth. Thus, the Christian scholar may not separate *theologia*, that knowledge which attends faith in its concrete existence, from piety. It was because of this separation that *theologia* got lost from theological education and from theology.[47] Its recovery is truly about the recovery of the Christian mind in the course of specialist concern. The Christian mind is about the mind of Christ. Professionals at the middle level and technical experts at the apex of the inverted pyramid together share with all the people of God at the grassroots level the challenge to strive constantly to be connected vitally to the Vine, even Christ.

While training at the professional level should not *primarily* be geared to specialist interest, training in action-reflection should, at the same time, help to cultivate the Christian mind as well as the discipline basic to the life of inquiry and scholarship. Only very few of those trained at the middle level ever go on into specialist areas. Indeed many who pass through seminaries "may be scholarly, but they can never become scholars."[48] For this reason, it is not justifiable to have a curriculum at the middle level that assumes everyone is training for a technical and specialist career. What tends to be missing at the middle level of training is the dialectic of reflection-action, and therefore the tendency of most middle-level seminary training is to concentrate primarily on reflection.

This same problem exists on a much more heightened degree at the level of specialist interests. A heart for God and a commitment to

---

[47]For an illustration of an attempt to recover spirituality in theology by seeking to bring praxis into systematic theology and drawing spiritual implications of the loci, see Simon Chan, *Spiritual Theology: A Systematic Study of the Christian Life* (Downers Grove, IL: InterVarsity, 1998). Using historical exemplars, Mark McIntosh addresses the same issues in Mark A. McIntosh, *Mystical Theology: The Integrity of Spirituality and Theology* (Malden, MA: Blackwell, 1998). See also Kenneth Leech, *Experiencing God: Theology as Spirituality* (San Francisco: Harper & Row, 1985).
[48]Harper, "Shall the Theological Curriculum Be Modified," 56.

the renewing of the mind do not come to us naturally, whether as lay believers or as Christian professionals or as Christian scholars. The tendency to shift focus is with all mortals, hence the injunction to be regularly transformed by the renewal of the mind (Rom. 12:2). That is a reason for the Pauline injunction, "train yourself to be godly" (1 Tim. 4:7)! This injunction goes to all—believers at the grass roots, professionals, and specialists alike.

The entire training continuum tends to operate under a domino effect: The professional, at the middle level, must first experience the practical Christian life in order to facilitate the same at the grass roots. The specialists, from whose ranks seminary professors are most often formed, must first experience the practical Christian life in order to facilitate the same in their students. Indeed seminary professors reproduce after their kind.

So the success of any fundamental proposal about renewal in holistic formation lies in the hands of those who educate men and women in the pivotal middle level. These constitute the "train engineers" who could either cause "derailments" or guide the train to its desired destination. That is why I propose this tripartite approach for theological education. The key in this approach is to have those operating at specialist and professional levels respectively relate purposefully to those in the level below them.

This means that specialist training must not only cater to esoteric knowledge but must equally recognize what is needed for those specialists who will go on to teach the professional cadres. In the same way, professional training must not only cater to the thrills of results of knowledge through specialist interests but must also recognize what is needed for those believers at the grass roots.

Assuming, as is often the case, that specialist interests in theological education must be remote to the ordinary Christian life does a great harm to Christian scholarship. Specialist level training will undoubtedly concern esoteric knowledge, which many at the grassroots level may not be concerned about. This, however, is not to suggest that such knowledge has no bearing on the Christian life and existence in the world. Archaeological expertise is needed to uncover the past as it relates to the Christian faith. Language expertise is needed, both to recover and to understand the sacred texts given through the medium of ancient human languages and preserved in variant manuscript forms. Socio-cultural expertise of different kinds is needed to help understand past and present peoples and situations-in-life to enhance our understanding of ministry challenges. Any one of these areas of expertise could be *both* esoteric *and* relevant to life where the ordinary Christian lives, moves, and has his or her being.

SUGGESTIONS FOR A HOLISTIC APPROACH TO THE CURRICULUM OF TRAINING FOR MINISTRY

First, I would recommend the introduction into the curriculum of theological *propaedeutics*, or introduction to theological studies. This would, at the beginning of the course of studies, give the student the big picture of the components of training, the core of the training program, and the interrelationships of the components of training. Such an overview would reveal the *ratio studiorum* as well as the ideals espoused in the course of studies. It would set forth the philosophy of theological education, and it would describe how the practical Christian life is integrated into the entire course of studies.

Second, I would suggest that there must be an *ecclesial* component in ministerial training. What is the church—what is its nature, its purpose, and its tasks? This component would also seek to provide an understanding of the nature of ministry, aspects of various grace gifts in the body of Christ, how to ascertain the nature of such gifts in the individual lives of learners, the ministerial offices, and the functional relationships of those offices to one another and to the Triune God.

To be sure, ecclesiology is a component in most expressions of the purely formal mode of theological training, but often in this mode ecclesiology is treated in a strictly compartmentalized way that divides the "theoretical" from the "practical." This means that often the supposed "theory" of the church is consigned to the region of dogmatics, while the supposed "practice" is reserved for the practical theology division. I am advocating the integration of things that obviously belong together, broadening the *ecclesial* component to cover the ministries and its offices, and developing in learners biblical and theological understanding of ministry and the minister in relation to the Triune God and fellow humans. All of these can and should be packaged into one continuous learning experience within and out of the classroom, in cooperation among teachers and professors in the school and in the faith community. These would all work in concert to provide an *ecclesial* understanding, both propositionally and in life settings that allow for mentoring, learning by firsthand experience, and observing live models as well.

Third, there must be a *relational* component in ministry training. The practical Christian life has to do with present existence, character, and development of Christian virtues; it has to do vitally with how to relate to God and others and so forth. This is the area most difficult to present well in the strictly formal mode of training. This is the component that is more easily caught than taught. And, therefore, this is where a combination of the three modes of training should vitally come together.

The *relational* component of ministerial training would be primarily concerned with the individual's *inner life* and relationship to the Triune God. Emphasis would be placed on at least the following—the discipline of ingesting the Word of God, prayer, meditation, obedience, penitence, the habit of "walking with God," and enjoying him.

But the *relational* component of ministerial training must also involve the individual's *outer life* and his or her relationship to the community of faith and to the world. With respect to the community of faith, the vital areas of how to cultivate reciprocal fellowship, care, love, service, human relations, and so forth must be part of the core curriculum. With respect to the world at large, theological education must involve understanding the "mundane" issues of injustice in whatever form it takes in a local setting and globally. It will also involve demonstration of God's love to the dying world, service to the world God so loved, developing human relations skills, understanding issues of interfaith relationships, and so forth. All of these should be directed toward understanding and exercising God's love, compassion, and the prophetic role of the church in the world.

These *relational* aspects are sometimes approached purely cognitively and formally. When this happens, teaching and learning begin and end in the classroom and library. But it is far better to approach this relational component holistically both in and out of the classroom. For this to happen successfully, learning must deliberately be contrived in partnership between school and church, and at times with the society at large. In this holistic approach, the role of the teacher extends beyond the traditional school setting. Also, those who function as "teachers" or "facilitators" would include those traditionally so designated in the school context, as well as others within the church setting, and at times even in the larger society. This then would allow for mentoring and apprenticeship of observation, as trainees learn from models in and out of school settings in any of the disciplines of relationships mentioned above.

A pedagogy of theological education that brings the original practical Christian life to the fore in a *relational* component must ensure that trainees are equipped as facilitators of the practical Christian life and existence within the faith community. The prevalent pedagogy strives to produce those who *tell* others, whether in teaching, preaching, or in therapeutic sessions. That pedagogy is very weak in producing facilitators who can empower the people of God to attain their potentials— whether in terms of Christian life and walk or in terms of the work of service or of doing the ministry. It is little wonder that the prevalent pedagogy is geared toward making the people of God spectators as the minister *tells* them what they need to know. The recovery of the practical Christian life in ministry education will ensure that learners become facilitators as they first experience the life of Christ and as they facilitate the same in others within the context of pilgrimage in the world. Training in facilitation of the practical Christian life can truly happen as school, church, and at times society interface.

Of the three areas suggested, the last two, the ecclesial and the relational, together constitute the practical Christian life. They deal with an understanding of the nature and purpose of the *ecclesial* community and its *relationship* to God, self, and humanity. These equally correlate positively with what ultimately matters to the life of the church and its leadership in the course of the Christian life, existence, and ministry. How the two components will be arranged in terms of space within the curriculum is not here prescribed, as situations and conditions differ around the world. However, it is vital that the space so created and the configuration of the practical Christian life together with the traditional fourfold divisions must utilize a combination of the formal, non-formal, and informal modes in the process of theological education.

Kelsey identifies the faculty and the traditional ethos of a seminary as the two elements that most often lead resistance to change in theological seminaries.[49] Both of these are vitally interconnected. School curricula tend to be self-perpetuating, and when needed change is regularly and successfully resisted, curricula eventually "fossilize." Hence, an ideal curriculum by itself cannot overcome the "countervailing power" (Kelsey) of an unresponsive faculty who play a vital role in the making of the "traditional ethos" of a theological school. That "ethos" is the institutional culture that gets transmitted across generations. Kelsey sees in this culture a mixture of "power relationships, patterns of behavior, and shared attitudes and dispositions."

Kelsey argues that "The faculty's potentialities for change in the educational process are defined by its actuality and not by the ideal possibilities for change sketched by a new curriculum." The totality of that "actuality" involves a delicate balance between the *explicit* and *implicit*, as well as the *null* curricula of a theological school. This balance inevitably rests with the faculty who must be open to change through in-service training, interfacing with church and society, learning to serve as facilitators in the process of teaching and teaching the same to their students, and above all modeling the life of Christ before students.

THE IMPLEMENTERS OF THE CURRICULUM OF STUDIES

Naturally, when issues such as we have explored here are raised, any number of red flags automatically appear, and understandably so. Three such I will consider here as I conclude.

First, if any proposal for ministerial formation renewal is to succeed, consideration must be given to the kind of background training that would-be implementers of the course of studies bring into the school. Those who have been trained strictly along the usual specialist interests tend to lack know-how other than in what they are used to. Renewal that could integrate spirituality in the formation process must, therefore, come through a combination of efforts at self-improvement, as well as in-service (re)training through formal modes and non-formal

---

[49]David H. Kelsey, "A Theological Curriculum About and Against the Church," in Joseph C. Hough and Barbara G. Wheeler, eds., *Beyond Clericalism* (Atlanta: Scholars Press, 1988), 39.

seminars and workshops arranged for seminary teachers and professors. When those who have been employed as professionals in their own rights, as *masters* of their areas of discipline, are now asked to integrate habits of the practical Christian life into their specialist areas, they will feel threatened. This calls for patient understanding on the part of those who are advocating renewal.

A second concern, which is related to the first, is that such ministry formation renewal as has been proposed appears to introduce increasing demands on professional (now in the technical sense) interests. There are grounds for this concern, and it would be wrong to dismiss out-of-hand the various expressions of this concern. But the benefits of the kind of renewal being suggested are enormous, and the ultimate recipient of those benefits is the church of Jesus Christ on earth. The benefits are clearly worth the cost. However, those who advocate such renewal must take adequate account of this additional cost and must assist in covering that cost. Again, patient understanding as well as appropriate support must characterize renewal advocates.

Third, the proposal appears threatening in several respects. First, it demands that the teacher or the professor practice what he or she teaches or professes and not just practice teaching only! Understandably, *telling* others is much easier than *showing* others how to live the practical Christian life. Second, it creates encroachment in the already entrenched fourfold divisions, as space is demanded for the inclusion of the habits of practical Christian life. Third, and on a related note to the previous concern, it requires specialists in the dialectic of action-reflection.

Responding first to the last of these threats, I would suggest that there is already the *basis* for the discipline of the practical Christian life in the present repertoire of theological knowledge. It should, therefore, not be too difficult to get individuals who will champion its cause in present institutional settings. These champions of the practical Christian life will then need to generate experiential and disciplinary knowledge as appropriate. What has been suggested as subject matter areas in this presentation is meant to serve only as starting point.

With respect to the matter of encroachment, I recognize that this is inevitable if renewal is to take place. Without taking something out of the curriculum, it will probably be impossible to introduce the new elements that have been suggested. But the whole exercise of exclusion and inclusion should be guided and informed by the desired training outcomes and not by power plays or "horse-trading" of subject matter. This too will be difficult. But the future of ministerial effectiveness is at stake, and the aim of what is being suggested is to infuse the practical Christian life into theological education, thus recovering authentic *theologia* in the course of studies.

Finally, asking that the teacher or the professor practice what he or she teaches or professes is certainly challenging in a way that even completion of a Ph.D. dissertation is not. This challenge, however, comes ultimately not from any human being but from the One in whose service all ministry (including ministerial training) is to be done. Throughout Scripture, all Christians, and *especially* teachers (see James 3:1), are commanded to live what they profess. If we who teach future ministers really desire that our students become models of godliness, then that is what we must be before them. And that, without question, will provide the most effective training in ministerial spiritual formation of all!

CHAPTER TWELVE

SHARING THE OPPORTUNITY OF THEOLOGICAL EDUCATION

WILSON CHOW

It is good to be connected to the worldwide Reformed family not only for myself or for the theological school from which I come and which I represent, but also for that part of the world where I live and serve. I refer to the Chinese-speaking Christian community in Asia.

For a long time, the Chinese churches in Mainland China, Hong Kong, Taiwan, and other places have been very much influenced by that branch of Christianity associated with dispensationalism and fundamentalism. This can be traced back to the days of the early missionaries who came with evangelistic zeal, preaching the gospel and establishing churches. But they came also with the specific theological traditions in which they were reared or which they acquired during their theological training.

Bible schools in the United States have thus played a significant role in the work of missions around the world. Many missionaries who came to China in the first half of the twentieth century were graduates of Bible schools and colleges in the United States that taught dispensational doctrines with a very fundamentalist Christian worldview. This was well accepted by the early Chinese converts who were mostly rural people and very limited in their education. They were attracted by the simple truth and the easy-to-remember charts and diagrams as Christian doctrines were explained to them. These Chinese converts then popularized dispensational and fundamentalist theology, which gradually became the mainstream theological perspective of most Chinese Protestant churches.

As the Chinese churches grew in the *diaspora*, beginning in the mid-fifties of the last century, a marked change took place in the outlook and the constituency of Chinese churches. As a result of a strong movement of the gospel ministry among students, many from the intelligentsia came to faith in Christ. The new believers, along with those growing up in their churches, were challenged by the Christian faith presented to them through Bible studies, lectures on campuses, and their own reading and investigation of God's Word.

Their newfound faith spoke powerfully to the minds, hearts, and souls of these converts, and many of them went on to in-depth biblical and theological study. Some went abroad to study in seminaries in the Reformed tradition. Thus a new door was opened for Chinese Christians to enter into a "Christian world" or "theological arena" much larger than their own confines. As a result, many Chinese believers have come to appreciate the depth and the richness of Reformed theology.

In Asian or Chinese cultures, Christians incline to dismiss labels and regard such descriptions as sectarian or partisan practices. The norm is to be "biblical." Yet things may go wrong under the disguise of being "biblical." In an age of theological confusion and diversity, it is important that churches in the developing world, the fast-growing Chinese churches in Mainland China included, should stand on a firm theological foundation with a system of truth derived from the Word of God, so that the church will grow to the full stature of Christ and be a witness to the world. I hope and pray that the World Reformed Fellowship will increasingly provide the opportunity for Chinese (and other) believers to build a network of fellowship, encouragement, and mutual help in the twenty-first century.

THE OPPORTUNITY OF THEOLOGICAL EDUCATION—THE VISION

In the context of the developments described above, I will address this question: Why and how should the evangelical Reformed church worldwide seize the opportunity to deliver appropriate education to growing and needy churches?

Obviously, theological education provides one of the things the church needs—ministers of the gospel. Qualified ministers are not naturally born or dropped from heaven as gifts. They become who and what they are after years of training. Theological education is the training, equipping, and preparing of God's people for the ministry. It is, as often spoken of nowadays, leadership development.

The church needs leaders. Or to put it humbly, I believe the church needs servant-leaders. These leaders are called, chosen, trained, tested, and proven to be such. Theological education plays the role of training and equipping these leaders. If it is true that the growth of a church depends on its leadership (such as its pastors, elders, and Christian workers), and if it is also true that the quality of that leadership in turn depends, at least partly, on adequate and appropriate training, then theological education holds the key to the well-being of the church. It rightly becomes a concern and an opportunity.

The church has a variety of ministries—Sunday school, children and youth ministry, music, ministry of mercy, evangelism, missions, and the list goes on. Theological education is often looked upon as one of those ministries. Indeed it is. But it is more than that. It is that ministry without which you normally do not have the trained personnel for the other ministries. Work needs to be done by people, and people need to be trained.

Many churches and their leaders have impressive and exciting plans—for expanding their ministries, adding new departments and programs, sending out more missionaries, and building more churches—while giving precious little thought to the necessary supply of trained workers to do all of that work. Many leaders do not even seem to care much about theological education.

It is both sad and destructive that few church leaders (lay Christians) seem to realize the vital importance of theological education. They fail to catch this vision and seize this kingdom opportunity. Massive resources are often put into projects, be they building projects, mission projects, or other appeals, and proportionally tiny amounts are committed to training the people without whom any kingdom project, no matter how grand, will come to naught.

It is, therefore, absolutely necessary, if the church is to be what it can and must be, for all Christians to recognize and publicly affirm this vision of the great and urgent need for leadership development.

Today, for example, there is great enthusiasm for mission to China. This land of 1.3 billion souls is a field ripe for harvest in the eyes of many western churches and mission groups. Since missionaries are not allowed to enter the country for religious activities, people go in for business, education, medical, and other professional services with the purpose of sharing the gospel and doing evangelism. In particular, teaching English is a favorite means to fulfill the missionary mandate.

While we who live in China admire these foreign efforts to evangelize our country, we must ask what is the greatest need in China today. The church in China is getting strong and growing, and the Chinese Christians are vibrant in their faith. They can do a better job in witnessing to their neighbors and sharing the Christian faith with their fellow countrymen than any outsiders. What we can contribute from outside is to help build the church in China by listening to them—to find out how they are doing and what are their needs.

It does not take long to realize that theological training is on the top of the list of urgent needs for the Christian church in China. The National China Christian Council reports that today there are twenty-two theological schools in the whole country (as compared to over five hundred in the United States). It is hard to believe that there are so few seminaries in China compared to the large number of its Christian population, estimated from a conservative figure of twenty million to as high as eighty million. There is a crying need for theological training in China. We must catch this vision when we think of world missions.

THE OPPORTUNITY OF THEOLOGICAL EDUCATION: THE MISSION

Here we come to the implementation of the vision. What is the task of theological education before us? What are we to do? I propose that we proceed along two lines.

THEOLOGICAL EDUCATION AS INSTITUTION

We must first consider theological education as an institution, a theological school, a seminary. There are different training models or patterns, with a wide range, from discipleship training centers of a handful of students to well-organized, large-scale schools that graduate hundreds of students each year. I will confine my remarks here to the more traditional formal model. By this I refer to that of a theological school, which has an organizational structure, a board, a president, leadership and an administration team, and a qualified faculty. It has a campus and a library. It operates with an annual budget. It has a standard procedure of admitting students. It offers different programs and grants degrees that are accredited, or in the process of being accredited, by a regional, national, or international accrediting agency.

Theological education understood in this sense as an institution usually features a strong theological foundation, clear objectives, and a measure of stability. Its theological stance is usually derived from its denominational affiliation or from some other constituency, its objectives and goals are set by the individual school, and its stability is determined by available resources such as personnel and finances. These are all responsibilities that the school must carry by itself. They are not imposed by others and cannot be fully shouldered by outsiders. But there may be—and there probably should be—consultation with similar organizations on all of these matters.

First of all, theological commitments cannot be changed without betraying the institution's essential identity, and the denomination or other constituency must fully support any such change. But suppose a question arises as to whether permitting a specific form of doctrine or behavior would, in fact, change that essential identity. While the institution's denomination or other constituency makes the final determination about such a question, interaction with other institutions can be crucial in discussions that will precede any such determination. This provides a wonderful opportunity for sharing perspectives among different institutions.

Likewise, each individual institution must carefully develop and regularly update specific pedagogical goals and objectives. While it bears the responsibility for doing this hard work, the institution surely should seek advice and support from similar institutions that have gone through this kind of planning process. What one institution has learned from its attempts to use technology to deliver parts of its educational package can be of enormous benefit to other schools. Again, this is an opportunity for cooperation and mutual support, which should not be missed.

The same basic principle applies to an institution's responsibility to develop adequate personnel and financial resources. To be sure, no "list" is protected more diligently than an institution's donor list. And no institution enjoys having its personnel poached by another school. But these critical areas of an institution's life may represent the best opportunity of all for evangelical Reformed schools to demonstrate that they really do believe that they and others are all *equally* part of the kingdom work of theological education. When items such as money and people are at the heart of so much perceived competition, finding ways to demonstrate kingdom unity in these matters will bear a powerful testimony both within and outside our institutions. And we who are leaders in Reformed theological education should not rest until we find these ways.

One of the keys to effective institutional theological education is contextualization. It carries with it the opportunity and responsibility for relevance and for meeting the actual needs of the church when it comes to training people for the ministry or any form of Christian service. If we take "Think Global, Act Local" as a maxim for theological education, then I would regard contextualization as the practice of "acting local." I shall discuss "think global" in my next section. A theological school is a localized means of developing leaders. It is for a particular context, in terms of geography, culture, and time. It is for the here and now. It is not for everywhere and everyone. It is not timeless. Each school in each place must work out what is best for itself, not blindly copying or imitating others. What works for those others probably will not work for us, and the reverse is true as well.

Let me illustrate. Before Hong Kong was reunited to China in 1997, there was much concern for its future. There were those who feared that as it returned to its motherland, Hong Kong would never again enjoy freedom as it did in the colonial days. Waves and waves of migration took place to Canada, the United States, Australia, and the UK. Many of those who left were Christians, pastors and leaders included. They thought the door for Christian ministry would be closed to them after the Communist takeover, and they would want to continue serving somewhere else. It was suggested to us at the China Graduate School of Theology (CGST) that we should consider relocating the school to serve the Chinese overseas, maybe in Canada, the U.S., or Australia. We were told there were great needs for theological training in those places where the Chinese population had significantly increased and Chinese churches were flourishing.

While we appreciated these kind thoughts and good intentions, and while we recognized there was an urgent need to establish training centers for Chinese Christian communities in the *diaspora*, my colleagues and I representing the school leadership were convicted that CGST would not be the same CGST if it were no longer in Hong Kong and were transplanted somewhere else. We serve in a particular context, and we face real issues and challenges arising from that situation. Our training, style, and content must reflect our commitment to serving our churches and community and to meeting the needs around us. We encouraged and supported theological schools to be launched in other places for Chinese churches, to be administered and operated by local leadership, but as for ourselves, we chose to remain in Hong Kong to continue the task that the Lord has entrusted to us.

Such an outlook is not to be taken as a provincial mentality. It does not exclude or antagonize. Rather it puts a focus on theological training that is not distracted or sidetracked. The emphasis is on seizing unique opportunities in the particular context where the Lord has placed us. This corresponds to what Paul teaches: "Each one should test his own actions. Then he can take pride in himself, without comparing himself to somebody else, for each one should carry his own load" (Gal. 6:4–5, NIV).

Yet this is only half of Paul's teaching, for he also says, "Carry each other's burdens, and in this way you will fulfill the law of Christ" (Gal. 6:2, NIV). Institutional theological education must also have a global perspective, taking interest in theological education as a whole beyond one's own institution. Our carrying the burden together has its limits or boundaries when it comes to individual schools, but we need to carry each other's burdens when we come to a wider context, when we begin to "think global," when we consider the needs and opportunities represented in our worldwide Reformed fellowship.

THEOLOGICAL EDUCATION AS MOVEMENT

But we also need to remember that theological education is not just a grouping of individual institutions. Theological education is also a movement. Our individual theological institutions are concrete expressions of this movement, and all of us who are involved in theological education participate in this movement in different places.

As a movement, theological education is a global phenomenon, not confined to one particular location. It is larger than any school or even the sum of all institutions. It is an ongoing process inviting like-minded people to join in to labor in order to nurture a new generation of ministers, passing on the baton, entrusting the gospel to reliable men who will also be qualified to teach others (2 Tim. 2:2), to maintain the core values, to keep the quality and standard of excellence, and to fulfill the mission. A movement is a driving force. It provides the dynamics to make a lasting impact. A movement does not die.

A movement does not exist by itself apart from its visible forms. It becomes visible in theological schools. But schools come into being, develop, grow, and as time goes on may become stagnant, degenerate, and eventually die off. Only a sense of the movement keeps a school running, getting revitalized, and bringing renewal. When the schools are left by themselves, they may be operating like machines, but they are not productive. Theological schools must not detach themselves from the movement. It is because theological education is a movement that we can enter into meaningful and fruitful discussion as to how we can best seize the opportunities together.

To be part of this movement means we have to "think global." We must look for ways to assist others in their attempts to seize the unique opportunities placed before them. In the words of the apostle Paul, "Each of you should look not only to your own interests, but also to the interests of others" (Phil. 2:4). It is out of our concern for theological education as a movement that we care for other schools and want to relate to them in whatever ways possible.

I mentioned briefly above the situation of theological education in China. The religious policy in China is such that theological schools are under the supervision of provincial Christian councils or the national council and are not free to work with outside organizations. Even for us in Hong Kong, being part of China, there is not much we can do directly with the institutions on the mainland, because, as a special administrative region of China, we in Hong Kong have to observe the "three mutual principles" of non-subordination, non-interference, and mutual respect.

But as a seminary in Hong Kong, we want to relate to our counterparts on the mainland because we belong to the same movement. We take the initiative to get to know the schools, to pay visits, and to express our goodwill. Then we look for opportunities to share with them our resources and experience. The door is now gradually opening. Our faculty have been invited to give lectures and teach short-term courses in China, and we are beginning to have students coming to our school from the mainland. We are learning to seize opportunities together, at least on our part, although these are still limited to a certain extent.

We need both institutional theological education and the movement of theological education. They go hand in hand. We work in schools, but we do not lose sight of the movement. Our individual school is a small piece of the jigsaw puzzle. We need to see the whole picture.

HOW TO SEIZE THE OPPORTUNITIES OF THEOLOGICAL EDUCATION

To me, what specifically we can and should do is actually a less important question. The specific things we do are like the paths we walk on. We make the paths. We can always come up with new roads. Yet we must know where we are going and have a sense of direction before we travel. We shall come to what I regard as more pertinent issues in the next section. Right now let me give some suggestions. I speak from the perspective of an Asian context with growing and needy churches. We have a relatively short history and hence limited experience in theological education.

Our starting point is not thinking about what we can get from other schools, what they can give us, or how we can help other schools, but what we can give them. It is not about needs in the first place. Rather we must see where we stand as a school as we take part in this global movement of theological education and ask ourselves what can we offer to the movement. It all comes down to the sharing of resources.

BUILD UP A NETWORK

To be responsible partners in the global work of theological education, we must first check our manpower. It is critical that we build up an international network of theological schools that are willing to come together to promote theological education, give mutual support, and work together. We are in the same "business" of theological education, and there are areas of common concern that we share—issues and challenges that we face. We need to talk about them, do our own homework, and compare our notes. We are not looking for an association or any formal organization. We need to be bonded or connected to institutions of similar theological persuasion, that embrace the same core values. Membership in the World Reformed Fellowship certainly provides such a network. Yet as the focus is on theological education, it may be well to form certain fellowships within the Fellowship. At any rate, the form is not important. It matters more for us to get to know other schools and be known to others. Only then can we build up channels of communication.

Faculty Exchange and Development

The pride of a theological school is its faculty. It will be a challenge to the participating schools to work out a scheme whereby schools can exchange faculty members for teaching at other institutions. There are certainly problems to solve and hindrances to overcome, but the difficulties are not insurmountable. The idea is not that the "haves" help out the "have nots," or that the strong meet the needs of the weak. Of course, there are schools that do not have enough faculty and thus need assistance. Yet faculty exchange is meant to be two-way traffic. It involves both give and take. It is for the mutual enrichment of the participating schools and for faculty who teach as well as for students who are taught.

Faculty are accustomed to the convenience of their offices, familiar environments, and adequate facilities. However, to spend some time at another school, another place, or even another country would provide opportunities for new discoveries and new experiences. This can only enrich faculty members for better service when they return to their home institutions. And this enrichment needs to be seen as the enrichment of the entire project of theological education worldwide. Because we are all part of Christ's one body, what enriches any part enriches the whole.

Imagine spending a month in Africa or two weeks in China. What seemed unlikely decades ago has become commonplace. Schools can always schedule modular courses for a two-week duration that would otherwise last the whole semester. Better still, a faculty member can stay in another school for a semester or quarter during his or her sabbatical.

Of course, language may be a problem. But for a graduate school in many parts of the world, including developing countries, the English proficiency of graduate students is such that they can understand teaching in English reasonably well without any major problem. If the situation requires it, an interpreter in the class can always be provided, although that is not the most ideal arrangement.

Many theological schools in the developing world have good scholars with their own areas of expertise. They have not attained to the fame and prestige of professors in many western seminaries. Yet they have significant contributions to make. If schools in the West bring these scholars onto their campuses as short-term visiting faculty, these instructors will surely bring new insights to all of the classrooms in which they teach.

There are practical problems that we need to consider, matters such as personal inclination, adjustability to new surroundings, family needs, and so on. Faculty exchange is not for every professor. It may not even be for every school, or at least it may not be for every school all of the time. But those who participate will definitely be enriched. However, faculty exchange will not just "happen." All of us must be intentional about it if it is to occur. But we can know this—the more we are involved in faculty exchanges, both as senders and as receivers, the better global theological education will be, and the better trained our graduates will be as they move to minister in our global culture.

Developing National Faculties

Another area in which we must be intentional involves the development of national faculty. This applies especially to schools in the developing countries. Theological education in these parts of the world has been upgraded from Bible schools to seminaries, from diploma to Bachelor's degrees and to graduate programs. Accordingly, there is the need for upgrading the faculties of these schools. Some such schools have plans to send their promising young faculty to study overseas for advanced degrees, despite great pressures of shortage of manpower and lack of funds. The choice of institutions is sometimes a matter of expediency, depending on acceptance and the offer of scholarships; sometimes the choice is made at random. It would be a great service to these schools if Reformed seminaries in the West were willing to partner with them in the development of their faculties.

But this should be done on a school-to-school basis. Application to pursue advanced degrees must come with the certification that the applicant is already a faculty member of the school or will be appointed to such a position. There should further be the recommendation from the school and the confirmation that the person will return to continue his service at the school upon completion of his study. This is to prevent the possibility of brain drain. The Langham Trust in the UK, now the Langham Partnership International, has enabled a good number of young scholars in the developing countries to finish their doctoral studies. Many of them today are professors in the leading seminaries in their own countries.

As with faculty exchange, this process must be intentional, and institutions in the West must be willing to work together. No single institution can meet the needs of developing churches in the entire world. But if a network of western evangelical Reformed seminaries were created, and together these institutions made sure that educational opportunities were available to churches in every part of the world, the global church would be strengthened, and the kingdom of Christ advanced. One possible implementation facilitator for this "dream" is the Theological Education Commission of the World Reformed Fellowship in consultation with the Langham Partnership International. There are other possibilities as well. The real question is whether western evangelical Reformed seminaries will *together* seize this global opportunity.

Student Exchange

Many educational institutions have student exchange programs. Let us start thinking about this possibility, first on an individual basis among our schools. Some years ago, the China Graduate School of Theology was offered a scholarship for one of our students to spend a semester at Wycliffe Hall at Oxford University. That created quite an excitement among the student body. We invited the students to apply. The student of our choice had to meet with the approval of Wycliffe. It turned out not only that the student who studied for a semester at Oxford herself benefited from the program, but also that her subsequent sharing of her experience enriched our whole community.

The key to the success of this experiment is, on the one hand, the generosity of the hosting school to offer adequate financial resources to the candidate and, on the other hand, the right choice of the student. If the number of students can be increased to a few more, that will be even more encouraging. But then the financial burden will be heavy. We must realize that a few students from another school, or from another country, in the midst of several hundred students of the local school amount to no big impact or influence. Yet they can be like sparks of fire that will glow and kindle. The important element is the "presence" of what represents another school in the life of the local school.

Our student's opportunity to spend a semester in Oxford was a wonderful means of enriching the entire enterprise of evangelical Reformed theological education. The same kind of enrichment will occur when students from schools in the West study at non-western institutions. Think of an American or European or Australian or Latin American student taking a semester to study in Asia. It will be like a short-term mission, but with the main purpose of theological study. The learning will not be confined to the classroom. It is a cross-cultural exchange. There will be a lot of adjustments, but the overall benefit is obvious.

Here again, forming a working network of schools that are willing both to send and to receive students will be crucial in making certain that the "wealth" is spread appropriately "for building up the body of Christ" (Eph. 4:12, ESV). And again the same question appears: Are evangelical Reformed schools, both in the developing world and in the developed world, willing to consider the big picture of global theological education and to act in a way that demonstrates that consideration? Are they genuinely willing to be a full and active part of a network of like-minded institutions?

SHARE OTHER RESOURCES

Theological Books

The West is greatly blessed in the availability of Christian literature, including Bible commentaries, reference works, textbooks on various courses, and many others. In comparison, theological schools in developing countries whose mother language is other than English suffer a great lack in published resources. In the Chinese-speaking context, for example, a good number of books have been translated into Chinese and are used as textbooks and reference works in seminaries. But there is a continuing urgent need to make available good Reformed theological writings.

The fact that publication has become a business sometimes complicates the issue. Bookstores, including Christian bookstores, are flooded with popular books and books that can sell well and fast. It is often difficult to find good evangelical, Reformed theological books. Until we have enough national faculty and scholars to write for our schools and students, we will continue to depend on books produced in the West. In the meantime, students who can read English can have free access to the kind of materials they want or need. For the benefit of non-English readers, it is crucial, therefore, for some network of evangelical Reformed theological educators to devise a plan to translate and publish more of the right kind of theological books from our tradition. Funding is, as always, a concern. But if resources could be found for such a publication program, a huge present gap in the global theological education movement could be filled. In the long run, of course, we must encourage national or local faculty to supply the books needed. But until that happens, we all must work together to supply the present need.

Conferences, Consultations, and Seminars

The movement of theological education can be enhanced, and theological schools can be strengthened, by gathering together faculty members to participate in theological conferences, consultations, and seminars. These could be held in conjunction with such regular events as the General Assemblies of the World Reformed Fellowship, or they could be held separately as annual or biennial events. However they are scheduled, the purpose will be to share information and to wrestle together with matters of theological educational method and with theological issues of current concern.

When such gatherings are regional rather than global, they should be hosted by the institutions within the network and meet where those institutions are located. In some cases, several schools in a region or country might join together to host the event. The themes of these regional conferences would be determined by the specific theological context of the location where the particular conference is being held. It may not be a common or general theme with which schools all over the world are familiar. And yet network institutions from around the world would be made aware of the regional conferences and would be invited to participate. The idea is that we would all come to that place and participate in discussing the issues that are especially urgent for our brothers and sisters in that area. We all have much to learn and much to teach.

In China today some of the key universities have departments of religious studies. This reflects the present generation's interest in academic pursuits. Some religious studies departments even offer Master's programs in Christian Studies. In one university in Hunan, there is a center for biblical studies. Some years ago they sponsored a conference on biblical studies and invited international biblical scholars as participants. All these activities are happening outside the church and the seminaries and are a challenge to the Christian church. That is because all these activities are conducted by non-Christian academia, and they present the Christian faith and Christian theology from their non-Christian perspective as a purely academic exercise. We do not want to see them as spokesmen for Christianity. However, they have access to resources in the West from Christian groups. This trend in China deserves our attention. We could hold a consultation or conference to probe the topic "The Challenge of Religious Studies to Theological Education."

SOME FINAL THOUGHTS ABOUT THE OPPORTUNITIES IN THEOLOGICAL EDUCATION

We can always come up with new ideas and new ways of doing what we want. But what do we want? What would we like to see accomplished? This is not only a matter of what opportunities of theological education we seize together, but also how we seize those opportunities. I suggest that our partnership in this endeavor should be characterized by four elements.

1. Our partnership must be *international in scope*. We work together across national and territorial borders. The church of Jesus Christ is universal, and we are a worldwide family. We may hear of what people call First World, Third World, Two-thirds World, majority world, but to us there is no division of east and west, north or south. God's world is one. We may let slip from our lips terms like the above, but they are merely of conventional usage. Being truly international means that all nations are equally well represented and respected in the work of theological education. The international character of working together means unity in diversity, acknowledging our differences, and paying attention to the needs and concerns in various places.

2. Our partnership must be *interdenominational in dimension*. Today the church in China claims that it has entered the post-denominational era. This is true because China has gone through a history of changes, of uprooting and tearing down, of building and planting. Even so, denominational tradition and heritage can still be observed today in China and are respected.

In many parts of the world, denominational divisions among Christians are still a reality. These divisions may be the result of historical development. But we need to realize that while the Reformed faith is particularly associated with certain denominations in the West, the situation is different in Asia. Among those who came under the influence of Reformed theology during their study in the West and have come to espouse the Reformed faith, not a few find themselves serving in non-Reformed denominations, churches, seminaries, and organizations. For these people, it is not church affiliation that identifies their theological loyalty. They may be a lone voice in their circles, and that is why a Reformed fellowship will be a means of support and encouragement to them and their ministry. Our working together in theological education must not forget those who do not serve in traditional Reformed circles. We must include them and be open to people in all denominations. It is to be interdenominational.

3. Our partnership must be *intercultural in perspective*. This fol-

lows naturally from the above two points. There has been fruitful study on the relationship between gospel and culture since Lausanne in 1974. Indigenization and then contextualization have been topics of much discussion in theological construction and theological education. In order to be relevant and meet the needs of local churches, theological training must be contextual. That applies to both form and content— that is, academic programs, curricula, courses, practicum, spiritual formation, etc. However, the practice of contextualization cannot be at the expense of biblical faith. There must be a clear distinction between the normative, the relative, and the relevant.

In our fellowship and in our working together, it is important that we keep an intercultural perspective. We must acknowledge that there may be a different way of looking at things and of doing things. It is not that one is better than or superior to the other. They are just different. We may not agree and accept the other ways, but they deserve our hearing and respect. One needs to be sensitive to cultural forms and expressions. This understanding is vital to working together. It is an enrichment of what we already possess.

4. Our partnership must be *interdependent in spirit*. Interdependence is the true spirit of fellowship and partnership. But for this to happen, theological schools in the developing countries must come out of their longtime dependence on western missions in the past. That is why the church in China over the past five decades has emphasized the three-self principles to attain to selfhood. These are the principles of self-governing, self-supporting, and self-propagating. The sign of a growing church is its self-reliance, maturity into adulthood. This is healthy growth. Today we see the implementation of the three-self principles and the fruits they bear in China.

We must mature from dependence to independence and then go beyond independence to interdependence. That is true maturity. There is no isolation from, no hostility toward, and no competition with others. In order to work together, it is good that we have a sense of need for the others but also feel needed by others. We are here to help one another. We are growing and fulfilling our mission together. We are all victors for Jesus Christ.

CHAPTER THIRTEEN

SHARING THE OPPORTUNITY OF RADIO MINISTRY

JIMMY LIN

First of all, I would like to make it clear that I am not an academic and that this presentation is more a narrative of my personal journey of learning while I was on the job over the past fifteen years.

My story begins on a bright sunny afternoon in June 1989. I remember sitting with thousands of others on the lawn in Victoria Park in Hong Kong. On a big-screen TV, we were watching what had happened the night before in Beijing when hundreds of young people were injured and killed by soldiers in what is now known as the June 4 Tiananmen Massacre. I saw anger and sadness on the faces of the young people, but above all I saw hopelessness. I could not sleep that night as the question came back to me again and again: only Jesus can give them real hope, but how can we tell all of them about the good news—there are so many of them—and the country is so big?

Radio!

That was the answer that came to mind in 1989, and it was the beginning of my journey that led to my becoming the Chinese Broadcast Minister and the Interim Administrative Director of *The Back to God Hour.*

RADIO IS IMPORTANT IN TODAY'S WORLD

In 1896, radio became a possibility through Marconi's discovery of wireless communication. Since then, we have witnessed the exponential growth in electronic communication in the past 110 years from radio to television to cell phones to Internet and beyond. But according to the data provided by the World Development Report as shown in Table 1, radio is still the most accessible among what is called "information connectivity." This is especially true among the middle- and low-income segments, the ones with whom our Lord is deeply and profoundly concerned (Luke 4:18–19).

Table 1:
Information and Communication Infrastructure Connectivity

Economy	Daily News-papers 1998	Radios 1997	Television Sets 1998	Telephone Mainlines 1998	Mobile Phones 1998	Personal Computers 1998	Internet hosts per 10,000 people January 2000
Low income		157	76	23	2	3.2	0.37
Lower middle income		322	250	90	18	13.6	2.83
Upper middle income	89	493	285	176	76	53.1	35.88
High income	286	1286	661	567	265	311.2	777.22
Low and middle income		263	172	69	17	15.6	5.4
East Asia & Pacific		302	228	70	25	14.1	2.69
Europe & Central Asia	102	442	353	200	23	34.6	18.87
Latin America & Caribbean	71	420	255	123	45	33.9	22.33
Middle East & North Africa	33	274	135	81	8	9.9	0.55
South Asia		112	61	19	1	2.9	0.22
Sub-Saharan Africa	12	198	52	14	5	7.5	2.73

Source: World Development Report 2000-2001, Table 19

The second point to note is the continuing extraordinary dramatic growth of the number of radio receivers through the years. According to the research done by Gray, even in a world seemingly dominated by the Internet and the iPod, the increase in the number of radio receivers has been more than tenfold since 1950, and there is no sign of a slowing down.[1] It is estimated that in 2002 there were 47,776 active radio stations in the world, providing seventy million hours of original programming.[2]

In the graph below, we see the considerable differences in the geographical distribution of radio receivers in the world.[3] This has important implications for Christian radio programs, and we will come to that later.

Table 2

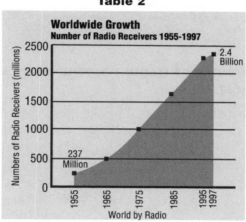

It is obvious from the graph above that the growth of ownership of radio is most dramatic in Asia. The next chart highlights the penetration of radio in the five most populous countries in Asia. Incidentally, among these five are China, India, and Indonesia.[4] These are three of the top four countries in the world in terms of 2005 population, totaling an amazing number of 2.6 billion people, almost 40 percent of the world population! Obviously, radio remains an extremely important mode of communication in the twenty-first century.

---

[1]Frank Gray, "The Unlikely Missionary," *Mission Frontiers,* U.S. Center for World Mission, December 2000.
[2]See the following website: http://www.sims.berkeley.edu/research/projects/how-much-info-2003/broadcast.
[3]Ibid.
[4]Ibid.

Table 3:
Access—Growth in the Number of Radio Receivers

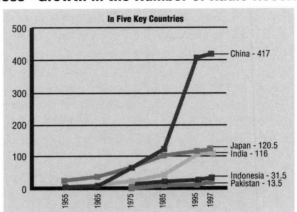

THE UNIQUENESS OF RADIO FOR THE WORK OF THE KINGDOM

Although Marconi's technological breakthrough came in 1896, it was not until ten years later on December 24, 1906 that we had the first successful voice transmission. On Christmas Eve of 1906, the first radio signal transmission was sent from the coast of Massachusetts to ships at sea. Incidentally the content was a religious service featuring readings from Luke and a violin solo of "O Holy Night." What a great start!

First, therefore, radio is uniquely suitable for the Christian message. I remember one time waiting for a bus in downtown Chicago with a blind friend. He suddenly said to me, "Why are there so many crickets here?" It was just unbelievable to me that he could hear the sound of crickets at such a busy street corner. The reason was, he was not distracted by what he saw (or could not see). Yes, we do need multimedia to satisfy the needs of all our senses, but when there is nothing to watch or smell or touch, one will concentrate a bit more on listening. The apostle Paul said that faith comes from hearing the message of the gospel (Rom. 10:17), and radio communicates and demands a concentration on the content of the message more than most other media.

Second, Christian radio programs are especially important to evangelism and church growth among the illiterate and in cultures with numerous language groups.

To mention just a couple of related examples, UNESCO says there were over eight hundred million illiterate people in the world in 2000, and Africa as a continent has a literacy rate of less than 60 percent. But even for those who can read, there is also the problem of too many language groups in Africa. Africa is home to almost 1,900 ethno-linguistic groups, one third of the world total. However only ninety-five of these groups have the entire Bible translated, and 179 groups have only the New Testament translated. This leaves more than 1,600 groups having no Bible of their own, not to mention other Christian literature. But the majority of these individuals can understand either French or English, and so radio is a critically important means of getting the Word of God to them in spoken form.

Third, Christian radio plays an important role even in the more technologically advanced parts of the world. One usually assumes that most people experience the Christian faith by attending a church service. However, according to a very recent nationwide survey done by the Barna Research Group in America, 67 percent of adults used at least one form of religious media in a month, while 63 percent attended a church service.[5]

Who Uses the Christian Media in a Typical Month

	All Adults
Listen to preaching, teaching, talk-oriented Christian radio	38 percent
Listen to Christian-music radio	43 percent
Listen to Christian radio, any format	52 percent
Watch Christian television	43 percent
Read Christian books, other than the Bible	33 percent
Use any of these three Christian media	67 percent
Attend a Christian church service	63 percent

Fourth, radio waves transcend geographic and political boundaries or restrictions. Shortwave signals theoretically can travel around

---

[5]*The Barna Update*, July 2002, The Barna Group, Ltd., California.

the world by reflections between the ground and the atmosphere. The third chart above demonstrated that Asia, North America, and Western Europe are far ahead of other regions in terms of numbers of radio receivers. However, according to research done in May 2000, the Middle East, Africa, Eastern Europe, and to a certain extent Latin America have very high percentages of ownership of shortwave radios as shown in the tables below.[6] Shortwave is common in these regions because some of these countries use shortwave as their main source of national transmission.

Europe	percent of radio households with shortwave
Albania	54
Bulgaria	81
Greece	77
Macedonia	50
Poland	94
Romania	68
Serbia & Montenegro	71
Slovakia	77
Turkey	53

Africa	percent of radio households with shortwave
Angola (Urban)	88
Burkina Faso (Urban)	92
Cameroon (Urban)	93
Ethiopia	82
Ivory Coast (Urban)	93
Ghana	94
Kenya	86
Mozambique	88

[6]See the following website: http://www.shortwave.org/Audience/Audience.htm.

Nigeria	93
Senegal (Dakar)	80
Senegal (National) (92)	89
Sudan	83
Tanzania	90
Uganda	88
Zambia	90
Zimbabwe	98
Middle East	
Egypt	61
Jordan	83

This high rate of ownership of shortwave radios enables international Christian networks to broadcast the message of Christ to places where Christian missionaries are not welcome. These include Muslim and Communist countries. Robert Fortner, an authority on international broadcasting, estimates that the three major international Christian networks (FEBC/BA, TWR, and HCJB) produce approximately 20,000 hours of programming each week in over 125 languages.[7]

According to a study done by Radio Monte Carlo in 2005, in the Arab-speaking world, 39 percent of the population is still illiterate, only 9 percent have access to television, and only 2 percent have access to the Internet. In contrast, 97 percent of the population own a shortwave radio. Obviously, radio is the way to go if we really want to reach out to the Muslim world.

Americas	percent of radio households with shortwave
Barbados	39
Brazil (Urban)	32
Brazil (Rural SP)	35

---

[7]Robert S. Fortner, "Cross-Cultural Aspects of Evangelical Broadcasting: Prospects and Difficulties," in *Evangelicals, the Mass Media, and American Culture*, Billy Graham Center, Wheaton College, 1988.

Guyana	41
Jamaica	9
Mexico	5
Peru	61
Trinidad	35

In Communist countries, governments often use jamming to interfere with unwelcome broadcasters like Voice of America or BBC. But in a sort of "gentleman's agreement," they usually leave religious radio programs alone. Representatives of *The Back to God Hour* have been told this by Chinese officials many times, especially with regard to our office in Hong Kong. As long as we broadcast strictly what they call religious material (the gospel), they won't jam our broadcasts, but if we stray into any areas that sound to them like politics, they will jam our broadcasts.

THE BACK TO GOD HOUR
CHINESE MINISTRY MODEL

The model that is presented below has evolved out of our past fifteen years of ministry. With the advance of technology, it is becoming harder and harder to define what radio is. Now, in addition to traditional transmission technologies, the Internet and cell phones can both deliver radio programs. Regardless of how radio transmissions are delivered, they remain the cornerstone of our ministry.

In our audio production, we use a three-pronged approach to programming: pre-evangelistic, evangelistic, and nurturing. To appeal to the desire of people in Communist China to learn English and to learn about the outside world, we are producing the bilingual *English World* and also the *Eye on the World* programs. *Sermon* is the backbone of our evangelistic programs. Our nurturing program is *Q & A*, which is based completely on the questions we receive from our audience. Most recently we have added the age dimension to our programming, producing programs especially for children.

Our finished programs are aired to China, Southeast Asia, Australia and New Zealand, Canada, the United States, and countries in Central America (Belize and Panama). We use FM, AM, and shortwave stations. We use commercial, Christian, and ethnic stations. Some stations are very local, while others are superpower transmitters more than a thousand miles away.

The Back To God Hour
Chinese Broadcast Ministry Model

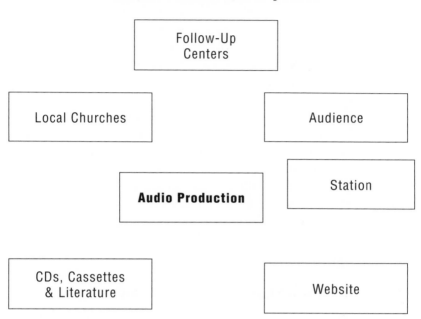

Follow-up is extremely important to radio ministry. Our staff at the follow-up center in Hong Kong handles the responses from our audience in China, Southeast Asia, and Australia/New Zealand. For responses from North and Central America, we do the follow-up from our main office in Chicago. In 2005 we received an average of five hundred responses per month, which include letters, phone calls, faxes, and e-mails.

The responses can generally be classified into several categories: requests for church referrals, questions about the Christian faith and life, requests for Christian materials, and feedback on the programs. We work with local churches for referrals whenever it is possible. As a result of these referrals, some of the churches come to know us better and start supporting our ministry. Some of these churches even buy airtime on the local stations for us, and some go even a step further and take over the follow-up work for us.

We make sure that every question is answered in a timely manner. As mentioned earlier, these questions form the basis of our very popular *Q & A* program. Once we have our audio programs recorded, the scripts can then be produced as literature. These are usually printed as small booklets to ensure delivery and to save postage. We also package our audio programs into series of cassettes and CDs; these are also sent to listeners to help them grow in the faith. We take all feedback from our listeners and from churches seriously, for this is one of the important ways that we can learn to improve.

Finally, the Internet has added an unprecedented dimension to audio outreach. It has given the ministry an extra channel of delivery and has enabled us to reach areas where no radio stations are available. We launched our web site in 2000, and in that year we had a total of about 20,000 user pages. But in 2005 our monthly average was over 25,000 user pages (the figure would be much, much higher if we had used hits), which translates into a 1,500 percent increase in five years. It is also important to note that during the same period the responses to radio kept on rising.

WHAT LIES AHEAD FOR CHRISTIAN RADIO?

Some predicted the demise of radio as television came to a dominant place in various international cultures, just as others predicted that books and libraries would disappear as soon as the Internet became globally available. Of course, we have not seen either prediction realized (yet), but there are surely many challenges that radio and audio programming has to face in the near future.

In 2003, the *NRB* magazine (of the National Religious Broadcasters) surveyed several media agencies, asking them to identify "the next big thing." One of the answers repeated often was "personalized media delivery."[8] This is already being realized in the phenomenon of MP3 players capable of downloading and storing thousands of programs that can be accessed at any time and any place. Listening will become much more listener-scheduled than provider-scheduled.

---

[8]See the following website: http://www.nrb.org/partner/Article_Display_Page/0,,PTID308776|CHID568024|CIID1582226,00.html.

Partially as a consequence of the above, radio stations may become more single-genre, such as all talk, all music, all preaching, all Bible studies, etc. There will be stations catering mainly to men, to women, to young people, to the old, to children, and to various other specific groups of listeners. This is another aspect of the "personalization" of media delivery systems.

Third, it is likely that radio programming will become much more interactive. Listeners will be able and encouraged to respond to programs through the Internet and through cell phone text messages. And as listeners respond, programmers will be able to develop "cookies" like those that exist on personal computers today. Listeners will then receive audio broadcasts according to the preferences that have emerged in the responses they have given. Conceivably, this would one day mean that no two individuals in the world would ever receive exactly the same radio program, that every "broadcast" would be targeted to a specific individual. And this would give radio unprecedented opportunity to mold and shape the lives of its audiences.

This brings us to a final opportunity/challenge. In addition to and because of the above-mentioned changes related to technology, Christian broadcasting must seize the opportunity to go beyond what it has done so well in the past. It must, of course, continue to teach biblical doctrine; but it must also begin to address, far more than has been the case thus far, issues of personal morality and ethics. And then it must go even a step further. Radio must seize the opportunity to address issues of corporate morality and must become directly involved in changing the communities in which its broadcasts are received. Faith and obedience do come by hearing, and because they do, the future opportunities of radio are even greater than its glorious past.

Although these opportunities and challenges will become reality at varying paces in different regions due to social, economic, cultural, and political differences, all broadcasters have to deal with them eventually. This means that many more resources (personnel and technical) will be needed for media ministries. It will only make sense for media ministries to join hands in tackling these complicated issues in order to play our important part in the Great Commission!

PART FOUR

A FINAL
CHALLENGE

SHARING KINGDOM BURDENS AND OPPORTUNITIES WITH "MAINLINE" AND "SEPARATED" BROTHERS AND SISTERS

RON SCATES

Back in the 1990s a certain American Presidential candidate ran on the unofficial slogan of "It's the economy, stupid!" For thoughtful Christians today, that should translate into, "It's the kingdom, disciples!"

Authentic biblical ministry is always kingdom ministry. Mark's Gospel reminds us that Jesus came preaching not the church, not a denomination, not political ideologies, not even doctrinal formulae. Instead, he came preaching the kingdom. It's all about the kingdom.

When I address our congregation's new-member classes, I always say, "You're not obligated to join Highland Park Presbyterian Church by going through this class. After going through the class, if you come to Christ, but then feel led to join Faith Lutheran Church—hooray! Our job is to get you into the kingdom and then help you find your way to a kingdom congregation. We'd love to have you here—if that's where the Lord is leading; but if not, we simply rejoice that you're in the kingdom." It's all about the kingdom.

I'm glad that the Executive Committee of the World Reformed Fellowship was kingdom-oriented enough to invite a "mainline (old-line) sideline" Presbyterian to be a part of this volume. I count it a real privilege to be part of this effort as we cross over racial, political, geographical, and denominational boundaries to embody *harambe* (Swahili for "coming together as one") in service to advancing the kingdom. I believe that being a Christian mandates me to look for what I have in common with other Christians rather than focusing on the differences.

John Frame in his book *Evangelical Reunion* says that a good way to foster a spirit of unity among diverse Christians is to tell three jokes about your own denomination. So here goes:

• How many Presbyterians does it take to change a light bulb? *Change*?!!

• A chronologically gifted (in other words, elderly) lady went to her Presbyterian Church USA pastor and asked if he would conduct a funeral for her recently deceased dog. The pastor graciously and gently explained why, theologically and biblically, he didn't do funerals for animals. Matter-of-factly, the lady replied, "Well, I guess I'll go down the street and talk to the Baptist pastor then and see if he'll do the funeral. If so, I'll give *him* the $500 honorarium." With that, the Presbyterian pastor exclaimed, "Why didn't you tell me the dog was a Presbyterian!"

• A Presbyterian pastor went bear hunting. He wandered into a blind canyon and suddenly found himself cornered by a giant, ferocious grizzly bear that was blocking the only way out. The pastor aimed his rifle, and the gun jammed. The grizzly rose upon his back legs and was poised to attack. The pastor dropped to his knees and began to pray, "Dear Lord, please turn this grizzly bear into a Christian." Suddenly a great miracle occurred. The bear dropped to his knees and began to also pray. "Father, for this food we are about to receive, we give you thanks. Amen."

Yes, believe it or not, there *are* evangelical, Reformed Christians still left in the mainline denominations. I am actually only one of millions. Lest you question my truly Reformed pedigree, let me state, "I'm a seven-point Calvinist. I found two that Calvin missed!" In all seriousness I left seminary priding myself on being a "four-point Calvinist," the problem being, of course, that thorny doctrine of "limited atonement." At a conference, early in my ministry, I made the providential "mistake" of sharing my stance with Professor John Gerstner of Pittsburgh Seminary. He stared right through me and said, "Son, I want to have dinner with you tonight." That night over dinner he put me in the "Calvinistic crucible" and helped me see that unless you're a universalist, everyone has a doctrine of limited atonement. The only question is, who limits it—we or God? If we do, then you and I are ultimately sovereign over our salvation, not God. His final words to me were, "Son, you're going to have to decide to either go with your gut or with the gospel of grace. You better make a choice soon." Haunted and convicted by Gerstner's manifesto, I decided to go with the gospel of grace and replaced my Elmer Fudd theology with John Calvin. I went from "TUIP" to "TULIP."

But if I've seen the light of evangelical, Reformed faith, why have I remained in a mainline denomination like the PCUSA? I won't rehearse here the dirty laundry of the PCUSA. Suffice it to say that if anyone is aware of the deep theological and moral crises that continually plague the PCUSA, it is I. Actually, I've tried to leave . . . twice, but the Lord won't let me go. Being wired missiologically at heart, my prayer has always been, "Lord, I'll go wherever you call me to go, or stay wherever you call me to stay." So far God has not let me leave what is a very spiritually dysfunctional denomination. Instead he's helped me see the PCUSA as a "mission field." I've never run from the mission field. Please pray for the PCUSA—and for those who stand for biblical orthodoxy within that denomination as well as in other mainline bodies. Each year it becomes increasingly harder to be an evangelical, Reformed Christian in the PCUSA. I go back and forth between wanting to cut and run and being "Athanasius *contra mundo*." I will stay until the Lord releases me. I believe the Lord *has* called others out of the PCUSA as a judgment against her, but so far I'm not one of them.

One crucial thing that helps me stay is the challenge of cultivating a kingdom vision versus wallowing in denominational myopia. Wherever I've gone in ministry—San Antonio, Baltimore, and Dallas—I've made a top priority out of remembering that my ministry is not chiefly about me, my church, or my denomination. It's supremely about the larger kingdom. This has caused me to seek out and forge relationships with pastors across denominational lines who have a similar kingdom vision.

In Dallas this has meant that for the past six years I have been in a covenant group with Jim Denison (Senior Pastor of Park Cities Baptist Church) and Skip Ryan (Senior Pastor of Park Cities Presbyterian Church). Every other Monday we meet for lunch to laugh and cry and pray together and hold ourselves accountable to our calling. There was an immediate chemistry among the three of us—three different denominations but only one faith. We've not let issues of polity or baptism keep us apart. As we have—by God's grace—modeled partnership among our churches, to our churches, to the larger church, and to the world, the laity of our three churches have observed the fun we have together and have grown—from the grass roots up—a ministry called "Churches Together" in which our three churches collaborate on kingdom ministry as a witness for the Lord. So that you know just how much of a God thing our covenant relationship is, never in six years have we three senior pastors ever talked worship attendance, membership, or budgets!

Please don't axe PCUSA and other mainline types from your map of the kingdom. We need you—and you need us. We need to be and to work together. Though nineteenth-century Presbyterian evangelist Charles Finney was not very Reformed, he did get it right when he said, "Whenever there's a Presbyterian General Assembly, there's a jubilee in hell!" Despite that reality, the two marks Calvin used to identify true churches still exist: (1) where there is true preaching of the Word; (2) where there *is* right administration of the sacraments.

As for the third mark—added *after* Calvin—the diligent exercise of church discipline, well, not a whole lot of discipline can be exercised in the PCUSA at present. When I was in the Baltimore Presbytery, I had four disciplinary cases involving church officers. In each case, rather than cooperate with the measure of discipline, each officer eventually jumped ship and went down the street to liberal Presbyterian churches, where they were welcomed with open arms despite their lifestyles. No church perfectly lives out the marks of a true church, but we should intentionally aspire in that direction. And I believe that it is Jesus' desire that churches that *do* aspire to that end team together for ministry, worship, fellowship, and service with other churches that have similar aspirations.

I am convinced that denominations are irrelevant to God as we head into a post-denominational twenty-first century. There is only one church of Jesus Christ, made up of all who truly bow the knee to Jesus and who seek to order their lives under the authority of God's Word. Jesus established only one church, not many denominations. We, over the centuries, have allowed race, politics, geography, cultural peccadilloes, economics, class, etc., along with theological pride, to slice the body of Christ into thousands of sinful pieces. We need to repent of our divisions and move past them into what Philip Jenkins is calling the "new Christendom." If you've read his book (*The Next Christendom: The Coming of Global Christianity*)—and I recommend you do so—then you know that God is bringing about a great realignment of the Christian church around the world.

During the nineteenth and twentieth centuries, Christendom's locus, power, and numbers were in the "First World." By the end of the twentieth century, we had seen the demise of First-World Christianity—the church in the West becoming largely captive to not only the winds of liberal theology, but also to affluence, power, and a northern European/North American cultural stiffness. That malaise is now being challenged by a Two-Thirds World church that is growing and worshiping and making disciples in ways that call into question our previously held First-World vision. As a whole, the First-World church is shrinking. The Two-Thirds World church is growing dramatically. If this is a typical year, my denomination (the PCUSA) will lose between forty thousand and fifty thousand members. The Rural Presbyterian Church in India is, by contrast, making disciples hand over fist. They alone will make up for PCUSA losses in about four months. You've heard the statistics before: somewhere around ten thousand people a day are becoming Christians in South America, Africa, and Asia. God has shifted the center of world Christianity back to the Two-Thirds World.

I really believe that God's plan for advancing his kingdom in the twenty-first century involves the "rescue" of the First-World church by the Two-Thirds World church. As I speak, we're seeing this unfold in the worldwide Anglican communion where Two-Thirds-World bishops and churches—who are orthodox and evangelical—are flexing their muscle (they have the votes!) and are trying to correct the aberrant course that the First-World Anglican churches have taken in the areas of human sexuality and theology. In my own denomination, one of the few bright spots and signs of growth is the planting of immigrant ethnic congregations who are looking at "Mother Church" and saying, "What's wrong with you? How did you get this way? Please come home!"

And their concern is not just with theology and human sexuality. The Two-Thirds World church has something to say to us affluent First-World types for whom money and power have sometimes displaced our passion for Christ. Every year I take a mission trip into the Two-Thirds World. Each time as I struggle to leave my First-World comforts and conveniences behind, I meet brothers and sisters in Christ who have so much less than I do (by the world's standards) but who have so much more when it comes to the joy of life in Christ. Every time I go on one of these mission trips, I come back wondering whether or not I'm even a Christian. Often among what God is doing in the Two-Thirds World I am unmasked as the one—even with my true-blue, evangelical, Reformed faith—who quietly bows the knee to the unholy trinity of "bodies, bucks, and buildings."

Back in the U.S., I sometimes throw a pity party for myself when I am "persecuted" for praying at a public event in the name of Jesus. But the party soon ends when I hear about Chinese pastors who have been beaten, imprisoned, threatened with death and when told that Christians in the First World are praying for the persecution to stop reply by saying, "Oh, no, please don't pray for the persecution to stop. It's the persecution that hones our faith. It's the persecution that keeps us close to Christ. It's the persecution that is advancing the kingdom in China."

In my own congregation, we have undergone a paradigm shift in terms of how we need to submit ourselves to Christ and our Two-Thirds-World brothers and sisters. Five years ago we decided to plant an African Presbyterian Church in Dallas because of the great number of African immigrants in our city. We brought an African pastor onto our staff. We gave him money and a place to meet in our building. The idea was for him to build the church up to the point where it could sustain itself as a viable congregation. We would then ceremonially launch the new church and pat ourselves on the back for advancing the kingdom.

But a strange, Holy Spirit thing has happened. Over the past five years, big, affluent Highland Park Presbyterian Church—once the evangelical flagship church for the old Southern Presbyterian Church (PCUS)—realized that perhaps we need the African church more than they need us. Both congregations realized that our staying together would better advance the kingdom. We realized that we need to be re-evangelized by our African brothers and sisters. We realized they have gifts of passion and joy that we lack and that we need to be re-discipled by them. We realized that if Highland Park Presbyterian Church was to ever approximate looking anything like the kingdom ("from every tribe and tongue . . ."), we'd better assimilate our African friends into who we are and vice versa so that we might all become who God wants us to be.

Parallel to that, we've also brought a Korean pastor onto our staff (this is radical for the Park Cities area of Dallas), but we are committed to advancing the kingdom by moving toward looking more like the kingdom. We joke and say that we are now a "mission church" of the Presbyterian Church of East Africa, but in reality it may be more serious than joking.

Two-Thirds World church, we need you to come and rescue us! The mainline church has gone a-whoring—we constantly toy with heterodoxies and aberrant sexual lifestyles, in addition to addiction to wealth and affluence that have led us to compromise the faith once delivered to the saints. All of these aberrations arise because, in our affluence, we have the luxury of toying with such idols. We need you to intervene, slap some sense into us, and show us through your lives of authenticity and integrity in Christ the heights from which we've fallen. There is hope for the mainline church. I don't believe the Lord has completely given up on her yet. One of the reasons I wanted to become involved with the World Reformed Fellowship was so I could be in more direct contact with Christians from the Two-Thirds World and in that contact issue a cry for help. Please pray for the western church. Please say no to our foolishness. Please send missionaries to re-evangelize the West.

Let's partner together for the kingdom's sake. I believe a Reformed, evangelical Christian is someone of any race, tribe, or nationality who believes:

1. that the Scriptures are our supreme authority and our infallible guide for faith and practice;

2. that Jesus is fully God and fully man and the only way to salvation;

3. that people have a need for personal conversion to Christ in order to be saved;

4. that the Holy Spirit is Lord over the process of election;

5. that missions and evangelism are priorities for the church; and

6. that people need to be a part of the Christian community for worship, fellowship, and service.

Wherever I go, I encounter countless people in mainline churches who affirm these six things. I find Anglican, Lutheran, even Roman Catholic evangelicals who assert and live out that—or a very similar—corpus of faith. In this increasingly post-denominational age, I find myself having more in common with people from all kinds of denominations who hold to "mere Christianity" than I do with many of my fellow PCUSA clergy. Both heresy and schisms are sin—one against truth, the other against unity and love. As we strive for an authentic, biblical kingdom vision, as we seek to advance the kingdom together by partnering with believers across all sorts of denominational, geographic, political, racial, and class boundaries, I believe we're headed where the Lord wants us to go. Whenever I want to draw the boundaries too tight, when I'm tempted to draw someone out of the circle over some fine point of theology, I'm reminded of what Francis Schaeffer calls "The Mark of the Christian." If we can't reach across our differences and diversities (those that do not compromise the core of evangelical, Reformed faith) and join hands and treat each other with love, then we give unbelievers, who observe us fussin' and fightin', the right to walk away from Christ.

The Lord has preserved a remnant in the First-World mainline churches. Don't write us off. Don't forget us. We want to partner with any and all who are about kingdom ministry. As I often tell my congregation, "'For God so loved the world . . . ,' and the only question remaining is, 'Will we allow God to love the world through us?'" I believe he can and will do that better if we're working *together*.

MEMBERS OF THE WORLD REFORMED FELLOWSHIP

(AS OF MAY 21, 2007)

DENOMINATIONAL MEMBERS

The Christian Reformed Church of South Africa
The Church of England in South Africa
The Evangelical Presbyterian Church (U.S.A.)
The Evangelical Presbyterian Church of Myanmar
The Evangelical Presbyterian Church of Peru
Grace Presbyterian Church of New Zealand
Mount Zion Presbyterian Church of Sierra Leone
The National Presbyterian Church of Mexico
The Presbyterian Church in America
The Presbyterian Church in India
The Presbyterian Church of Australia
The Presbyterian Church of Bolivia
The Presbyterian Church of Brazil
The Reformed Church of Latin America
The Reformed Churches in South Africa
The Reformed Evangelical Church of Indonesia
The Reformed Presbyterian Church of India
The Reformed Presbyterian Church of Uganda
The United Baptist Church of Christ (Colombia)
The United Presbyterian Church of Pakistan
The United Reformed Churches in Myanmar

(Total of 21)

CONGREGATIONAL MEMBERS

Bedford Presbyterian Church (Nova Scotia, Canada)

Bundibugyo Community Worship Center (Bundibugyo, Uganda)

Chattanooga Valley PCA (Flintstone, Georgia, USA)

Christ the King Presbyterian Church of Argentina (Rosario, Argentina)

Covenant Fellowship Church (Glen Mills, Pennsylvania, USA)

Covenant Presbyterian Church (Tullahoma, Tennessee, USA)

Cresheim Valley Church (Chestnut Hill, Pennsylvania, USA)

Duke Street Baptist Church (Richmond, Surrey, England)

The Evangelical Christian Mission (Yangon, Myanmar)

The Free Reformed Church of Kenya (Ogembo, Southern Kish, Kenya)

Grace Fellowship (Kampala, Uganda)

The Jinja Reformed Presbyterian Church (Jinja, Uganda)

Lexington Presbyterian Church (Lexington, South Carolina, USA)

New City Presbyterian Church (Margate, Florida, USA)

The Protestant Church of Smyrna (Izmir, Turkey)

Redeemer Church (Louisville, Kentucky, USA)

The Reformed Presbyterian Church of Togo

Trinity Presbyterian Church (Rye, New York, USA)

(Total of 18)

ORGANIZATIONAL MEMBERS

Akademie fur Reformatoriesch Theologie (Hannover, Germany)

Aletheia Theological Institute (Lawang, Jatim, Indonesia)

The Apologetics Group (Draper, Virginia, USA)

The Back to God Evangelistic Association (Kampala, Uganda)

Bandung Theological Seminary (Bandung, Indonesia)

CHAIM Mission to the Jews (Glenside, Pennsylvania, USA)

Chongshin University and Theological Seminary (Seoul, South Korea)

The Christian Counseling and Educational Foundation (Glenside, Pennsylvania, USA)

Covenant Theological Seminary (St. Louis, Missouri, USA)

Covenant Theological Seminary of Myanmar (Yangon, Myanmar)

Faculté Libre de Théologie Réformée, Aix-en-Provence, France

Haddington House (Charlottetown, Prince Edward Island, Canada)

Highland Theological College (Dingwall, Scotland)

IgniteUS, Inc. (Columbia, South Carolina, USA)

Istituto di Formazione Evangelica e Documentazione (Padova, Italy)

International Theological Seminary (El Monte, California, USA)

Iyani Bible School (Sibasa, South Africa)

The Jackson Institute (Atlanta, Georgia, USA)

Knox Fellowship (Burlingame, California, USA)

Martin Bucer Theological Seminary (Berlin/Bonn, Germany)

Miami International Seminary (Miami, Florida, USA)

Mukhayo Theological College (KwaMhlanga, South Africa)

The Presbyterian Lay Committee (Lenoir, North Carolina, USA)

Presbyterian Mission International (St. Louis, Missouri, USA)

The Redeemer Church Planting Center (New York, New York, USA)

Reformed Evangelical Theological Seminary of Indonesia (Jakarta, Indonesia)

Reformed Presbyterian Theological Seminary (Pittsburgh, Pennsylvania, USA)

Reformed Theological Seminary (Orlando, Florida, USA)

Reformed Theological Seminary of Colombia (Barranquilla, Colombia)

Save Souls Ministries (Karachi City, Pakistan)

The Society of Biblical Christian Churches of Pakistan (Gujranwala, Pakistan)

TE3 (Theological Education for Eastern Europe) (Sofia, Bulgaria)

Westminster Seminary California (Escondido, California, USA)

Westminster Theological Seminary (Philadelphia, Pennsylvania, USA)

Whitefield College and Theological Seminary (Lakeland, Florida, USA)

The World Reformed Fellowship of Sierra Leone (Bo, Sierra Leone)

(Total of 36)

INDIVIDUAL MEMBERS

Pbro. Felipe de Jesus Buenfil Alcocer (Haciendas del Caribe, Mexico)

The Rev. Stanislav Alexiev (Sofia, Bulgaria)

Dr. John Armstrong (Carol Stream, Illinois, USA)

Rev. Tom Ascol (Cape Coral, Florida, USA)

Mr. Chris Attaway (Winter Springs, Florida, USA)

Dr. Mariano Avila (Grand Rapids, Michigan, USA)

Rev. Moses M. Bamai (Kaduna State, Nigeria)

Rev. Martin Ban (Santa Fe, New Mexico, USA)

Dr. William S. Barker (Webster Groves, Missouri, USA)

Dr. Tucker Bartholomew (Philadelphia, Pennsylvania, USA)

Dr. Joel Beeke (Grand Rapids, Michigan, USA)

Professor Pierre Berthoud (Aix-en-Provence, France)

Mr. Alwyn Bezuidenhout (Seoul, South Korea)

Mrs. Cora Bezuidenhout (Seoul, South Korea)

Mr. Noel Bowers (Randburg, South Africa)

Mr. Roy Boyd (Atlanta, Georgia, USA)

Dr. Lawrence Bray (Boothwyn, Pennsylvania, USA)

Rev. Matthew Paul Buccheri (New York, New York, USA)

Dr. P. J. (Flip) Buys (Rayton, South Africa)

Rev. Victor Elias Gaete Caceres (Vregion, Chile)

Dr. David Calhoun (St. Louis, Missouri, USA)

Rev. Robert Calvert (Rotterdam, The Netherlands)

Dr. Steven Casselli (Tampa, Florida, USA)

V. Ravi Chandran (Nasayanur, India)

Rev. Craig Chapman (Rye, New York, USA)

Dr. Leonardo De Chirico (Padova, Italy)

Dr. Wilson Chow (Hong Kong)

Dr. T. Gordon Coleman (Alison Park, New South Wales, Australia)

Mr. Russell Copeland (Essex, Massachusetts, USA)

Mrs. Sally Cummings (Malvern, Pennsylvania, USA)

Mr. Mark Dalbey (St. Charles, Missouri, USA)

Rt. Rev. Dr. Glenn N. Davies (New South Wales, Australia)

Mr. Rodney Davila (Santiago, Chile)

Rev. Phaswana Dembe (Dzanani, South Africa)

Dr. Robert Den Dulk (Cannonsburg, Michigan, USA)

Dr. David Dively (Louisville, Kentucky, USA)

Rev. Emiliano Donoso (Quito, Ecuador)

Mr. Bill Douglas (Midland, Georgia, USA)

The Rev. Dr. Matthew Ebenezer (Moratuwa, Sri Lanka)

Mrs. Barbara Edgar (Glenside, Pennsylvania, USA)

Dr. William Edgar (Glenside, Pennsylvania, USA)

Rev. Carl Ellis (Chattanooga, Tennessee, USA)

Dr. Peter Enns (Lansdale, Pennsylvania, USA)

Rev. David Farrow (Toftwood, Dereham, Norfolk, England)

Dr. Aldo Fontao (Kihei, Hawaii, USA)

Mrs. Sally Fravel (Chapin, South Carolina, USA)

Mr. William Fravel (Chapin, South Carolina, USA)

Dr. David Garner (Sofia, Bulgaria)

The Rev. Dr. Seth Gbewonyo (Legon, Ghana)

Dr. Timothy George (Birmingham, Alabama, USA)

Dr. Paul Gilchrist (Buford, Georgia, USA)

Rev. Liam Goligher (Richmond, Surrey, England)

Rev. Jason Goroncy (St. Andrews, Scotland)

Dr. Douglas Green (Glenside, Pennsylvania, USA)

Rev. William Green (Wyoming, Michigan, USA)

Rev. Yusuf Gunawan (Semarang, Indonesia)

David R. Haburchak, M.D. (Augusta, Georgia, USA)

Rev. Tim Hanley (Chapin, South Carolina, USA)

Dr. Allan Harman (Ocean Grove, Victoria, Australia)

Dr. Mairi Harman (Ocean Grove, Victoria, Australia)

Mrs. Peggy Hedden (Columbus, Ohio, USA)

Mrs. Mary Heerdt (Glenside, Pennsylvania, USA)

Mr. Robert Heerdt (Glenside, Pennsylvania, USA)

Rev. Len Hendrix (Tullahoma, Tennessee, USA)

Rev. Walter Henegar (Atlanta, Georgia, USA)

Dr. Craig Higgins (Rye, New York, USA)

Rev. Ismael Hilerio (Cherry Hill, New Jersey, USA)

Dr. Rick Horne (Chester, Pennsylvania, USA)

Mr. Robert Hornick (Pensacola, Florida, USA)

Rev. Bruce Howes (Heritage, Delaware, USA)

Dr. Benyamin Intan (Jakarta, Indonesia)

Dr. David R. Jackson (Werrington, Australia)

Rev. Michael Jarrett (Marion, Iowa, USA)

Archbishop Peter Jensen (Sydney, Australia)

Dr. Thomas Johnson (Prague, The Czech Republic)

Dr. Peter Jones (Escondido, California, USA)

Mrs. Rebecca Jones (Escondido, California, USA)

Mr. Nicholas Vaca Justiniano (Cochabamba, Bolivia)

Professor Michael Kelly (Philadelphia, Pennsylvania, USA)

Mrs. Renee Kenny (York, Pennsylvania, USA)

Mr. Ross Kenny (York, Pennsylvania, USA)

Dr. In Whan Kim (Seoul, South Korea)

Rev. Frank Kovacs (Richmond Hill, Ontario, Canada)

Rev. Yakubu M. Kutai (Ambler, Pennsylvania, USA)

Dr. Woody Lajara (Lawrenceville, Georgia, USA)

Dr. Tim Lane (Jenkintown, Pennsylvania, USA)

Dr. Diane Langberg (Jenkintown, Pennsylvania, USA)

The Rev. Rafael Enrique Leal (Barranquilla, Colombia)

Dr. John Leonard (Glenside, Pennsylvania, USA)

Rev. Dercy de Lima (Belo Horizonte, Minas Gerais, Brazil)

Rev. Tshililo Liphadzi (Gauteng, South Africa)

Dr. Samuel Logan (Glenside, Pennsylvania, USA)

Mrs. Susan Logan (Glenside, Pennsylvania, USA)

Dr. Kin Yip Louie (Kowloon, Hong Kong)

Mr. Wykus Louw (Carlton Centre, South Africa)

Rev. John Maloma (Veneeming, South Africa)

Rev. Paul Manuel (Parkland, Florida, USA)

Dr. Thinandavha Derrick Mashau (Potchefstroom, South Africa)

Rev. Sam Mateer (Santiago, Chile)

Rev. William Mayk (Pottstown, Pennsylvania, USA)

Rev Professor A.T.B. McGowan (Dingwall, Scotland)

Professor David McKay (Belfast, Northern Ireland)

Mr. Jeff McMullen (Ellicott City, Maryland, USA)

Mr. Fernando Meister (Higienopolis, Sao Paulo, Brazil)

Mr. Elias Mendes-Gomes (Mauritania, West Africa)

Mr. Richard Mercer (Calgary, Alberta, Canada)

Mr. Harry Miller (Conyers, Georgia, USA)

Mrs. Julia Miller (Conyers, Georgia, USA)

Rev. Larry C. Mills (Jackson, Mississippi, USA)

Rev. Cornelius Molenaar (Petauke, Zambia)

Rev. T. M. Moore (Concord, Tennessee, USA)

Dr. Richard Mouw (La Canada, California, USA)

Rev. Mbulaheni Simon Muhali (Makonde, South Africa)

Rev. Isaac Ndivhaleni Mundalamo (Seshego, South Africa)

Dr. John Musselman (Atlanta, Georgia, USA)

Mrs. Irene Newell (Bellingham, Washington, USA)

Dr. Robert Newell (Bellingham, Washington, USA)

Dr. Wai-Yee Ng (Kowloon, Hong Kong)

Dr. John Nicholls (London, England)

Rev. David M. O'Dowd (Tulsa, Oklahoma, USA)

The Rev Timothy O. Olonade (Jos, Plateau State, Nigeria)

Dr. Manuel Ortiz (Philadelphia, Pennsylvania, USA)

Dr. Peterus Pamudji (Malang, Jatim, Indonesia)

Rev. Dr. Dennis Paris (Urb. El Conquistador, Puerto Rico)

Rev. Isaias Lobao Pereira, Jr. (Brasilia, Brazil)

Mrs. Barbara Perrin (Irmo, South Carolina, USA)

Dr. K. Eric Perrin (Columbia, South Carolina, USA)

Ms. Susan Post (Philadelphia, Pennsylvania, USA)

Rev. Cecil Charles Prescod (Portland, Oregon, USA)

Professor T. C. Rabali (Vanderbijlpark, South Africa)

Dr. Harry Reeder (Birmingham, Alabama, USA)

Bishop Frank Retief (Bergvliet, South Africa)

Mr. Mark E. Robinson (Jersey City, New Jersey, USA)

Dr. Ron Scates (Dallas, Texas, USA)

Dr. Thomas Schirrmacher (Bonn, Germany)

Rev. Ian Schoonwater (Grafton, New South Wales, Australia)

Rev. Leo Schuster (Houston, Texas, USA)

Rev. John Shane (Tokai, South Africa)

Rev. Michael Sharrett (Lynchburg, Virginia, USA)

Rev. Roberto Brasileiro Silva (Minas Gerais, Brazil)

Dr. Adrian Smith (Dallas, Texas, USA)

Rev. Peterson Sozi (Kampala, Uganda)

Rev. Wayne Sparkman (St. Louis, Missouri, USA)

Dr. T. Grady Spires (Beverly, Massachusetts, USA)

Dr. Chul Won Suh (Seoul, South Korea)

Rev. Robert Tanzie (Delray Beach, Florida, USA)

Rev. John Calvin Taylor VII (Tulsa, Oklahoma, USA)

Professor Steve Taylor (Melrose Park, Pennsylvania, USA)

Rev. Ken Thompson (Duluth, Georgia, USA)

Rev. Lian C. Tombing (Manipur, India)

Dr. Joseph Tong (El Monte, California, USA)

Mr. Mark Traphagen (Glenside, Pennsylvania, USA)

Mr. Thomas Troxell (Sun City West, Arizona, USA)

Dr. Tim Trumper (Grand Rapids, Michigan, USA)

Dr. Yusufu Turaki (Nairobi, Kenya)

Judge Rollin Van Broekhoven (Manassas, Virginia, USA)

Mrs. Laurie Vanden Heuvel (Fennville, Michigan, USA)

Rev. Tom Vanden Heuvel (Fennville, Michigan, USA)

Mr. Steven Vanderhill (Dallas, Texas, USA)

Rev. Richard Verreynne (Cape Town, South Africa)

Rev. Andre Visagie (Durbanville, South Africa)

Dr. Paul Wells (Aix-en-Provence, France)

Mr. Alan White (Glenside, Pennsylvania, USA)

Dr. Luder Whitlock (Orlando, Florida, USA)

Dr. Jack Whytock (Charlottetown, Prince Edward Island, Canada)

Dr. Parker Williamson (Lenoir, North Carolina, USA)

Dr. Charles Wingard (Huntsville, Alabama, USA)

Mrs. Lynne Wingard (Huntsville, Alabama, USA)

Dr. Timothy Witmer (Upper Darby, Pennsylvania, USA)

Dr. Carver Tatsum Yu (Kowloon, Hong Kong)

(Total of 170)

INDEX